What Others Are S

MW01623911

Little Moments, Big Magic

"Like Yahoo!, Big Brothers Big Sisters is about inventing new possibilities for people and allowing each of us to be part of the magic of transforming lives and communities. At the heart of Big Brothers Big Sisters are its extraordinary people who give of their time and their energy to make a difference in children's lives. These stories are an inspiration to us all."

Jerry Yang
Co-founder & Chief Yahoo!

"We had more Big Brothers Big Sisters stories in *Chicken Soup for the Volunteer's Soul* than any other charitable organization. This book is further evidence why! One hundred years of touching children's lives has resulted in some incredible stories—heartwarming, inspiring tales that will make you laugh, touch your soul and leave you misty eyed."

Arline Oberst
Co-author *Chicken Soup for the Volunteer's Soul*

"Big Brothers Big Sisters is an organization that I have supported for more than two decades. This book is a testament to the power of the Big Brothers Big Sisters one-to-one form of mentoring, and the ability of one person to change a child's life. Each story touched me with the impact that a Big Brother or Big Sister has had and the difference that one person can make."

Lynn Swann
Former Pittsburgh Steeler and NFL Hall of Fame

United Way's dedication to the spirit of volunteerism comes to life through Big Brothers and Big Sisters everyday. We salute our partnership with Big Brothers Big Sisters and we salute with admiration the special partnerships that last a lifetime as told so beautifully in this book."

Brian A. Gallagher
President and CEO, United Way of America

"These inspirational stories by former Big and Little Brothers and Sisters illustrate why Arby's has been a proud community partner with Big Brothers Big Sisters for over seventeen years. As you read their stories, you'll understand the many ways Big Brothers Big Sisters Makes a Difference in the lives of young people across the nation. We are proud to salute the efforts of BBBSA in their Centennial year."

Doug Benham
CEO and President, Arby's Inc.

"Ken Blanchard and I were excited about including Big Brothers Big Sisters in the story-line of our book, *The On-Time, On-Target Manager*. The reason is that BBBS is all about sticking to the mission and making a positive impact. Everyone benefits from participation—not just the "Littles," but every bit as much the "Bigs." These wonderful true stories are clear proof!"

Steve Gottry
Coauthor of *The On-Time, On-Target Manager*

"The Centennial Book demonstrates an old truism—that it is better to give than to receive—and illustrates why Big Brothers and Sisters believe that they get back so much more than they give. If you are not already a Big Brother or Sister before you start reading this book, you will be!"

Helen Ostrowski
Global CEO, Porter Novelli

Little Moments BIG MAGIC

Inspirational Stories of Big Brothers and Big Sisters and the Magic They Create

Beth Barrett
Alan Annis
Denice Riffey

100 Great Stories Celebrating the First 100 Years of Big Brothers Big Sisters

Magical Moments Publishing, LLC
Gilbert, Arizona
www.magicalpublishing.com

Published by:
Magical Moments Publishing, LLC
Gilbert, Arizona U.S.A.
www.magicalpublishing.com
Phone: 877.778.5958
Fax: 203.267.7142
E-mail: info@magicalpublishing.com

ISBN: 0-9749130-0-6

Printed in the United States of America.

Cover design: Kathi Dunn, Dunn + Associates Design

Cover photos courtesy of: Buena Vista Television, Linda Laird, and Kurt Inderbitzen.

Back cover wording: Susan Kendrick Writing

Chapter title artwork: Nancy V. Barrett

This book is dedicated to the millions of
Big Brothers, Big Sisters,
Little Brothers, Little Sisters,
employees, volunteers, and donors
who made the 100th Anniversary
of Big Brothers Big Sisters possible.
We dedicate this with love to all of you
and hope these stories inspire you
to continue to spread the magic.

To my Little Sister Karen, without whom this would not have been possible, and to the rest of my family—my mom, Nancy, Cindy, Nathalie, Bill, Pam, Michael, Karen, Sara, Mike, and Linden—with much love.
Beth

To my father Roy, who recently passed onto a better place. Thanks for bringing little moments and big magic into my life.
Alan

Art by Little Brother Conner Aikman and Big Sister Nikki Arsenault

Table of Contents

3. We Are Family

4. On Angel's Wings

5. The Magic Continues

6. Dream Weavers

7. A Little Inspiration

8. The Family's Perspective

9. Leaving A Legacy

10. Speaking From The Heart

11. Little Moments, Big Rewards

Acknowledgements

Sometimes little events, things that seem insignificant at the time, turn out to be life-changing experiences. *Little Moments, Big Magic*, the slogan for Big Brother Big Sisters, is a fitting title for this book. Just as little moments create big magic in a child's life, similar little moments created the big magic of this book. We want to acknowledge a few of the many people who helped directly and indirectly in making *Little Moments* a reality.

Judy Vredenburgh, Mack Koonce, Robin Palley, Joe Radelet, Noreen Shanfelter, Jammie O'Brien, Nicola Atherstone, and everyone else at BBBSA with whom we worked: Thank you for believing in our vision, for all of your hard work, and for placing your trust in us to pull this momentous project together.

Linda Searfoss: Your thirty-one years of service to the BBBS organization is truly inspirational, and your conversation with Alan inspired this book. Thank you for your wonderful soul and for being a Big Sister to all of us!

Laura Capello, for being instrumental in putting the authors together and for listening and offering advice and help all along the way; your passion and commitment is always inspiring!

John Boal, for listening to Alan's idea and giving him Beth's name. Your generosity of spirit became the fertilizer that made it possible for the seed to reach its full potential.

Cindy Camargo and Nathalie Durand: This book would never have been finished on time without your incredibly kind energy supporting it. From editing, to IT assistance, book design, and layout, you were with us for every step of the process, and no words can express the gratitude we feel for the immense help you gave to birth this book.

We would like to thank a wonderful group of people who offered us their time, opinions, and valuable advice on selecting the final stories and improving them, including Tom Ambrose, Desi Annis, Eloise Annis, Monica Annis, Karen Barrett, Linden Barrett, Nancy Barrett, Alexis Bevington, Karina Bland, Lila Coddington, Claire Combs, Renee Cudhea, Rick DeBruhl, James Diesing, Derrick Dolphin, Chad Ettmueller, Penny Feldstein, Tom Ferrick, Ray Freeman, Sophie Freeman, Zoe Freeman, Doug Fulton, Pia Garcia, Meg Garlinghouse, Marilyn Greco, Candy Hawkins, Karen Hays, Arnel Kasmally, Sally Laurel, Donni LeBoeuf, Emily Lines, Morgan Lyons, Ph.D., Nicole Magnuson, Mickey McGuyre, Tom McKenna, Amy McSheffre, Jeanne Mealey, Michael Nofal, Mary Beth O'Brien, Song Paek, Jacquelyn Park, Dr. Daniel Perkins, Dave Persichini, Scott B. Peterson, Barbara Quaintance, Ben Shamburger, Honorable Barbara J. Sheedy, Maurie Beth Smith, Vicky Solot, Pamela Van Zandt, JoAnn Verrier, Ruth Wooden, and Lynn Ziegenfuss, and a double thank you to Scott Peterson for participating in the panel and helping us select additional panel members. We couldn't have made the final selections without you! Thanks for squeezing a lot of stories into your hectic lives.

A very special thank you to B. J. Sheedy, who went so far beyond giving valuable advice that she actually helped us edit the stories. You are an extraordinary woman and a great help!

Nancy Barrett: Your drawings are charming, and your editorial review and never-ending emotional support and belief in this project were much needed and appreciated!

Kathi Dunn and Hobie Hobart of Dunn Designs, for

working so patiently with us and giving us such a creative cover, and to Susan Kendrick for your terrific back cover wordsmithing skills.

Sybil Sosin, you are the best copy editor there is! We really appreciate your incredibly prompt turnaround and all your advice.

Al Sandler, and United Book Press: You are a great guy, and United Book Press is a great company to work with. Thank you for taking the time to teach us what we needed to know, and for your patience with our learning curve.

Pia Garcia and Lisa Lochner, our PR team extraordinaire at Porter Novelli: Thanks for your assistance with stories, quotes, and getting the word out about the book, so more people will know about the magic of this incredible program!

Each of the authors has particular people to thank:

Beth thanks, first and foremost, Cindy Camargo and Nathalie Durand for keeping me fed both physically and emotionally during this incredibly intense time, and for being the best friends a woman could ever ask for. I am eternally indebted to you.

Thank you to some of the mentors who changed my own life: Sister Renee Cudhea and Father Edward Fitzpatrick for believing in me and supporting my goals when I was an adolescent; Joyce Galante, Esq., who was my role model as a woman lawyer and, perhaps not coincidentally, also a Big Sister; and the most important mentor I have had as an adult—Jack Canfield. You showed me who I could be and how I could get there. I struggled for so many years trying to find my life purpose, and you simply opened the door and showed me. When the student is ready, the teacher really does appear!

To my Little Sister Karen Hays: As I've watched you

grow the last thirteen years, I have grown next to you. Thank you for all the joy you have given me! You are my gift from God.

To all of my family and friends for your incredible belief that this was my mission, for your unending support, and for loving me despite the fact I haven't returned your calls for months!

Alan wishes to thank Anthony Robbins. You created a Little Moment and inspired me to become a Big Brother and get involved with this amazing organization. Thank you, Tony, for being a great inspiration and coach.

Suzy, my loving wife: You gave me support and helped me during my stressful times. Your love for people and of life makes you a shining example of the goodness of all mankind. You are truly the heart of my life.

Denice wishes to thank Mrs. Susan Lane, my fourth-grade teacher, for helping me through the death of my mother. I am forever indebted to you for seeing my personal needs and addressing them with love and understanding.

To the man who challenged me to rise above mediocrity through my college years, Frank Keller: Thanks for expecting more from me than I did from myself. You raised the bar and opened my eyes to new possibilities—thank you!

To BBBSAZ CEO, Brian Hassett: I've gained a renewed passion for BBBS through your enthusiasm, sincerity, and talented leadership.

To my dad, Jim Wardlaw: Your example has taught me that a work ethic, integrity, honesty, and sacrifice never go out of style! And to Patty Wardlaw: Thank you for being a cheerleader and supporting my every endeavor.

To Tim Larsen: Thank you for helping my husband and me to better juggle careers, family, and dreams!

To my husband, Matt: Thank you for taking on more,

sleeping less, and believing in a mere possibility. You are my life and my love, and I'm eternally grateful for the sacrifices you make daily for me and for our wonderful family.

To my daughters, Rachel, Madison, and Rebecca: Remember that following your dreams in order to help others is never a selfish endeavor. Thank you for helping out more at home while I pounded away at the computer. I appreciate, adore, and love you all to pieces.

The authors would like the thank the incredible employees of the 470 BBBS agencies around the country who shared the leads, the stories, and the magical moments that they have experienced, so that we could learn about the great stories from the first hundred years.

This was a bigger project than any of us had expected when we dreamed this book into fruition. Due to its enormity, we may have neglected to mention people who deserve special thanks. If you aren't included, please accept our sincere apologies. We greatly appreciate all the people who helped make this book a reality.

We give special thanks to all the people who submitted stories for the book, whether they were printed or not. This book would never have existed if you weren't willing to open your hearts and share the beauty, warmth, and inspiration of your experiences!

Foreword

By Wayne Brady

Big Brothers Big Sisters celebrates its 100th anniversary by sharing 100 personal narratives from men and women who experienced *"Little Moments" and "Big Magic"* through mentoring. This inspiring collection reveals the power of mentoring through stories from various points of view — the mother who credits her son's Big Brother with giving him guidance and friendship in the absence of his father, the Little Sister who learned there are no limits to how far she can go despite being legally blind, the Big Brother who found joy, self-awareness and a life-long friend through mentoring a young boy.

I'm pleased to introduce *"Little Moments, Big Magic: Inspirational Stories of Big Brothers and Big Sisters and the Magic They Create"* not only because I believe in the power of mentoring, but also because I experienced it first hand.

I was blessed to have been born with a wonderful role model in my life—my mother, Valerie. She's the most unselfish person I know and a big source of inspiration for me. She'll sometimes give jobs to ex-drug dealers or guys who have just had really bad breaks. She gave this one sketchy guy a job cutting the lawn. I was freaking out about it, but I realized that where I see this hardened criminal who could snap your neck and run amok, she sees somebody's son. It scares me, but on the other hand I think we could all use some of her vision.

The lessons I learned from my mother about reaching out are what inspired me to become a Big Brother about twelve years ago. I was working at a theater in Orlando, and they helped me get in touch with a kid named Mike; I hung out with him for a few months, until he moved away. I'll never know how much I helped him, but I know he taught me a lesson that helped me both personally and professionally and has stayed with me to this day.

Mike made me feel very thankful for what I had been given. I grew up with a mother who absolutely adored me, and I was very fortunate with my schooling and my work. This kid didn't have the best of anything, but he had this attitude that said: "Nothing can hold me back. Nothing is going to keep me down." He wanted to be a doctor.

I brought him over to the theater one night after I'd had a really poor show. In my very selfish, actor-y way, I was venting to him about it. I remember him looking at me and saying "I don't know what you're talking about. These people love you. I wish I had people love me like that. I want to be like you."

At first I thought he was talking about the show, but then I realized he was talking about my family, because he had been spending time with us. When he said he wanted to be like me, I was absolutely floored. It finally made me conscious of all I had that I didn't appreciate. After that, I vowed never, ever, to be a whiny actor or a whiny person. I really think I was on my way to being a brat, and he curbed it. I don't take anything for granted anymore. I try to be humble and very grateful for everything that comes across my plate, and to not get so caught up in the I-I-I, me-me-me of it.

I look at my baby daughter and want her to realize that there's value in other people's lives as well. It's not just about you. And that's why you need to try to make a difference. I'm not saying you should run out and save the world, because most people can't. But if you can help one other person and start a chain reaction, do it. It's so important to remember the world is bigger than you.

A great way to start that chain reaction is to mentor a child. Thanks to Big Brothers Big Sisters, the oldest and largest mentoring organization in our country, more than two million children over the last one-hundred years have experienced a meaningful relationship with their own personal hero, a Big Brother or Big Sister.

Today Big Brothers Big Sisters serves youth ages 6 to 18 in 5,000 communities across all 50 states, and continues to transform lives through the simple act of matching caring adults with children in need. Many of the people you will read about in this collection, who received the benefit of a Big Brother or Sister, have gone on to give back what they received. The stories in this book speak volumes about the lasting impact many have had on the lives of the young.

Now that's a really *big* chain reaction!

Art by Little Sister Rachel Funk

Introduction

One hundred years ago, a young clerk named Ernest Coulter was appalled by the suffering of the thousands of children who passed through his court. He recognized that "There is only one possible way to influence this youngster, and that is to have some earnest, true man volunteer to be his big brother." In 1904, Big Brothers Big Sisters was born.

Today, Big Brother Big Sisters is the oldest and largest youth mentoring organization in the United States, serving more than 200,000 children in 5,000 communities across the country.

Offering up their time, energy, and resources, our volunteers have changed the lives of individual children forever by revealing the beauty, richness and magic in everyday moments.

Big Brothers Big Sisters has a positive ripple effect throughout the community. By broadening children's horizons, showing them what's possible and helping them reach their full potential, often in partnership with the schools, the environment for teaching and learning is greatly improved. When we reach many children in an individual school, not only do those children go on to become contributing, productive citizens but the educational experience and attainment for all the children is enhanced.

As president and CEO, I have the privilege of championing Big Brothers Big Sisters' life-changing mission for every child who wants or needs a Big Brother or Big Sister. But I also play another important role: I am a Big Sister to sixteen-year-old Sherice. Through my friendship with her, I get to see the world in a fresh new way and share her delight in new experiences and widened horizons. Our friendship is not all about helping her, although she may never know the many ways in which she has totally changed my life.

The stories featured in these pages are a snapshot of the millions of touching and poignant moments that Bigs and Littles have shared over the past century and demonstrate the measurable impact of our work. This book is a tribute to all the volunteers and donors who give of themselves so wholeheartedly, and to the children whose lives they have changed. Their relationships truly are the magic that Big Brothers Big Sisters creates everyday.

Judy Vredenburgh,
President & CEO
Big Brothers Big Sisters

Chapter 1

A World of Possibilities

The Turning Point

Big Brother H. Kenneth Hamill and Little Brother Kenneth Saladin

At the time I first met Ken Hamill in 1963, I was a boy in crisis—the oldest child in a family recently split by divorce. With my mother thrown into the workforce for the first time in her life, working both day and evening jobs, my brother, sister, and I were latchkey children before that expression was coined. I was lonely and angry, wistful and rebellious, disoriented and confused about my place and possibilities in life.

In such a turbulent state of mind, a child will do unwise things. When you do unwise things, you start getting into trouble. And so, from time to time, a police officer would bring me home from one of my misadventures and have a talk with my mother. If I had continued down that path, I could well have spent my adolescence in detention.

But my crisis was also a time of opportunity. What comforts I could not find in society, I sought in nature. I passed my time hiking the woods and fields near home, wading in streams, climbing trees to eat wild cherries and peek into birds' nests, and collecting insects and fossils. Fortunately, certain teachers and counselors recognized both my potential and my peril and referred my mother and me to Big Brothers for help.

When Ken Hamill volunteered to be a Big Brother, his life was at a turning point as well. He had suffered a stroke that paralyzed his left arm and leg. Even though he regained the ability to walk to some extent, the paralysis took away his love of participatory sports. He and his wife Berenice had adopted a daughter, but in lieu of a son, Ken turned to Big Brothers of Greater Kalamazoo, Michigan. He once confided he was hesitant about volunteering. He worried about what kind of boy he might be matched with, and, because of his paralysis, he was unsure how much he could do for a boy. Ken took a chance on me.

For five years, until I graduated from high school, Ken was a regular presence in my life. We saw each other once or twice a week—often just to go out for dinner or a sundae. But simple things like this mean a lot to many of the kids served by Big Brothers Big Sisters. Other pleasures included visiting his home, doing little yard jobs, and having lunch or dinner with Ken and his wife. Through them I saw that there was a more solid way of life to strive for. Their home and friendship were a buffer against the mindless hostility of the world outside.

Ken Hamill and my early science teachers were the most influential people in putting me on the road to my career. Many winter evenings Ken took me to Audubon Society lectures and slide shows. He leaned on me to negotiate the icy sidewalks, and I helped him get his winter coat off and on, over his lame arm, in what became a familiar little ritual between us. These outings were the most memorable cultural experience of my early teens. Just to be among educated, well-dressed people in a fancy lecture hall made me feel vicariously rich for an evening, while the Audubon programs deepened my love of nature and my desire to understand it.

In 1964 Ken gave me a subscription to a weekly

magazine called *Science Newsletter*, which I continue to subscribe to today. He also gave me a subscription to something called "Things of Science"—a monthly package that contained supplies and instructions for carrying out simple science experiments at home. Ken drove me all over the county to collect jars of pond water for microscopic study. This exploration evolved into a series of projects that I entered in the county science fair, where I hoped to win a trophy in zoology.

His efforts paid off for me. I won the grand prize for the entire science fair two years running! I was sent to International Science Fairs in St. Louis and Dallas. That was a heady experience indeed—a glamorous exposure to prize-winning science and a world of fine hotels, restaurants, banquets, and scholarly honors—such a different life from the unhappy one I knew at home! On my second try in Dallas, I won fourth prize. This time, when my copy of *Science Newsletter* arrived, my name was in it.

The United Way made me a poster child for their campaign that year. Strangers recognized and congratulated me in stores and on the street, and, for the first time, I saw science as a way of earning public respect. At last, I began to feel some self-esteem, some sense of potential, some possibility of going somewhere with my life beyond high school.

I began to set my sights on college, but I didn't get much encouragement from home. I heard "college is for rich people"—there was no point to considering it because there was no way we could afford it. I assumed that kids from poor families could not go to college—college was for somebody else. But Ken kept telling me I could do it. I received a financial aid package, earned a B.S. in zoology from Michigan State University, and received my Ph.D.

from Florida State. Now, this kid who once could scarcely imagine even *attending* college has been a college professor for twenty-seven years. In 2001 I was honored with the title of Distinguished Professor.

Ken and I remained friends long after our match officially ended. My children became his honorary grandchildren, and, just before he died, he got to see galley proofs of my first book, a college textbook of anatomy and physiology. Ken was one of those few invaluable people who made me realize that such things were possible. He rescued me from the brink of self-destruction, gave me control over my own life, and started me down the path I'm still exploring. In tribute I gave him a plaque engraved, "To a Saturday hero and lifelong friend."

Because of Ken, I know how important the influence of one adult can be to a young person. I have been a Big Brother to boys in Florida and Georgia.

To me, the meaning of immortality is the way our lives echo through the people we touch and reverberate in unpredictable ways for generation after generation. I have tried to make my own life a continuation of Ken's and to ensure that what he did for me will live on through the things I do for others. The Saturday heroes of Big Brothers Big Sisters deserve no less.

By Dr. Kenneth S. Saladin

No Limits

Big Sister Beth Barrett and Little Sister Karen Hays

I always thought the Big Brothers Big Sisters program sounded very worthwhile, and I knew that one day, when I wasn't such a busy trial lawyer, I would volunteer to be a Big Sister. Then one month in the local bar association newsletter there was a desperate plea for people to volunteer because many children were waiting several years to get a Big Brother or Sister. Even though I was very busy and could come up with a million reasons why I didn't have the time to volunteer, I also got a very clear message in my heart that I had to volunteer.

I immediately called the BBBS office in Waterbury, Connecticut. It was only when I was dialing the phone that the thought occurred to me that maybe they wouldn't want me because I have a nerve disease in my legs and walk with crutches or use a wheelchair to get around.

The caseworker assured me that a perfect physical condition wasn't necessary and that BBBS could work with a volunteer's limitations. After I went through the application process, Mandy, the caseworker, called me one day at work and said, "I have the perfect Little Sister for you. Her name is Karen, and she is eight years old."

Perfect, I thought. What a great age—young enough for Disney movies but old enough to have amusing conversations.

Then Mandy said, “And the reason I think Karen is a perfect match for you is because she is legally blind”.

“Legally blind!” I blurted. “Mandy, are you insane? The blind leading the lame? What kind of match is that? I don’t even have a hand to hold her hand because my hands are on crutches.”

Mandy said, “I knew you would say that, Beth, but let me explain why I know you are the perfect Big Sister for Karen. Her mother is blind, her two older sisters are legally blind, and her father has cerebral palsy. I want Karen exposed to someone who has a physical challenge that doesn’t let it interfere with the quality of her life. You would be such a good role model for her. You can show her that she can be anything she wants to be and do anything that she wants to do despite a physical challenge.”

That is a pretty hard rationale to resist, so I agreed to meet with Karen. While drinking a soda, this adorable little eight-year-old with thick magnifying glasses and I discussed how we could adapt our special needs to each other. Could she hang on to my shirt or coat instead of my hand and promise she would never run away from me, since I couldn’t catch her? With great seriousness, Karen promised me she would always stay by my side.

I then asked Karen what special adaptations she would need from me. She asked me if I would tell her if stairs went up or down, and then she said, “Well actually, you only have to tell me if the stairs go down because I don’t mind falling up stairs, but it really hurts when you fall down them!” I promised I would always tell her whether stairs went up *or* down. She also asked if I could tell her if there was a curb or if the land was uneven. That seemed reasonable enough for me so, on a handshake of agreement we became sisters.

When Karen was ten, she said to me one day, "Do you know why we get along so well, Beth?" I asked what she thought. "We both have the same haircut, we both love art, we both wear glasses, and we're both handicapped and we don't even care!" she answered with a smile. That is when I was positive that Mandy made a wise choice in this unlikely pairing of the blind and the lame.

During our years together, Karen and I have had a lot of fun. We have tasted different foods of the world at ethnic restaurants and fairs, attended concerts ranging from classical to jazz and rock, gone on marine biology and rock-hunting expeditions, and visited museums and zoos. We've done countless other activities ranging from the more mundane tasks of planting gardens and cooking to the excitement of day-trips to explore New York City.

When Karen was almost sixteen, she asked me one day, "Do you think if someone has had a Big Sister for a long time and they are getting to the age when the Big Sister program ends that they will ever see their Big Sister again?" I asked "Are you talking about us?" "No," she said hesitantly. "Well," I responded, "I can't answer that hypothetical question because I can't speak for what other people may do. But if you are talking about us, Honey, I'm going to be at your wedding. I'm going to be Big Sister to your kids." "No!" she stated emphatically. "You're *my* Big Sister!" "Okay," I said with a smile, "then I'll be an aunt to your children."

She was grinning from ear to ear, and I had the heart-filling realization that all the little moments I had spent with her over those many years were indeed magical to her.

When I first met Karen, she was an excruciatingly shy child. She didn't know how to talk to people, so I taught her how to have a conversation and make friends. She had been told she was stupid and would never amount to anything. It was presumed she was destined to live a life on disability. I was told by our caseworker that, if I could give Karen the confidence to believe she could graduate from high school, it would be a great achievement.

At Karen's high school graduation, I cried with joy as I watched this young woman receive her diploma. In the card I gave her, I wrote, "I have done many things in my life that I am proud of but the very best is helping you become the person you were born to be."

Karen merely required a little support from an extroverted mentor to find her own extroverted personality. She just needed to see someone who has a physical challenge who accepts it as a simple fact of life to realize there are no limits to how far she can go unless she limits herself.

In May 2004 Karen will graduate from college as an English major with excellent grades. I'm bringing a box of tissues. I'll need them.

My Little Sister, a college graduate ready to take on the world! Who would have believed thirteen years ago that this child with limited eyesight would grow into a beautiful, confident young woman with a clear vision of her promising future!

By Beth Barrett

Food for Thought

Big Brother Bruce Cross and Little Brother Todd English

My father sat me and my younger sister down one day in our suburban Atlanta home to tell us that he and my mother were getting a divorce. He looked at me and said, "Todd, you are the man of the house now. Take care of everyone." I was nine years old.

That was the end of our family as we knew it. My father left and had virtually no more contact with us. What he left behind was a boy in need of a positive male role model.

Fortunately for me, that man, Bruce Cross, entered my life as my Big Brother. The first time I met Bruce, he came to my house and met me, my mother, my grandmother, and my sister. Bruce tells a funny story about that first meeting. He says he asked me three questions. My mother answered the first one, my grandmother answered the second, and my sister answered the third. He knew right there that I needed a man in my life!

Bruce asked me if I would like to go somewhere and talk man to man. I was so happy to have a man to talk to. Our first outing was to McDonald's, and Bruce jokingly credits my passion for food and the restaurant business to his taking me for that initial meal.

Initially, our common ground was sports. We loved any kind of sports. It was great having Bruce on the sidelines cheering me on at my baseball and soccer games. We were both avid Atlanta Braves fans, and we were there for the historical moment on April 8, 1974, when Hank Aaron hit his 715th home run and broke Babe Ruth's record. What a great memory that was for both of us!

But the nicest part of our relationship was my ability to talk to Bruce about anything. Nothing was off limits. Bruce was totally cool about the little missteps all of us make when we are young. If I veered too far off course, Bruce would say, "Hey, Todd! What are you doing?" But even in those times, he was never judgmental. He was just offering a little wisdom to keep me on the right path. Bruce imparted advice in a laid-back, caring way. He would say things like "This is how I would handle it" or "I would look at it like this," but then he left it up to me to make the decisions. The really important thing to me was knowing that Bruce stood behind me to pat me on the back or catch me if I fell.

When I was around fourteen, my mom remarried, and we moved to Connecticut. Coincidentally, at around the same time, Bruce and his family moved to Indianapolis. But the physical distance between us didn't affect the emotional connection we had. I went out to visit Bruce each summer, and we remained Big Brother and Little Brother. Bruce was my safe harbor of constancy in the sometimes turbulent seas of adolescence.

Once, when I was sixteen, in an episode of extreme adolescent angst, I ran away by taking a bus headed, I thought, for Indianapolis. Somehow I got on the wrong bus and ended up in some godforsaken place nowhere near Indianapolis. I called Bruce, and he said, "Hang on. I'll get in the car and pick you up."

Bruce found me sitting on the edge of a cornfield waiting for him, and we drove the six hours back to his home in Indianapolis. In my distraught state, I had ended up six hours away from Indianapolis, but Bruce thought nothing of getting in the car and driving to pick me up and bring me to the safety of his home.

So many of the memories of my life involve food. I don't remember where I was stranded on that bus escapade, but I have a wonderful memory of the ride back to Bruce's home. We stopped at a place to eat where I had deep fried bread served with a crock of homemade apple butter. It was a fantastic meal! I actually serve a similar dish in my restaurants today, except I don't deep fry the bread.

That trip was a turning point for me—one of those life-altering moments that, depending on what kind of support you have in your life, can either break you or make you. During my struggle to find myself, I discovered the passion of my life—food. That is when I started cooking.

Always the supportive Big Brother, Bruce wanted to help me in any way that he could. One of his neighbors managed probably the best restaurant in the city—the restaurant at the top of the Indianapolis National Bank building. He gave me a tour of the restaurant, brought me into the kitchen where we had lunch, and introduced me to the chef. The chef's name was Wolfgang Puck. Of course, anyone who knows food knows that Wolfgang Puck became one of the first true celebrity chefs. But I met him at his first job in America.

Wolfgang and I are still friends. I admire him and have emulated him in my own professional career as a chef and restaurateur. I like to tease Wolfgang when I see him and remind him that I know where he came from, long before he became a Hollywood celebrity chef.

And I know where I came from, long before my own

success blossomed. I know that I would not be the man I am today had Bruce Cross not volunteered to be my Big Brother.

I am so grateful that I was blessed by many mentors in my life, the first and most fundamental being Bruce, that I have made it a mission in my own life to support mentoring in any way that I can. From mentoring youngsters ranging from inner-city children to young chefs, I know that it is vital to support the development of our young. It literally makes the difference between having a society of successful adults versus a society of people who never reach, or even know, their potential.

More than thirty years later, Bruce is still my Big Brother, and he always will be. We are close friends; we still hang out together several times a year, despite the fact he lives in Arizona and I live in Massachusetts and travel all over the world on business.

Physical distance has never been an issue for Bruce and me. We have an emotional bond that has always far surpassed the miles between us.

By Todd English as told to Beth Barrett

Giving Us a Future

Big Brother Patrick Newall and Little Brothers Manuel Carrasco and Ernesto Carrasco

My mother left our village in Mexico and headed for America with nothing more than my little brother and me and the clothes on our backs. She knew her sons didn't have a future in Mexico and she didn't have a future with her husband, so we left. My father stayed behind.

While America is the land of opportunity, opportunities are limited for a Mexican immigrant who never graduated from high school and speaks little English. The only job my mother could find was as a live-in housekeeper. Because my brother Ernesto and I couldn't live with her, she left us in the care of my aunt. Mom could only visit us on Sundays, and sometimes she could sneak in an additional visit during the week. Despite the restrictive nature of her job, she still managed to make sure we stayed healthy by taking us to the doctor, the dentist, and anything else we needed.

But my mother's absence left my brother and me alone a lot, with no one to guide us. My aunt did her best to help raise us and teach us how to behave, but in some ways we were raising ourselves. I didn't have any male role model, so I did my best to observe the way men were supposed to be and passed these lessons onto my younger brother. I think we were gender confused as to how we were supposed to act, since all we knew came from the perspective of women.

It was upsetting to me to listen to other kids talk about what kind of weekend they had with their fathers. I couldn't relate to their stories, and I felt unable to bond with guys since I couldn't talk about cars or sports, or relate to anything that would be called manly.

Even though she didn't live with us, my mom saw the struggles and difficulties we were going through. She decided to give Big Brothers Big Sisters a chance to see if they could give her a helping hand. She prayed she would not have to work as a live-in housekeeper for the rest of her life, but until that time, she had faith that Big Brothers Big Sisters would be able to give this little eight year old an additional adult in his life who could help him grow into a man.

I was on a waiting list for two years, but finally, when I was ten, I was introduced to Patrick Newall. Patrick had recently arrived in Los Angeles to pursue his dream of becoming an actor. Meeting Patrick for the first time was a shock. I had seen his picture, but never imagined how tall he would be. At first, Patrick appears intimidating because he is very tall and a body builder. Once you get past his tremendous arms, though, he's kind-hearted and a gentleman. My mom got a nice sense of the type of person Patrick was and consented to our match.

At first, just Patrick and I would go out, but my little brother Ernesto, who is four years younger than me, felt left out. It wasn't too long before Patrick realized that it would be in my family's best interest if he became Ernesto's Big Brother too. Sure enough, soon after he was taking us both to the zoo, the museums, the park, anywhere we wanted to go. He did his best to teach us everything he knew about life, about health, and about proper English, and every once in a while he would sneak in a lecture or two. He helped us out financially by paying for us whenever we went out.

Wanting the best for us, Patrick helped my mom move us to a better neighborhood and to better schools. Our old neighborhood schools were full of gangs and drugs, and Patrick strived to help us avoid their influence and obtain a good education. He helped both Ernesto and me enroll in magnet school programs, where we developed our own love of education and started getting good grades.

Knowing very little English, my mom needed help at parent-teacher nights. Patrick did his best to accompany my mom to every single one of them. During high school, Ernesto and I could look forward to seeing Patrick at almost every football game and wrestling match we had. Win or lose, Patrick would greet us afterward with a thumbs up.

Our formal Big Brothers relationship with Patrick ended when we each graduated from high school. But even without the formal commitment, Patrick still managed to take the time to push us to get into the best college possible. I am currently in my fourth year of college with a major in electrical engineering. Ernesto is a freshman pursuing a career in international business, with Japanese as a third language after Spanish. After completing his first independent film, *Borough of Kings*, Patrick has moved on to producing as well as directing movies.

I have learned some wonderful life lessons from my Big Brother. He has taught me to be sincere and respectful of other people. He has taught me how much first impressions count and to have a strong work ethic. The things Patrick has taught us are not superficial things like how to have machismo. His lessons are bigger and more important than that. He has taught us how to achieve our goals in life and in our careers. My mom brought us to

America to give us a future, and Patrick's influence has shown us how bright those futures are.

The most valuable thing I cherish from this ongoing relationship is that, no matter how bad things seem at times, I know Patrick will always be there to point us in the right direction and give my mom a helping hand. Before Patrick, I had no idea what it would be like to have a male role model. Now that we have him in our lives, my mom, Ernesto, and I have no idea how we would live without him.

By Manuel Carrasco

The Little with Big Dreams

Big Brother Silvio Proano and Little Brother Ty Eiland

Growing up in Westchester County, New York, was an adventure, first because of the challenges that would present themselves, and second because of the victories that would supersede the pain of being an abandoned child. My mom was young and single. Not knowing the identity of my father was a major struggle for daily affirmation and social acceptance.

As I grew older, I withdrew from family members, classmates, and teachers. I felt I was a victim of circumstance. Often I would not speak in public because of a stuttering problem. My speech impairment only worsened my already low self-esteem and negative self-image. My mother applied to a program she heard of that mentored young minorities. I was only ten or eleven at the time, and the only thing I remember was going to a party at Pace University and waiting to meet my new Big Brother.

Silvio Proano walked up to me and greeted me with a firm handshake and a warm smile. Having little interaction with male figures, I honestly did not know how to handle that type of attention. As time went on, Silvio became one of the most influential people in my life. He allowed me into his world more than most would expect.

I often wondered why this recently divorced man with no children would spend so much time with a kid like me. I can recall him coming to my school to pick me up—just to spend quality time with me before he had to make his business trips for IBM. Silvio would often allow me to plan our outings, giving me some freedom to dream and explore things on my own terms. Silvio inspired my interest in higher education through his actions, not merely his words.

We went to four major universities on tours before I was even able to apply for college. The funniest trip was our excursion to West Point Academy in New York. On our way to the campus, Silvio and I were listening to Muddy Waters (his favorite artist), and he was speeding. He was pulled over by the local authorities, who let him go with only a warning, mainly because of his truthfulness and sincerity. Instead of being upset and disgruntled, he showed, by example, how a man handles serious situations with poise and ease.

At West Point, I recall sitting in the chapel, seriously talking about God and how much I wanted to do good in my life and make him and my mother proud. He told me to stay true to my beliefs, whatever they may be, and never let my circumstances dictate my future.

On our trip to Yale University, I became interested in going to college away from home to pursue the field of architecture. As we walked through the halls of this beautiful institute of higher learning, Silvio spoke about the buildings and what he loved about them. His talk inspired my hobby of photographing buildings.

Most of my time with Silvio was spent learning about various things in his life that I would later mimic as an adult. From choosing the proper suit for interviews and meetings, to picking quality watches and learning the skills of dining etiquette, Silvio gave me a head start on the tools of adulthood that I now pass on to my peers.

Silvio gave me a sense of belonging and unconditional love. He often spoke words of encouragement and prayed for my successes. He was very candid about his personal life and clearly expressed his expectations of me as a maturing youth. He taught me to accept responsibility for my actions. I took his instructions and suggestions to heart and began to apply those things to my everyday life. I soon became a strong voice in my community and was invited to serve on both national and international boards for agencies such as the United Way and the American Red Cross.

Silvio moved away for business reasons, and I lost contact with him my last two years in high school. Though visibly absent, his virtue was a constant mirror of what I was to do and how I would accomplish the tasks at hand. I applied to twenty-two colleges and universities to study architecture. Nineteen of them accepted me. I attended Howard University in Washington, D.C., and completed an MBA degree program in the United Kingdom.

Throughout my academic tenure, the drive I saw in Silvio became my push toward professional success. From interning with then Secretary Madeleine Albright at the U.S. Department of State to interning at the Allstate Insurance Headquarters in suburban Chicago, I saw his spirit imparted in the things I did as a way of respecting the impact he made in my adolescence.

Soon I will begin a special doctoral program in international development with a major emphasis in Middle Eastern and African affairs. My life has really paralleled Silvio's in that I travel internationally to countries like the Czech Republic and the United Kingdom, and the Middle East. I adopted his interest in business, and I have been named the international chair for a special campaign that will seek to raise $10 million dollars to help Ethiopian children beginning in 2004.

Although I lost touch with Silvio for a few years, we later reconnected. Silvio and I still speak at least once every few weeks, and I am often caught telling stories of my Big Brother and how great an influence he was on me. At twenty-six, I still aspire to achieve and succeed and be like my Big Brother.

Silvio now has a new wife and two young children who mean as much to me as he does. I consider them family because they are an extension of someone who considers me his family.

One of Silvio's dreams is to own a BMW. My plan is to make his wish a reality so he can say that his Little Brother made his dreams come true, like he did for me.

By Ty Le'Var Eiland

Caring from the Heart

Big Sister Nancy Meister Doty and Little Sister Brenda Clark

I first met my Big Sister on June 3, 1970. My grandmother Shirley took my three older sisters and me to her church that evening to meet our own Big Sisters. The church basement was decorated like a big birthday party. This had extra special meaning for me because it really was my birthday. It was my sixth birthday and one that I'll always remember.

The room was filled with lots of woman and excited young girls like me. I still recall the ice cream sundae that I ate with my new Big Sister Nancy. She told me how extra special I was at the table because it was my birthday.

What I didn't know then was that I would still have my Big Sister in my life thirty-three years later to share things with and grow old together.

I was born the youngest of four girls and was being raised by a single father. My parents were divorced at a young age. When I met my Big Sister, I was too young to realize what having a Big Sister really meant.

My older sisters were then eleven, ten, and eight. Their relationships with their Big Sisters did not last as long as mine, but this was due to various life events. Some matches evolve with marriage, family, and career changes, and others do not. Either way, the impact that a Big Sister makes can last years—even a lifetime.

My match with Nancy opened a new world for me. She introduced me to her family and showed me what true family values were. I still fondly refer to her parents as Aunt Lill and Uncle Joe. We shared many great conversations on trips to visit them, and we would attend church on Sunday. Nancy adored me, and she always let me know she was there for me.

When I was ten, Nancy enrolled me in charm school. There I learned proper manners and how to carry myself as a young lady. Nancy knew what I needed, and I always admired and aspired to be like her.

Nancy's husband-to-be, Art Doty, took my charm school graduation photo. That photo represents my transition from a tomboy to a little lady and makes me smile every time I see it.

Even after her marriage, Nancy continued to make me a part of her life. She was essential to my growth as a teenager when I was learning about independence and responsibility.

Her own career was inspiring to me because she worked hard but had always taken a few hours a week to spend with me, even if it was just a trip to McDonald's or a movie at home. She had taken me to work with her on career day. Now they call it Bring Your Daughter to Work Day, but I'd much prefer Bring Your Little Sister (or Brother) to Work Day!

It was very reassuring to know that Nancy would never give up on me. I was included in her family vacations and was always excited to go camping and skiing.

My father was not always able to afford vacations, but he was always thankful for my Big Sister and for her involvement with me. My father, Nancy and Art are good friends. My father and Nancy are the two most important people in my life.

At the age of eighteen, I moved to Florida. There were sometimes long periods of time when we didn't always call or write, but whenever we did, it was so easy to catch up on lost time. In my mind and in my heart, Nancy has always cared about me and given me advice when asked.

Every visit to Michigan always included a visit with Nancy and Art. It was always a special vacation from Florida when I could also visit with Aunt Lill and Uncle Joe. I still have the pink elephant piggy bank that they bought for me at the Detroit Zoo when I was a little girl. Her parents are elderly now, and the time I get to visit with them is even more important with each passing year.

My life has been forever changed as a result of my relationship and match with this wonderful lady. She always remembers my birthday and brings a smile to my face with her Valentine, Halloween, and Christmas card greetings and packages. She's been my role model and helped me become the woman that I am today.

I now live in San Francisco where I am a successful, single, career woman. I have been working in the hospital industry for the last fifteen years and now work for one of the top ten hospitals in the country. My career and profession are very important achievements in my life, but I feel that I am the confident and strong person I am today because of my Big Sister.

As a tribute to Nancy, I've recently applied to the local chapter in San Francisco to become a Big Sister. I know there is a young girl who will benefit from all that I have learned about the bond of friendship and true caring from the heart.

By Brenda Clark

Service Before Self

Big Brother Brian Bednar and Little Brother Peter Grossenbach

When I was nine, my mom, my brother, and I moved to Arizona from Florida without my dad. I was lonely, scared, and sad. I had some pretty tough transition issues, as I had a hard time fitting into school, received poor grades, and even had my arm broken by bullies. As I look back, I don't remember life being fun and carefree like most kids my age. I guess I needed more than what my mom could offer at the time but didn't know what that really meant or how to fill the void that left me feeling hopeless.

Fortunately, my mom recognized my struggles and enrolled my brother Dan and me in the Big Brothers Big Sisters program. I could never have known then what a difference it would make in my life. I just knew I wanted a cool guy to hang out and do fun stuff with. Any guy would do as long as we went camping, played some sports, and hung out.

As it turned out, I got more than just any guy as my Big Brother, and we experienced a friendship much bigger than just two guys hanging out. Since 1989 I have been a part of my Big Brother Brian's life, and he has been a central part of my life, and my brother's and my mom's lives also. When Brian married, I was one of his groomsmen, and, when I graduated from high school and the Air Force Academy, Brian was there. Both of my parents (each of whom had remarried) were also there, and it was a lifetime dream to have realized my personal goal with the most important people in my life present.

I look back now as a twenty-two-year-old Air Force pilot, and I can say that every aspect of my life was affected by Brian—from digging out of that original gloom where grades meant nothing to me to becoming the Spanish Honor Society president and the senior class treasurer. In our everyday activities, from carving pumpkins to camping, fishing, and running marathons, Brian taught me the impact of personal sacrifice and service as well as to believe in long-term friendships.

The biggest effect Brian and Big Brothers Big Sisters had on my life was to literally chart my future career path. Brian and I attended an agency-sponsored event at Luke Air Force Base. When I sat in the seat of a jet simulator, I knew immediately that one day I would be a pilot for the U.S. Air Force. And here I am—an Air Force pilot!

It's amazing how many thousands of hours Brian has spent with me and my family. He never once made me feel like a burden or an obligation. In fact, Brian has always treated me like his best friend and has always made me feel like he is constantly thinking of me. Even when we had weekly outings already planned, Brian would call during the week just to say hi.

He always encouraged me to do good things and make the right choices. Through his friendship, I learned early on what the Air Force Core Values expect of me today: *Integrity first, service before self, and excellence in all you do.* I could not have been better prepared for military service than to have lived the value system Brian made my own.

How could I repay such a dear friend for making that commitment fifteen years ago? Hopefully, along the way Brian has seen my successes as a direct response to his influence. I now fully realize the importance of giving back, and I look forward to becoming a Big Brother myself.

Time will allow Brian and me to continue growing in our friendship and, perhaps, one day I will be the one whom Brian can lean on for advice, compassion, and strength. In the next fifteen years, I intend to make Brian proud of me as I become a man, a husband, and a father who cares deeply for others and puts service before self.

Thank you Brian for seeing me through my growing years, for sending me off into adulthood ready for challenges, and for preparing me to give of myself to improve the lives of others. I am eternally grateful.

By Peter Grossenbach as told to Denice Riffey

The Road to Success

Big Brother Ron Butler and Little Brother Sashe Dimitroff

In 1970 my mother and I emigrated from Yugoslavia to the United States. We spoke little English, had little money, and had no family support other than each other. We lived in a poor neighborhood in Flint, Michigan, where there was a high crime rate. To put it in perspective, the police regularly searched my junior high school for weapons. I remember walking home from school using a different route because my friends and I had been mugged so many times. When I tried to defend myself, I was twice suspended from school for fighting.

Understanding the value of an education and strong role models, my mother enrolled herself in college and me in the Big Brothers Big Sisters program. Ron Butler, my Big Brother, was a young man with a family of his own and an active career as a banker. He volunteered to be a Big Brother and took a genuine interest in my welfare. We got together about once a week. Sometimes we would go to a movie or a ballgame, and other times we would just talk. There were no great speeches, no life lessons. Rather, in the few hours we spent together each week, Ron simply gave me his friendship. He also gave me perspective by showing me that the poverty I saw around me, the fights, and the drugs did not have to be part of my future.

Ron's companionship gave me a great foundation when I was a teenager. We had a lot of firsts together; for example, he gave me my first talk about girls. Ron's family had a very pretty neighbor who was about my age. She came over to talk when I went to Ron's house. I remember trying to muster up all of my thirteen-year-old coolness to find the right thing to say. Like every other thirteen year old, I felt awkward rather than cool. My most vivid memory is that while I was posturing, all I could think was "why did you say *that*?" She was gracious; I was mortified.

To his credit, Ron watched from the porch and mercifully did not utter a word. After she left, he told me that I was cool when I was myself. He said girls felt as awkward and insecure as boys (which was news to me) and that treating them with kindness and having fun, just like with other friends, was all the coolness needed. It took several more years for that lesson to sink in, but I will give the same advice to my sons when they are old enough.

As I grew up, Big Brothers Big Sisters would visit every few months to see how my mother and I were doing. Over the years, the agency gave me several bicycles because my mother could not afford to buy one. She was a proud woman who refused to take welfare, despite the fact that in the mid-1970s her monthly paychecks from her two jobs were only about $100 more than the rent. Big Brothers had to give me several bikes because crime was so bad in our neighborhood that five of them were stolen. The current CEO tells me that while the agency still gives out bikes, it now also provides locks and helmets.

Big Brothers was a great influence at a critical time in my life. About a decade later, I graduated from the University of Texas with a degree in finance and then moved to New York to work on Wall Street for Merrill

Lynch. In 1988 I returned to Texas, enrolled at the University of Houston, and graduated magna cum laude with a law degree and an MBA. Today, I am a partner at a major law firm. I have been married for seventeen years to a wonderful woman who is the love of my life, and we have three beautiful children. I am an active member of the board of directors of Big Brothers Big Sisters here in Houston.

I have been somewhat introspective about my life lately. I think we all receive different gifts, but it sometimes takes us a while to recognize them and even longer to appreciate them. The other day, I was watching my oldest son's Little League game. The mother of one of the other boys learned that I was from Yugoslavia and that I am a lawyer. She asked me if I thought it was difficult for people to succeed in America. My gut reaction was "Yes, of course it is." She then asked how I think it happens—is it luck, do you have to be really smart, do you have to work hard, or do you just have to be born into the right family? I realized there is no easy answer; success is very different for everyone. Even defining success is hard. For me, it takes several forms.

It is a success that we broke away from poverty and violence—but I didn't do that by myself. That success is due to my mother's foresight to leave Yugoslavia because we had no future there, to come to the United States, and to understand the value of an education. My success is due to the constant help we received from Big Brothers Big Sisters. And in an intangible yet invaluable form, success came from the everyday common sense and good judgment I received from my day-to-day interaction with my Big Brother Ron.

It is a success that I received a good education—but that was also not due solely to me. I worked several jobs in college, but I also played sports, performed in theater, and was a member of a fraternity. It was a time of trial and error (I went through six majors in five years), and I got a lot of second chances from my family, professors, and friends. Importantly, I had the opportunity to discover who I was, what I believed, and the fact that choosing a career that would make me happy was more important than choosing one that would make everyone else happy.

It is a success that I have a wonderful family—but that, most of all, is largely due to others, not me. For seventeen years, my wife loved me even when I was not the easiest person to live with, when I had to spend more time at work than at home, and when I often needed her shoulder more than she needed mine.

Success is not easy—it takes hard work, it takes persistence, and, in the best of all circumstances, it takes relationships. That's my conclusion—that life is all about relationships—the ones that you form and the ones that form you. I feel strongly that Big Brothers Big Sisters helped me personally by giving me tremendous direction and the first, yet most important, tools for a productive future. I wouldn't be here enjoying the blessings of a wonderful family, career, and life without Ron Butler and Big Brothers Big Sisters, and for that I will always be grateful.

By Sashe Dimitroff

A Beautiful World

Big Brother Congressman Adam Schiff and Little Brother David McMillan

Sometimes it is the quality of our dreams that pulls others to us.

For Adam Schiff, a Harvard law school grad new to Los Angeles, the dreams of a small boy reached right off an aging page to grab him. They were the words of five-year-old David McMillan on an application asking what he would want if he had three wishes. His mother had put words to paper for him: "A Big Brother. A puppy. A beautiful world."

"I was struck by any five-year-old child who would use one of his three precious wishes on something as philosophical as a beautiful world," said Adam, now a congressman from California who splits his time between the West Coast and the nation's capital. "I would have gone for the skateboard or the train set, never a beautiful world."

It was that wish that convinced Adam he had to meet David, who had been waiting for a Big Brother for nearly two years. Then, as now, there is often a shortage of men volunteering to be Big Brothers.

"The agency had told me that at that time, kids were facing a two-year wait for Big Brothers, and they asked me how I'd feel about having an African American Little

Brother because for minority Littles, the wait was four years," Adam recalls.

"I told them I thought it would be a wonderful idea. I'd learn more from the experience that way. The next thing I knew, they gave me three Little Brother applications and launched into a four-hour interview about my entire life."

After he was paired up with David, they went off to Venice Beach on their first outing. David was seven years old. "We went out into the surf and it was really cold." It was so cold that, then and there, they decided to dub themselves "the survivors."

"And we're still the survivors today. Our relationship goes on, and when we talk about being Brothers, it is not in the past tense." The day their match was supposed to be formally closed, when David reached eighteen, they got a call from the caseworker. Neither wanted the file closed. "We put off coming in time after time after time, and finally we didn't get calls anymore. We still consider ourselves an open match."

It's been quite a road: seeing David through his degree from Yale in history and English and then on to film school at USC, and for Adam the path to Congress, with David serving as the narrator on a commercial for him in his first campaign in 2000. Adam, a Democrat, represents California's Twenty-ninth Congressional District. He has focused his legislative attention on strengthening communities, national security, and introducing a kids-first agenda of initiatives to improve education, safety, and health care for kids.

David was being raised by his mother and was very close to his aunts and grandmother when the pair first met. The family wanted a man's influence in his life.

Adam recalls that they'd always talk about current events, movies, and music. David loved to razz Adam for his taste in music. Such old-fashioned choices, David would say of Billy Joel and Steely Dan. Now Adam chuckles, saying that when David listens to today's pop music he "doesn't get it either."

But it wasn't the music part of their relationship that stuck; it was the movies. "Lunch or dinner and the movies were our favorite times out. We saw just about everything—animated movies in the beginning, then everything. We only walked out of one, and David never let me forget that it was a movie I'd picked."

Sometimes it's those little moments that really make all the magic. David was active in drama classes through school and always interested in movies and theater. And now, after film school, he's working in the film industry.

It wasn't a straight shot to the top. Once Adam got tickets to the Emmys in L.A. and was all excited to take his Little. "That's how I discovered that there are two Emmys: national and local," Adam recalls of the night of the rude awakening. They were really excited about going to the Emmys and dressed for the occasion, in black tie. But right from the start something seemed odd. The front of the auditorium was relatively empty, and the pair scooted up and sat right up front. The MC "was some local unknown talent. We were wondering what was going on." It became clear soon enough: the front rows were empty at the no-big-deal local awards because once each winner collected an award, he or she (and family) promptly departed! No one wanted to sit up front and be seen leaving so soon. At the earliest possible opportunity, David and Adam scooted out too—off to take in another movie.

Looking back, Adam recalls the moment in 1986 when he first got involved. His friend, a Big Brother, had shared how much he enjoyed his experience. This inspired Adam to make a real difference in someone's life, "not something intangible and abstract, but a very real participation." And that is indeed what he found.

Adam shares his favorite joke about David. "People are always asking me how he would have grown up without my influence. He was always a unique spirit, a very bright, precocious kid. Impressive. Without my influence, would he have gone to Yale? That's simple. But for my influence, he would have gone to Harvard!"

And what's David's funniest story about Adam? "Many years ago, Adam called me and my mom up and told us he had some exciting news, but that he wanted to tell us in person. We assumed this meant he and Eve had finally gotten engaged. The next evening, Adam came over, face beaming. Mom and I were full of anticipation; we both sensed this was going to be a very special moment. 'You'll never believe it,' he said, full of pride. 'But I just got a job assignment in Czechoslovakia !' Needless to say, we were happy for Adam, but it certainly wasn't the news we were expecting. And we all had to wait a few more years before Adam *finally* popped the question."

Adam offers words of advice to anyone who wants to become a Big. "It will be the best thing you ever do. Unlike a lot of other wonderful causes out there, on this one you get to see the tangible difference that you make every day. You get as much or more out of it than the Little."

Now, living a bicoastal life that splits his time between his constituents in California and his work in Washington, Adam is still making a real difference—in Congress and as a national board member of Big Brothers Big Sisters.

It's not too far from the dreams of a little boy who sought a Big Brother he could join in making a beautiful world.

By Robin Palley

Words from a Little

Big Brother Josh Young and Little Brother Darius Murray

I come from a family of five women—mom and four sisters. My dad passed away before I was born, and the neighborhood we live in can be pretty tough.

I used to be what they call a bad kid. I would get up and walk out of the classroom in the middle of class; I got into fights with other kids; I didn't do well in school at all. I didn't care. The teachers and principal tried to get my mom to change me, but it didn't work. I remember her begging me to change, but I didn't. Then, all of a sudden, I found myself in an alternative school; an alternative school is your last chance before being expelled from the public school system. If you had met me then, you would have known I was definitely headed for trouble.

While I was in alternative school, my mom enrolled me in Big Brothers Big Sisters. I remember wanting a Big Brother, but I also remember waiting a long time. I know now it is because there are so many kids waiting for a Big, but, back then, I swear I thought they had forgotten me.

Then I met my Big Brother Josh. Josh took me out to do all kinds of fun things. I think the first thing we did together was go bowling, and there have been many firsts since then. I don't believe I have been bored since; Josh won't let me be.

My Big Brother opened up a whole new world for me—one that I would have never had the opportunity to experience otherwise. One of the most valuable lessons he has taught me is to appreciate the opportunity to learn new things, and, in a place like Miami with all its diversity, it's a great skill to have.

I'm not the same person today as I was when I went to the alternative school. The opportunities I have had through Josh and Big Brothers Big Sisters have shaped who I am today and who I will be tomorrow. Somewhere along the way, I've learned to take those opportunities and really make things happen.

I graduated from that alternative school with the honor of Outstanding Student of the Year and went on to attend regular high school. Since then, and thanks to Big Brothers Big Sisters' science program, known as Tripod, I now attend Coral Park High School's magnet robotics program. I love engineering, but I've also learned that I love animals and biology. I volunteer my time at the Museum of Science every Saturday, where I work with kids in the Wildlife Center. Not only have I learned a lot about animals, but I am also learning a lot about people, and I love that.

My Big Brother would proudly tell you I recently won the President's Service Award for volunteerism, but I don't know if that's really true, since Josh has my award hanging in *his* office, and I've really never seen it myself. It means a lot that he's so proud of me. Because of my great experience volunteering at the Wildlife Center, I am thinking about majoring in veterinary science when I attend college next year.

I know in my heart that I would not be the same person writing this if it weren't for Josh and Big Brothers Big Sisters. The same is true for so many thousands of other kids. I don't believe you can change a person, but I do believe you can influence that person to want to make a change. This program had that influence on me; it gave me a lot of great opportunities and experiences to help me change.

I can't tell you how different my life is from that of some of my friends. I've been able to do things they haven't, and I've learned things they may never learn—all because of Josh and Big Brothers Big Sisters.

When we started the program seven years ago, they gave us the titles of Big Brother and Little Brother. Today I think we are really best friends, and ten years from now I know we will be family.

I don't believe there are bad kids, just kids with potential who need opportunities. No organization believes more in the potential of children than Big Brothers Big Sisters. This program has permanently changed my life, and if every kid who wanted a Big Brother or Big Sister could get one, America would be a much better place. On behalf of all those kids with potential, thanks for giving us opportunities, and thanks for making a difference.

By Darius Murray

Chapter 2

Magical Moments

My TV Star

Big Brother Matt Lauer and Little Brother Todd Kulaga

No matter what the circumstances, being matched with a Big Brother is an exciting experience for any ten-year-old boy. Imagine how much more interesting it all turns out to be when your Big Brother also happens to be a local television personality. All in all, it is pretty thrilling stuff!

That's what happened to me twenty-one years ago. I was living a nice life in Providence, Rhode Island, when tragedy struck. My dad died when I was only seven, and, eventually, my mom, a great single parent, thought I needed someone else in my life. Even though we had a solid family structure with my wonderful older sister and many local relatives to help out, she believed I needed more. It's not unlike many other Big Brother stories you hear, but mine had an interesting twist.

My first and only Big Brother was a guy named Matt Lauer, who at the time was cohost of a local daily TV show called *P.M. Magazine*. It was typically cohosted by two good-looking, energetic TV personalities, one male and one female. Of course, most of you know that Matt now cohosts, along with Katie Couric, NBC's *Today Show*.

As a ten-year-old who didn't watch much of *P.M. Magazine*, I wasn't impressed with Matt's celebrity in

Providence. If he had been a Boston Red Sox or New England Patriots star, it would have been a different story!

From the start, Matt and I shared many interests, especially the Red Sox, and Patriots. We were two sports nuts. I still remember the day we first met at a local ice cream parlor. My mom was especially happy that Matt chose me because his TV career helped lessen her fears from a security standpoint. At that time, Matt was twenty-three years old, so he really was like a big brother age-wise.

We got together every week; sometimes Matt would pick me up several times during the week. I'd go to a TV shoot at a local park or get to watch as Matt interviewed someone. I even got to be on the show a lot—as a stand-in or whatever they needed me to be. I didn't do any major acting, but, for Providence, I was pretty famous as a child. I even did two public service commercials for the local Big Brothers organization.

Matt was married, had a great life with plenty of income, and did exciting things. People in Providence recognized us everywhere we went together.

When Matt landed a new job in Boston three years into our match, the arrangement had to slow down considerably. I was getting to the age where girls started to be of interest, but Matt stayed in contact even though it was getting harder for him. He came to Providence when he could to catch a game of mine.

We eventually lost touch when Matt got a new job. As far as I knew, he disappeared from the New England area. Six years ago, around the time Matt began the *Today Show,* we briefly reconnected and spoke on the phone.

That brings me to another good story that came out of our shared history. Last year, I got a call from the *Today Show* producers. They were planning a *This Is Your Life*-

type reunion show for the cast and wanted me to appear as a surprise guest from Matt's past. My wife Erin and I didn't hesitate to make the journey to New York City.

When we arrived, we got the real star treatment. Matt and I had only spoken by phone that one time, and my big thing was I never wanted him to think that I was star-hunting, so I always kept my distance.

When I came from backstage at the *Today Show* reunion, I think Matt was stunned to see how his skinny Little Brother had become a 6-2, 240-pound bodybuilder.

Matt said, "I guess the days of picking on you are over."

"Yes, they are," I responded as the audience laughed and applauded.

When I think back, I always admired Matt's energy. He was always outgoing, always happy. I never remember seeing him upset—ever. He was under control, which was the right type of personality for being a Big Brother (though my wife will tell you I didn't turn out that way). Nevertheless, Matt had a special impact on me, one I will never forget.

Perhaps Matt's most awkward moment as my Big Brother came when my mom insisted he instruct me about the birds and the bees. I know it was more uncomfortable for him than it was for me.

The fact that Matt originally took the time is still amazing to me. Here he was, a local celebrity, someone who had everything in the world going for him. He didn't have to spend time with a kid like me. But he did.

As far as I'm concerned, he's one of the nicest guys around. He really is. I wasn't part of any hard-luck, down-and-out story. But it certainly was nice to grow up having Matt as my Big Brother.

By Todd Kulaga as told to Tom Starner

Big Impact

Big Brother John Wells and Little Brother Loren Sargent

When John Wells, executive producer of the mega-hits NBC dramas *ER* and *West Wing,* decided to call Big Brothers of Greater Los Angeles seven years ago, he knew something was missing from his life. Even though he was putting in sixty to eighty hours a week, he still had Saturday afternoons free. While John felt very lucky about his accomplishments, which also include writing and producing the critically acclaimed ABC series *China Beach*, he wanted to give something back to the community in a personal way, not just by writing checks.

John wanted to give something back because he understands the value of one-to-one friendships. Back in college, one of John's professors, Fred Yeouns, took the time to give John some much needed attention. "I was pretty confused about what I wanted to do, and Fred took the time to look at me specifically and individually in what I was good at. He encouraged me in very specific ways that made a huge difference in my life because I wasn't seeing myself the way he did. When somebody sees you and shows up like that, you start to say to yourself, 'I must be worthwhile.'"

John got matched with LA, a nickname for Loren, when

LA was seven years old. LA's father had died of AIDS when he was five, and later his uncle also died of AIDS. Most of the male figures in LA's life slipped away, and his mother Dorothea began noticing behavior problems in LA, especially at school.

"Before John, I had a really bad reputation. I was always starting trouble. But recently I've pulled it together, and I'm on the high honor roll at school. I'm on the student council, and I've won two awards for my artwork. I am a leader in my class."

Now a freshman in high school, LA's future goals include going to college and becoming an actor. He has already taken several acting classes.

John didn't realize how different the Big Brothers experience would be from what he had imagined. "It's completely different than I thought it would be. I thought we'd be flying a kite with my hand on his shoulder. I was also afraid that I would fail or that he would be unmanageable—none of which has been the case. It's been much simpler than that."

It took John about a year to realize that just showing up was the most important thing. "I had in my own head an agenda of stuff to do and ways to make it all work, but I kept getting a little disappointed in that it didn't seem to make much difference to him if we were doing something that I thought was going to be special or not. After about a year, I realized his attitude changed toward me, not because of anything special we did, but because he started to believe that I was going to keep showing up. It was just the consistency." After awhile, John realized that on the occasional weeks when he didn't see LA, "I was amazed by how little I would actually accomplish on a Saturday afternoon."

John believes being a Big Brother helps create a much

needed connection in society. "The collective responsibility of men raising boys is increasingly missing in our culture, much to our great loss as a society. I think there's a lack of connection we all feel in the modern world. Some of that has to do with the dissolution of the nuclear family and the fact that people's families are spread out all over the country. Becoming a Big Brother creates that extended family. It's very much like we're family. We get involved in birthdays and Christmas, and I'm a better person for it."

For LA, John is "like a part of my family. Even when he's away he always calls or sends postcards."

John advises other men not to look at being a Big Brother as any type of burden. "I've found it easy and have made certain things a habit. Of all the things I do in my life, I get the most back for putting in the least amount of time. It's some of the most relaxing time I have, given the amount of time I work. It's like my planned recreation. It keeps me from being in the office on Saturdays, and it's not like anyone is going to say that I don't have my priorities straight."

The relationship has had a big impact on John. "It's changed me profoundly. In watching LA grow up, I feel like I've grown a lot and now have a different view of what it is to be a man. It has forced me to look at my responsibilities as an adult. I think it's hard for men to figure out what their identity is. I see little things that LA has gotten from me, like gestures and speech patterns. In some ways, I feel like I've gotten a parenting class without having to be a parent. I've learned a lot about myself and setting boundaries. I've also learned the most important ingredient in a family—constant love and approval. And at the same time, I've learned that there have to be standards and requirements."

For LA's mom Dorothea, the relationship has been a

blessing. "What a wonderful relationship to be part of and watch," she says. "I can't imagine LA's life without John."

Certainly, being the Little Brother of a Hollywood producer has its perks. LA has had a guest role on *ER* and has been to the Screen Actors' Guild Awards. But John and LA mostly do everyday activities, like going to the movies, running errands, and just talking. For John, being with LA is like "watching a tree grow. You don't notice the difference day to day, but over time you notice a substantial change."

John encourages other men to become Big Brothers because of how rewarding it is. "Having a car and a house and earning a living is all nice, but it's not all that fulfilling. You can't have a relationship with your car. There's something more to be had from life; being a Big Brother is one of those things that make life worth living."

LA and John have made a Big Impact on each other's lives.

By Richard S. Greif

Editor's note: This was previously printed in Richard Greif's book Big Impact: Big Brothers Making a Difference. *© 1997 available at Amazon.com.*

LA, who is now twenty years old, has decided to take a few years off and work in the film industry before attending college. He and John remain friends despite John's very hectic work schedule as the executive producer of the television shows West Wing *and* ER *and multiple other projects.*

Beautiful Colors

Big Sister Dorothy Flynn and Little Sister Jossette Kelly

I was eight years old when I was introduced to my Big Sister Dorothy Flynn in 1975. I am now thirty-four years old, a wife, a mother to four beautiful children, and a pediatric nurse residing in Kissimmee, Florida. The memories I have about my special relationship with Dorothy are as fresh today as they were during the eight years my Big Sister was a part of my daily life.

When Dorothy and I first met, she was in her mid-twenties, a stage in life when you find yourself racing toward an established career goal—or away from home. It is the time when you try to figure out who you are, what you would like to become, and what kind of influence you might have on society. I call it the self-made stage of life and attitude, where you are self-reliant, self-centered, self-conscious, and self-assured.

Dorothy was working for the Big Sisters Association when she decided to become a mentor. She was attending Boston University and then went to MIT for her master's degree. She became a Big Sister to me, an eight-year-old inner-city girl whose single, divorced mom was working full-time and going to school full-time, earning a master's degree from Boston State College and Lesley College.

My Big had an exceptional, unconditional love for me regardless of what I did or said. I look back at some of the questions I asked then and the way she gracefully handled them. I remember that I wanted a black Big Sister, one just like my sister Yvette. It was difficult for me, as a young black girl with a white Big Sister, to handle the glances and unspoken stares of people on the street or bus.

Even back then, Dorothy was blessed with a unique gift to see the world in beautiful colors; she had an artist's eye. I believe that's why her hobby was photography; everywhere we traveled, Dorothy's camera went with us, and, to be honest, every picture she took mirrored her views on life. They were beautiful pictures of everything and everyone. I learned from Dorothy that being black was a beauty, joy, strength, and secret cup of gladness.

Dorothy shared the world with me. Together, we set out on many adventures—from campaigning for the Democratic Party to watching performances of the ballet and the Boston Pops at Symphony Hall, whale-watching at Cape Cod, and learning how rock candy is made on Martha's Vineyard. Together we drove to New York for the West Indian Carnival, took in outdoor concerts in the Boston Common, went to see Broadway plays, marched with the Rainbow Coalition, and went to the Museum of Science, the Franklin Park Zoo, and the New England Aquarium.

Dorothy was an impressionable, blessed assurance that was placed in my life at the right time. Her adventure for life, I know, was a positive influence that led me to join the Army. Dorothy gave me a thirst and hunger for life, and she let me borrow her rose-colored glasses indefinitely. My mother's stress at being a single parent and provider, and her desire to achieve all she was capable of, were greatly eased knowing that her daughter was loved by someone as wonderful as Dorothy.

Dorothy may not be blood-related, but she will always be a member of my family, my Big Sister, and for that I am forever grateful to the Big Sisters Association of Greater Boston. May this organization continue to influence and change the lives of young girls and color their world with beauty and love.

By Jossette Kelly

Ray, Me, and Fee

Big Brother Robert Drozda and Little Brother Raymund Hawley

Unpacking a sack of Santa Claus proportions, my Little Brother Raymund, his eyes sparkling, states matter-of-factly, "I brought plenty to do." We have just returned from watching a college hockey game, and already it is 11 P.M. Six months into our match, this is our first overnighter.

As midnight nears, Ray is not thinking about bedtime; he's unpacking. A book on Jupiter; another on animals; children's magazines with games, puzzles, riddles, and short stories are among the treasures he has brought to share. I'm starting to get the impression that this nine year old thinks overnighter means all-nighter.

I had talked of becoming a Big Brother for years. As a youngster growing up with four older sisters, I desperately wanted a brother. As an adult, I still felt that void. My wife encouraged me to finally get involved. I was thirty-seven years old and thought less of being a role model than of simply having a young friend to pal around with.

On the day we were matched, Ray and I became instant friends; as he reached for my hand, he grabbed hold of my heart. I had no idea then that I would become not just a friend and mentor but truly a brother of the heart.

Raymund had his hidden side, his private side, his past.

I gently tried to help but often did not know what was going on inside of him. He was very shy and had significant fears. I tried to expose him to many different experiences. I became active with his school and teachers. He taught me to play the clarinet when I had never read music before. We hiked and swam, and he helped me garden and do household chores. But above all other activities, our relationship centered on dogs and dog mushing.

On our first outing I brought him to our house. I wanted him to see how and where I lived, to meet my wife Lenore, and to introduce him to the dogs. I was surprised to discover he was afraid of dogs. So I picked one especially friendly and gentle dog named Feebo to help break the ice. I put a harness on Fee, and we hooked him to a small plastic sled and hiked up the hill behind our house. Ray and I rode the sled downhill, with Fee excitedly running along.

Soon we began dog mushing, first sharing one sled as Ray learned how to handle it and the dogs. Later Ray would get his own sled and begin racing with our local Junior Mushing club. We took hundred-mile wilderness camping trips traveling from cabin to cabin. A major rite of passage for Ray occurred at age fifteen when he completed a two-day, 120-mile wilderness race.

One day early in our match, while running on our local trails, the dogs suddenly picked up their pace. A large cow moose was just ahead in the trail. The dogs were so excited that we could not hold them. We were running six dogs; three were pulling toward the moose, now just off the trail, while the other three were trying to pull down the trail past the huge animal.

We were caught between the cow on one side of the trail and her calf on the other. Quickly the cow turned and made a full charge at the dogs, stopping within inches of them. I could feel my heart beating in my chest as I unconsciously, protectively wrapped my arms around Raymund, who was standing on the sled runners in front of me.

The adult moose made a second charge, this time approaching from the rear; I could hear her snorting and feel her breath on the back of my neck. Ray looked up at me and, in what seemed like an unbelievably calm voice, said, "Robert, I'm scared."

I said, as calmly as I could, "I'm scared too, buddy." And then I screamed at my lead dogs to "get up, get up, HIKE, let's go!"

I turned to see the calf and mother moving away from us. We dropped the sled down a little bank and onto a lake and stopped. Now safe, we huddled together on the sled and tried to calm down. Ray asked me why I had pushed him against the handlebar, but I hadn't even been aware of it; it was an instinctive move, a protective shielding of him just as the mother moose was protecting her child.

The night of our first overnighter, Ray read aloud for nearly two hours. I interrupted occasionally, acting silly, illustrating stories, giving him the house rules. I was blurry eyed and sleepy, but I let him go on. He was so glowingly alive, a wonder-filled child.

"Let's brush our teeth, and you put on your pajamas." I said. "But I'm not tired," came the protest. "But I am; it's late; 1:30 A.M.," I replied.

We had no plumbing, so before bed we had to go outside. Raymund led with a flashlight and three dogs for security. He announced, "Robert, I'm not scared at all." I knew he was referring to his prior fear of darkness. Then he added, "I'm telling myself not to be scared." Hearing these words, I am warmed and I feel as if I am the one overcoming my fears.

Back in the cabin, I ask him where he wants to sleep.

"Wherever it is safer" is the reply.

"Well, upstairs is where the dogs like to sleep." There are four inside tonight.

Ray chooses to sleep upstairs, and I make up the couch for myself. When he's all tucked in, we stay up a bit longer talking. Mostly we talk about the dogs, and he hugs them and gets kisses from them in return. I find myself observing how tiny and fragile he seems and wonder how this feels from his perspective.

Finally, we say good night. A little while later, just before I turn off my reading light, I go upstairs to check on him. In the dim light I see his head propped up, and he's looking at me. "You all right?" I ask.

"I can't move Fee," he says.

Feebo has taken four-fifths of the bed. I am amused, and Ray seems only mildly distressed. With some effort on my part and much reluctance on Fee's, I move the dog. I start to leave, then stop, kneel down on the floor, and say, "I want to tell you something. It might embarrass you."

"What is it?"

And I say, "You are a wonderful boy. I'm so glad that you are here and happy and proud that you're my Little Brother." We hug and say good night.

Eventually, with the blessing of Ray's mother, my wife and I became his legal guardians, and he came to live in our house. Our relationship changed; I, by necessity, became more parental, but I always kept it in my mind to be a friend and brother first.

This past fall, with an air of confidence, Ray moved on to college. Real luggage has replaced the Santa Claus sack of old. But he still brought plenty to do and has learned a new meaning of an all-nighter.

By Robert Drozda

Our Common Language

Big Sister Arlene Schneider and Little Sister Becky Annacone

The written word has always been a very powerful bond in the match between my Little Sister Becky and me. The first phone call from the social worker seventeen years ago told me of a troubled child who was terribly smart, who loved language and escaped to books. There were other children waiting for matches, but this was the one for me, someone so steeped in books and words that I had become an editor.

We met in 1987, and things were awkward at first. Becky was much too smart to be won over easily, and gaining her trust was going to take work. Years of being rejected had taught her to protect herself from pain; I was warned that getting her to open up might take a while. She pushed at me, and I was hurt. But I was also stubborn, so I stayed. And then one day, as we were about to cross a street, she took my hand. I knew that I was in.

We were never an openly affectionate pair, and that sometimes set us apart from the other matches and worried me. But we developed a deep trust and understanding and began to take each other for granted in the best sense of the words.

We read together, wrote together, searched bookstores,

and later comic book stores, together. She wrote and illustrated books and made cards for me. We also made cookies, went to the movies, and relaxed on the beach. But words anchored us, in a fundamental way. Even on vacation in London, I found myself scouring comic book stores for her favorite issues.

We were the perfect nonathletic pair. It was all we could do to get through the annual bowl-a-thon without rolling down the gutter with the ball. But we were fearless in other ways, willing to ride every roller coaster at Great Adventure and, more importantly, to sit in the first and then the last cars. Over and over.

As our friendship grew, so did Becky's relationships with boys and girls her age. She met my friends, and I met hers. It was thrilling to see a child who had once been so alone be invited to sleepovers, perform with the flag team, and march across her high school stage to be inducted into the National Honor Society. She had to juggle to fit all the proms (and prom dates!) into her busy senior schedule.

I missed Becky's graduation from high school in 1995 because I was in another state with my father, who was dying. I will forever cherish the condolence note she sent. Could she ever know how much it meant to me to read these lines: "I'm sure that your father was very proud of you" and "I'll never forget you."

When Becky went to college in another state, we still kept in touch with letters. They were followed by a wonderful assortment of postcards from European capitals as she studied and then worked abroad for years. It was hard to believe that such a shy and withdrawn child had become so wonderfully continental. Clearly her love of language was not limited to English.

Our letters turned to e-mails after she returned to New Jersey and then moved again, this time to be with the man she loved.

Though our match had ended years before, Becky honored me by asking me to be a part of her wedding on October 19, 2001. The bride I saw that day was an amazing woman in every way—beautiful, funny, confident, warm, and giving. For those of us who had known her as a child, she was even more amazing. That once lonely child was surrounded by her many friends and the members of her family. And in her husband's family, she had found a whole new source of love and support.

The latest e-mails from Becky come with photos of the newest man in her life, her son Daniel, born October 27, 2003. She has again allowed me to be a part of her exciting life, and I am happy to be a "grand-big."

The most important gift I ever gave Becky, at least in my eyes, is a gift of words, the letter I wrote to her before she went off to college. I am never quite sure what lessons I may have taught her, but I am certain of some of the gifts she gave me. As I told her then:

"You've taught me some very big lessons—about love, about strength of character, about dedication, and about myself. I was so afraid when we first met that you would reject me, that I would fail. But you helped me overcome my fears when you let me into your life."

I hope I have done the same for her.

By Arlene Schneider

My Little Brother Pete

Big Brother George Wood and Little Brother Pete Soriano

Since 1968 I have been a Big Brother to five boys, and I am approaching ten years in my match with my current Little Brother. As you can imagine, I have a lot of stories from thirty-six years of involvement in this program, but I want to share the story about my former Little Brother, Pete.

Pete and I met soon after he turned thirteen. He was living with his handicapped grandmother and assorted younger siblings. On the day we met I took Pete for a walk to a McDonald's near his house. Once we had our orders, we found a table where we could eat and get to know a little something about each other. I told him that I was married and lived over in the next town, about ten miles away, and that we would get together about once a week for various activities. Then I asked him what he liked to do, and if he had any questions.

His first question took me by surprise. He wanted to know if there were Big Sisters, too, and if his older sister could get one. When I asked why he thought she might need one, he said because she was a drug dealer and a gang member. I agreed that she could use a Big Sister, but due to her age of seventeen and the fact she was living on her own without even a fixed address, it was unlikely that we could be of help.

We continued our conversation and finished our meal. Pete was personable and easy to talk with. I discovered that he was struggling in school, and he liked the idea of getting some help with his reading and math. I told him I liked sailing, but he had never been out on a boat and didn't know how to swim.

Over the first summer I got to meet his teachers because Pete was on a year-round school track, and I got material for us to work on together. He made rapid progress, though school never came easily. He learned to swim at a community pool, and to celebrate his achievement I took him sailing and camping on Catalina Island the following summer.

But the gang thing came back to haunt us. He was being heavily recruited by his older sister and other gang members. He experimented with tagging and took to wearing gang-style clothing. On two occasions I arrived at his house to find him in the backseat of a patrol car after neighbors reported that they had seen him climbing over fences. Happily, because of my years as a volunteer with the youth probation service, I knew the officers and was able to get Pete released into my custody. I told him that he could join a gang—I couldn't stop him—or he could have a Big Brother, but he couldn't have both. He knew that I was serious.

We entered counseling together and were able to make it work. The Responsible Teen Program offered by our local Big Brothers Big Sisters agency was a big help, as was the ongoing support I received from my case manager. Pete continued to struggle in school, but he kept at it. He had a wonderful work ethic, and if he understood a task, he completed it with little or no supervision.

Over the years, when Pete saw that I was truly committed to him, his behavior improved, and we became fast friends. That was ten years ago. Pete is now a fine young man of twenty-three with a full-time job in construction, and he is married with a newborn son.

Pete and I are still in regular contact, as I am with each of my former Little Brothers. All my Little Brothers, including my current Little Brother, sixteen-year-old Erik, know each other.

Pete is a perfect example of how important it is to reach out to a boy by a certain age. If we had never met, and if he had never gotten a Big Brother or other mentor, I have no doubt that Pete would have followed his sister's path into drugs and gangs, and probably would have dropped out of school and gotten into trouble with the law.

When Pete, my current Little Brother Erik, and I were having lunch last week, Pete told us that his life would never have worked out the successful way it has without the influence of his Big Brother. That made me feel good, but the very best part of the conversation was knowing that Pete was sharing his experience with Erik in the same way that a Big Brother would. Clearly, Erik has been welcomed into a family of Big Brothers.

By George D. Wood

The Little Brown Porsche

Big Brother Paul Sandler and Little Brother James Copes

In Philadelphia, the place where I grew up and still call home, it isn't always easy to escape from the inner city. But as an eleven-year-old growing up in the tough South Philadelphia projects, thanks to my mom Marion, I got the chance to escape and took advantage of it.

In fact, until my mom brought me to the Big Brothers Big Sisters of Southeastern Pennsylvania agency back in the early 1980s—hoping to match me up with a strong male role model—I definitely was headed down the wrong road. I quickly steered clear of that highway to nowhere, however, the day I saw a certain Porsche.

The Porsche, a small brown model, belonged to Paul Sandler, a young Philadelphia attorney who had come to the Big Brothers Big Sisters agency to offer his time as a volunteer.

I guess I was what you could call a rebellious kid. Not only didn't I want a Big Brother, but I also wanted to be left alone to live my life the way I wanted to. I wanted it to be just me and my mom—and my friends, of course.

But my mom stood firm, hoping to find me some much-needed guidance. She insisted we visit the BBBS agency. My dad was long gone, and I had no positive male role models in my life. I needed some help, and she knew it.

When I first met Paul, I was more interested in his Porsche than in his guidance. But with my mom's encouragement, I decided to give Paul a chance. Paul and I came from entirely different worlds. I was a black kid growing up in a tough neighborhood. He was a white, Jewish lawyer who had worked hard and was heading in the right direction professionally.

Despite those differences, it turned out that we had a lot in common. For starters, we both were major sports fanatics. Much of our time together in the early days was centered on sports. We would go to a Phillies game, or a Sixers game, or an Eagles game, and no matter where we went, Paul always managed to get good seats. For me, it was heaven!

Being a busy attorney, Paul couldn't always set aside a specific day or even a time of day for us to do things together, so many times he'd just call and say, "Hey, I have to go shopping. Want to come along?" Of course, I'd say yes, never knowing what new adventure lay ahead.

He also took me to many social events, either with his family, where I learned all about Jewish food, or with his law firm. I met all kinds of interesting people, and I know it helped me as I moved through my teenage years.

Thanks to Paul's idea that I should be exposed to all types of people, my social skills today are excellent, or at least that's what Paul says! There's no doubt in my mind that without that experience, I wouldn't have been able to move into the workforce and do the things I can do.

Looking back, the racial and cultural differences between us never presented any kind of roadblock to success. I never heard a single negative word from anyone about it. People on both sides simply accepted it. And why shouldn't they? Paul's a great guy. He put up with me in the early days, when I was a bit of a handful. Here I was, a young black guy from a much different part of town, and Paul's friends and family loved me. They really reached out to me. Early in our match, Paul and I met once a week, but there were times when we saw each other more often. I think I was as much a surrogate son as I was a Little Brother.

At one point, I asked Paul why he got involved as a Big Brother. He said he was a successful single guy in his early thirties, building a law practice. He felt that he wanted to give something to the community. Having heard about Big Brothers Big Sisters, he called the agency, and they started the search for a match.

There were more young black kids who needed help in Philadelphia than white kids, and Paul wasn't concerned about race. He was comfortable with the situation as long as my family agreed. My mom had no problems at all with it.

I hated going to school, and consequently I skipped many days. But Paul didn't lecture me about it. He simply went to the school and spoke to people there, trying to see if he could get me into a special program, one that provided extra reading and other skills he knew I would need to get a decent job someday. Before he went, he checked with my mom, who was always supportive and appreciative of Paul's efforts on my behalf.

And of course, there was always the sports connection. I'll never forget my first Sixers game. I was so excited that I didn't sit down for the entire four quarters. Paul says I must have been the inspiration for a team marketing campaign that used the tagline "Seats You'll Never Sit In." Apart from going to sporting events, we also played in a basketball league with the BBBS agency, and we shot hoops with regularity.

Our match officially ended nineteen years ago, but our friendship didn't end. For me, the biggest moment in our post-match friendship came last June, when Paul was best man at my wedding. Having him there made it an extra special event for my wife Laura and me. Paul told me how proud he was when I asked him to stand up for me. The feeling was mutual.

When we talk about our match, we both have great memories of the times we hung out together. But nothing will top my wedding day. For me, having Paul there to help us celebrate made it the best day of my life.

By James Copes as told to Tom Starner

The Haircut

Big Brother Don Mathewson and Little Brother Shane Miskell

As I sat in the barber's chair watching a man who must have hated children run his shears down the middle of my head, leaving mere stubble, I shuddered to think about the horror of going to school the next day. I looked like I had just experienced the first day of boot camp. How was I going to face my schoolmates?

It was 1971; I was eleven years old; and my father had left us months earlier. What could have been a tough time was really a positive turning point. Sadly, the only real emotion I ever felt around my dad was fear. When he left, the fear left. What remained, however, was a confused, insecure kid who had been called stupid so many times that he believed it.

Mom wanted her four sons to have Big Brothers. I was matched with Don, a twenty-three-year-old shoe store manager who had just finished a tour in the Army. Soon after our match, he married Lynn, and later they had a daughter, Dawn Marie. Little did I know then how important this family would become to me.

We went fishing, hunting, on picnics, and on Sunday drives. Don and I went on weekend camping trips, did chores, worked on cars, and built things. It seemed that

Don could do just about anything.

One night, after obtaining permission, we pretended to be behind enemy lines as we invaded a farmer's cornfield and slipped away with some of the tastiest sweet corn to be had. What a blast that was!

We did a lot of things together over the years, and many of those times are the best memories of my life. Don and Lynn told me they loved me and thought I was a great kid. More than once, though, Don sat me down and told me he was disappointed in my behavior and expected more from me. When Lynn knew I was coming over for dinner, she would cook my favorite meal of beef patties smothered in her awesome brown gravy. I can still taste that gravy!

Drugs became part of my life when I was fifteen, and by seventeen I was in trouble in school and consumed with partying. I kept up a good front with Don, though, because he would have been too hurt if he knew the truth. Don had a lot of hope for me, and I knew I was letting him down.

The parents of my generation, including my mom, never knew what hit them when the drug culture arrived. By the time she realized what was happening, the damage had been done. I quit school at seventeen and stopped calling Don. I didn't want him to know what was going on in my life.

A few months later I was busing tables at the Country Kitchen when Don walked in. He asked my boss if I could take a twenty-minute break. Don was upset and hurt that I had quit school, but he was most disappointed that I didn't come to talk to him. He said our relationship was too important to let the present circumstances end it. I agreed we would stay in touch.

Over the next few years, I bounced from job to job without any real plan or purpose. Twice when I needed a place to stay, Don and Lynn let me stay with them. I knew it was hard for them to watch me struggle, but they never gave up on me.

Going back to high school in 1986 was a huge turning point in my life. In 1988, at the age of twenty-eight, I graduated with a 4.0 GPA. I was on top of the world, and knew I could really be somebody and do something. I joined the Navy Submarine Force as a sonar tech. Advanced electronics school was difficult, and I struggled. I worked hard over the next year and a half to get through my Navy schooling, but I never gave up. I was determined to never again be a quitter.

In 1990 I married my beautiful wife Barbara, and we have three terrific kids. After leaving the Navy in 1994, I started working for my present employer, and I am now the lead electrical engineer on my company's mining and timber harvesting equipment. I have come a long way in my life and am extremely grateful for the way it turned out.

My life wasn't a fairy tale simply because I met Don and Lynn. I had many storms to travel through, but Don and Lynn were with me, believing in me and encouraging me to keep trying and never give up. They have been true friends. I will always consider Don my Big Brother with a big heart, and his beautiful wife Lynn as my special bonus Big Sister.

I asked Don once, "Why did you choose me for a Little Brother out of all the other kids?" His response was, "We had a lot of the same interests, but most of all, I thought you had a great haircut." Wow! What I had considered one of the most embarrassing days of my life was actually the best.

By Shane Miskell

Double O Little Bro'

Big Brother Greg Balogh and Little Brother Chris Gold

Chris was a Zen master of understatement. He had a 007 level of coolness about him. If I said something like, "Take the controls, buddy, and tell me how you like flying ultralights through the Andes Mountains," his reply would likely be "S'all right."

"Is this better than when we went over Niagara Falls in that barrel?"

"I dunno, I guess."

"How about when you hooked into that nine-foot mako shark on your fly rod?"

"Yeah, that was all right, too."

We didn't really do these things, mind you. I present the scenarios to make a point. Chris would never, for anything in the world, reveal that he was truly excited about something—except perhaps the prospect of playing video games in which things blew up.

I think his coolness started out as a defense mechanism, a way to maintain distance from this strange guy who suddenly waltzed into his life and started taking him places. But, over the years, Chris dropped his guard around me. I suppose he eventually realized that, no matter how he acted, he would still look supremely cool as long as I stood nearby for comparison. Even so, you can't take the Zen master out of the boy. He forever continued with his habit of supreme understatement. He just added a wry little knowing smile at the end of each muted declaration.

Maybe it was kind of a Zen thing that got me into Big Brothers in the first place, come to think of it. Ask yourself the question, "What is the sound of one person having fun?" It's not as difficult to imagine as the sound of one hand clapping, but it's also not nearly as pleasing as the sound of two people having fun. Fun is a finite resource, and maybe we ought to make the best use of it by sharing it.

But there I was, a wildlife biologist in Alaska in my early thirties. I was doing a lot of cool stuff solo, and it seemed like a real waste. So I called Big Brothers Big Sisters one day out of the blue and asked to be hooked up with someone who could use a little extra fun in his life.

Soon thereafter, Chris and I were driving down the highway in my pickup truck. He broke the ice between us as only Chris who had just eaten three huge bean burritos could. I don't know why, but nothing eases tension and makes a twelve-year-old boy laugh better than a fart.

Having (barely) survived his gaseous rite of initiation, Chris and I proceeded to take in movies and hit the trails around Anchorage. Typical Big/Little stuff.

But he was obviously uncomfortable with the idea of having a Big Brother whenever we would encounter his peers. So early on he asked if he could introduce me as his bodyguard. I understood his discomfort and did my best to behave as a good bodyguard would. I went stone-faced and kept my arms folded when we encountered his buddies. But I wasn't on guard duty for all that long.

After about a year of playing bodyguard, Chris asked me how much they paid me to be his Big Brother. Now, there was an awkward moment for you. I can honestly say that he caught me completely off guard. He thought that, for the past twelve months, I was being paid to be his friend.

I thought, "C'mon man, cut me some slack here! Ask me about girls or drugs or something easy like that."

It took me several weeks to convince him that I was his friend because I wanted to be and that no money was changing hands, unless it was me slipping him quarters for some video game. I don't think he believed me until he heard the same thing from our caseworker.

Our friendship reached a higher level when we finally had a mutual understanding that we were a Big/Little team because we wanted to be—not because we were expected or paid to be. It was about that time that I stopped being his bodyguard.

Over the years, Chris and I had the opportunity to partake in less-than-typical Big/Little activities like mountain biking, dog training, skijoring (being pulled by my dog while cross-country skiing), canoe camping, fly tying, fly fishing, and duck hunting.

I remember one time glissading down a mountainside with him in the Alaskan spring sunshine. We were sitting on our raincoats and flying down a snow-covered slope. I thought, "Jeez, I hope we both live to tell about this." I don't think there was much hazard of an avalanche on that slope, but there was a huge snow ramp at the bottom that wasn't obvious from above. We had sailed through the air for about twenty feet.

Chris and I had the opportunity to do something that I'll bet no other BBBS team has ever done; we ran a duck-banding camp in the wilds of Alaska for three weeks. Just us and the ducks and the mud as far as the eye could see. And what's more, while in the middle of banding ducks, we had a surprise visit by an Air Force Blackhawk helicopter on a training mission. Part of its mission, apparently, was to deliver a couple pizzas to us out in the middle of Mudville, Alaska. I'm supposed to be writing about magic moments here, and, while that particular moment maybe wasn't magical, it sure as heck was loud. Kind of surreal, too. What do you tip a guy who drives a $25 million pizza delivery vehicle?

My magic moment came at the end of our three-week experience when Chris told me that he wanted to be a duck bander when he grew up. I took this as a sign he thought our time together had been "all right." I also advised him not to close the door on other career opportunities just yet—what with duck banding being seasonal work and all.

Our match officially ended prematurely when I moved away from Alaska. But I was miserable living far from the place that truly felt like home to me. Within ten months, I was back in Anchorage. Chris and I saw no need to drag the Big Brother program back into our relationship. We didn't really need a caseworker anymore. We were just friends picking up where we left off. We continued hanging out until it was Chris's turn to leave home.

I have a photo hanging in my house of Chris asleep with my dog in front of a blazing wood stove. The photo exudes an aura of peace. There's another photo of Chris carrying a gunnysack full of ducks through the mud from a duck trap to our duck-banding station, a kid on a mission.

These days, Chris is part of our nation's peacekeeping mission in Korea. I'm not sure what he does over there. I think maybe if he told me, he'd have to kill me. But whatever it is, I'm pretty sure he must think that it's "all right."

By Greg Balogh

Chapter 3

We Are Family

Worth Fighting For

Big Brother John Sias and Little Brother Chris McMullen

On a Sunday afternoon in the fall of 1977, five-year-old Chris McMullen, his mother Sharon, and his father were watching a football game. At halftime, his father nonchalantly said, "I'm going out for cigarettes." He never returned.

The abandonment seriously affected Chris. Although very intelligent, his grades were mediocre. He was lonely, lacked self-confidence, and wasn't reaching his potential.

In 1981 Sharon learned that a Big Brothers Big Sisters agency had opened in Nashua, New Hampshire. Deciding that a Big Brother might be a good role model and friend for her son, she enrolled Chris. As the first president of the newly organized agency, I wanted to set an example, so I volunteered as a Big. Chris and I were the agency's first match.

My wife Marie and I took Chris places his mother did not have the opportunity to take him. He'd never been to New York or Boston, never seen the Red Sox play, and certainly had never been to Disney World. We played lots of baseball and took him skiing, camping, to museums, and to the library. We even took him to my thirty-fifth Colgate University reunion.

When he was twelve, his mother remarried. Since he was no longer in a single-parent home, our match should have been over. But he and I had formed such a close relationship that we asked to continue our match. By the time he graduated from high school, he had become an integral member of our family, often spending weekends in our home and helping us celebrate family holidays.

Chris graduated near the top of his high school class. He was accepted at Boston University and was awarded an annual scholarship. Four years later in 1995, he graduated cum laude.

By the time he started college, he and I were addressing each other as Dad and Son, and Chris never explained to his friends that I was not his "real" father. For four years, they all called me Mr. McMullen. For Christmas during his junior year, I wrote a values book for him: *Dear Son: There Are No Free Lunches*, which has since sold thousands of copies across the country.

After college, Chris worked for a year in Boston, got the urge to tackle the Big Apple, and left one day for New York with no job and no place to live. He landed a sales position with a leading dot-com firm and, for four years, before the dot-com industry crashed, he lived very well.

In the spring of 1998, when Chris was twenty-four, my wife Marie suggested, "You and Chris are so close; you have no son, and he has no father. Why don't you adopt him?" To be honest, I had never thought of it before, but it seemed like a wonderful idea. But what would my two daughters think? How would his mother feel about it? His grandmother? His stepfather?

With a great deal of care, I approached them each, one at a time. To my relief and joy, they all approved. Then I broached the idea to Chris, and he was overjoyed. I phoned my attorney, and in a few days he called back. "Adopting

Chris will be a piece of cake!" he said happily.

He set a May date before a Superior Court judge. Chris, Sharon, Marie, and I were all smiles as we walked into court, until the judge said gravely, "I would love to grant this adoption, but the state law won't allow it. The law says you cannot adopt him alone; both you and your wife must adopt him." But of course this was not an option. His mother Sharon is caring and devoted, the best mother a boy could have.

A few hours later, dumbfounded and dejected, Chris climbed aboard a bus back to New York, as fatherless as he had been for the last nineteen years.

I was not going to take this disappointment lying down. I figured we had three options. One was to do nothing. This was not acceptable. A second option was to take the judge's decision to the Supreme Court and hope they would overturn it. A third option was to change the state law. This seemed to be our best bet.

I contacted my state senator, Jim Squires, and asked if he would be willing to sponsor a bill in the next session of the legislature that would enable me, and others in my situation, to singly adopt a child over the age of eighteen. Jim said, "I'd love to, but first I have to get reelected in November!"

In January 1999, his bill was one of the first in the new legislative year. In February, Chris, his mother, my wife, and I spoke convincingly to the Senate Judiciary Committee that was considering the bill. Our story clearly touched the committee, and they unanimously approved the bill immediately, a highly unusual procedure in legislative bodies.

In April, we were asked to go before the House committee, but Marie and I were unable to testify due to a pre-planned trip. Chris testified alone and carried the day.

The bill passed, and the governor signed it into law.

Armed with this new law, we made a second appointment to appear before a Superior Court judge. This time it really was a piece of cake! An Associated Press reporter who had been following our efforts wrote a story, and soon the entire nation became aware of our exploit.

The Today Show invited us to be guests , and we spent an exciting seven minutes being interviewed by Katie Couric in her New York studio, where we related our experience to 15 million people.

While living in Manhattan, Chris was in a program similar to the BBBS school-based program, in which he mentored a boy, one of seven in his family. This experience led Chris to decide he wanted to be an elementary school teacher. He returned to Boston and enrolled in a two-year program at Boston University, where he earned his masters degree in elementary education in May 2003. He's now an elementary school teacher in Chelsea, Massachusetts, where he is both a teacher and a role model for low-income and underprivileged children.

It is great having Chris back in the area near us. Last Saturday we went skiing; two weeks ago we played pond hockey with my grandson; last night he came over for dinner. Life is good. Little Brothers are great, but when they turn into sons, they're even better.

By John Sias

Friendships for a Lifetime

Big Brother Jack Ellis and six Little Brothers

Jack Ellis was a successful businessman. He had traveled to exotic destinations and even owned a home in St Croix. Life was good for Jack professionally and socially, but he still felt there was something missing. When he was forty-five, during a midlife assessment, he realized that he had experienced so much, yet he had never given anything back to society.

That week, while leafing through the newspaper, Jack noticed an ad for a new organization—Protestant Big Brothers. He decided to get involved. That was 1961. Since then, Jack has mentored six boys and continues to be a strong advocate for what is now called Big Brothers Big Sisters of Greater Cleveland.

Jack's decision to become a mentor was based in part on his own life experience of growing up without a father. His mother raised him alone since the age of eight, when his father passed away. Knowing firsthand the significance of a male role model to a young boy, Jack wanted to help make a difference in the life of not only one child—but six.

One of Jack's most significant memories from his childhood was of driving "from the time his feet reached the pedals." Driving was a passion of Jack's that he wanted to share with his Little Brothers. He chose to mentor older children who were close to driving age.

From the time they received their licenses, Jack had them on the road, racking up miles behind the wheel. It was his goal to have each boy drive at least five thousand miles before they graduated from high school. They took road trips to Sandusky, Ohio, where Jack had business, and drove once a year to Florida to see the sights. "Knowing how to drive," Jack said, "is one of the most important things for a child to learn. These boys did not have someone to take them out on a regular basis. It was important to me to make sure they got the practice."

Recently, Jack was honored for his lifetime of achievements and service to the Big Brothers Big Sisters program. Four of his six Little Brothers and their wives attended the ceremony to honor their mentor, and a fifth sent a note that was read there. The comments and demeanor of the men all spoke of the deep relationship they have with their Big Brother.

His first Little Brother, Charles Wilson, said, "They say you learn by example, and Jack has been a kind, caring, patient, compassionate, and loving role model. He taught me that every different experience was part of my education. We started as Big Brother and Little Brother, and I am proud to call him my surrogate father and best friend."

Gerhard Hoffman, his second Little Brother, recalled, "What I remember most about Jack is his even demeanor. He was a constant in an up and down environment for me. That was the biggest influence on me. Of course, all of his Little Brothers know the Jack-line, 'It's all part of your education.' He gave us so many experiences that we may never have had the opportunity to experience without him."

Jack's third Little Brother, Michael Cheetham, reflected

on the scope of his Big Brother's influence in his life. "If there is any treasure that Jack has enriched my life with, it can best be imparted in the following thoughts: First, the most important thing that any of us can do in this life is to get along with others. That—and that reason alone—is why God created us and why we are here. We are our brothers' keepers. Second, there is nothing that can be kept from any of us—from the most humble to the wealthiest—through education and hard work. Finally, never let any opportunity to learn about the wonders of this world pass you by—and always hold the wonders of this world in reverent awe."

Michael's biological little brother, Chris Cheetham, became Jack's fourth Little Brother. Chris commented, "Throughout the many wonderful experiences he has shared with me, Jack has taught me about life. He's been there to pick me up, and he's been there to pat me on the back. I love him dearly. He's been a father, a best friend, and the biggest influence in my life. If I could have designed a custom relationship, I could not have created one better than the one I have with Jack."

The youngest member of this family of brothers was Steve Pack, Jack's sixth Little Brother. He feels, "Jack has shown me that life is a vast map. It has many destinations and innumerable ways to get places. Jack taught me how to read that map and how to chart my course. He taught me how to avoid trouble spots and, most importantly, how to learn from and enjoy the journey."

At eighty-seven, Jack Ellis is starting to slow down a little. But his friendships are stronger than ever with his Little Brothers. They regularly talk on the phone about their families, business, and life in general. Gatherings occur as often as possible. At a party celebrating the millennium, Jack and all six of his Little Brothers and their families gathered together. "It was great to have all my boys together in one place. I'm so proud of each one of them." Jack remarked.

The bonds of friendship that Jack and his Little Brothers forged over the past forty years run very deep. Every Friday evening, Chris still comes over to pick up Jack and take him to dinner. Jack is Chris's best friend, and they love spending time together. In addition to the normal conversations friends have, they reminisce about the memories and moments they had together—as Jack does with all six of his Little Brothers.

A simple effort, to give something back to society, has developed into more than forty years of life-altering effect on seven men. Jack doesn't worry anymore about his legacy to society. When he looks at the faces of his six "boys," he knows exactly what he has given the world.

By Julie Johnson

Our Vietnamese Brother

Big Couple David and Heather Denman and Little Brother Hung Huynh

While attending university in the late 1960s in Canada, where I was born and raised, I had been a Big Brother. My wife Heather and I did not have children when we settled in Harrisonburg, Virginia, in 1983. I became interested in becoming a Big Brother again not only to help a young person but also to fill a void I felt from being so far away from family.

In the meantime, a Vietnamese family had also settled in Harrisonburg and they needed the services of Big Brothers Big Sisters.

In 1982 several families were attempting to flee South Vietnam. The plan was to leave in small groups at different times in order to avoid the suspicion of authorities. Hoang Troung managed to escape with her two nephews, Hung Huynh and Hein Ho, her sister, her brother, and his wife. Many family members, including Hung's mother and an older brother, were left behind when police heard about the plan and cordoned off the village, thus preventing their escape. Hoang and her entourage became the proverbial boat people, landing in Indonesia, where they lived in a refugee camp for the next thirteen months.

Refugees left the camp as sponsors came forward who

would help them get established in the United States or other countries. Hoang's brother and his wife were sponsored by a church in Texas, her sister by a church in Fairfax, Virginia, and Hoang, Hung, and Hein were sponsored by our local Blessed Sacrament Church. They moved to Harrisonburg in 1983, when Hung was seven and Hein was five. The congregation helped them move into an apartment as they became integrated into the Harrisonburg community.

Hoang got a job at RR Donnelly and started her new life. She worked overtime to make ends meet. Hung and Hein often spent time home alone and had few social opportunities. Through the promotion of the United Way campaign at work, Hoang learned about the Big Brothers Big Sisters program and recognized that it would be good to have a male role model involved in the boys' lives and to get them some added adult attention.

I worked with people of different cultures in my job, which was one of the reasons the BBBS caseworker thought that Hung and I would be a good match. My travel schedule of approximately a hundred days a year was a detriment, though, as it made it difficult for me to meet the commitment of weekly contact with Hung. After further discussions, I asked about a possible couples match, whereby Heather could pitch in while I was traveling. We became the first couples match out of our agency when we were matched with nine-year-old Hung in 1985.

As a Big Brother and Big Sister, we spent time with Hung almost every week and enjoyed watching him grow up and learn to adapt to his new country. We taught Hung to play tennis, helped him with his English, took him with us to the beach, attended special occasions with Hoang, other relatives, and friends, and shared many of our special times with them.

Our biggest achievement was helping Hung learn to have fun and providing opportunities for him to play. The experiences of being a refugee and being separated from his mother and the responsibility of making his life in America a success made Hung wise and serious beyond his years. It brought us great satisfaction to introduce some of the joys of childhood to this sober youngster who had been through so much.

In 1994 Hung became a U.S. citizen. In the same year, Heather and I were blessed with the birth of our daughter Molly. It felt to all of us like Hung now had a little sister.

Hung graduated in 1995 from high school and joined the Navy. After boot camp, he was stationed in San Diego where he studied and worked as a medical technician. His mother, who had come to the United States three years earlier, joined him there.

After his five-year contract, Hung left the Navy and started studying computer technology. About two years into his studies, the tech industry went through enormous changes, and Hung joined the Navy reserve and went back into the medical profession. In early 2003 Hung was called up to active duty and was sent to Iraq. He returned to the United States in September 2003 and is currently studying to be an X-ray technician.

We have known Hung for eighteen years, and he always visits us when he comes back east for Christmas. In 2000 we visited him in San Diego and plan to go back in 2005. We still communicate regularly by e-mail and phone, and Hung often seeks and sometimes even follows our advice. He became a part of our family, as did his aunt Hoang, who routinely delivers homemade Vietnamese egg rolls to us and enjoys making dresses for our daughter Molly.

The couples match gave Hung the opportunity to observe a realistic model on which to base future relationships, an opportunity to learn and share American culture and values, and opportunities his family did not have the time or means to provide. We, on the other hand, gained a new family when ours was far away and developed parenting skills that we used later in raising our daughter.

We thank Big Brothers Big Sisters for a very successful match that has led to a lifelong relationship that enriches us all. We may not look alike, but there isn't any doubt we are family!

By David Denman

I Am Blessed

Big Brother Hoagan Powell and Little Brother Chuck Williams

How many times have you heard that inner voice urging you to do something? How many times have you listened, and how many times have you ignored it? Around twenty-six years ago, my inner voice was telling me I should become a Big Brother. Thank God I listened, for that decision blessed my life.

I was nothing special (happily, my wife disagrees!) except maybe to God. I had no money or special talents. In fact, I was a somewhat lost senior at the University of Houston. Despite all of my shortcomings, that inner voice continued to urge me to become a Big Brother.

Chuck and his sister were being raised by their grandparents. After her husband passed away, Granny wanted Chuck to have another positive male role model. She signed Chuck up to get a Big Brother. That's where I came in. At our first meeting, I still remember this shy, big-eyed, little nine-year-old boy with a huge smile peeking out from behind his Granny's dress. He was excited but apprehensive. We went to the zoo and had a great afternoon together.

As I got to know the family, I wanted to try to figure out a way to help Granny with her income. They were scraping by on the $4 per hour she earned working at Woolworth's. Call it divine intervention or whatever you choose, but I felt moved to investigate at the Social Security Administration.

On my first two trips to the local Social Security office, I was told by two different representatives that there were no benefits available for them. Despite this gloomy history, I felt compelled to go back a third time. This time the Social Security employee said there was a way, but time was of the essence. The children could qualify for Social Security Survivor's Benefits if Granny adopted her grandchildren within two years of her husband's death. We had four weeks to get it done.

I went to the Big Brother's office in Houston and explained our challenge. My caseworker called a local judge who called a law professor at the University of Houston, Bates College of Law. He recruited two law students to draft the legal papers. They all helped get the adoptions completed in record time. The children qualified for the Social Security benefits, and Granny had a little more income to help raise them. I think everyone involved in helping this struggling family felt blessed to have participated in this expedited process.

Chuck and I did a number of things together over the years, but sometimes the greatest joy came from seeing him blossom when I went to see his daily activities. I remember attending one of his peewee baseball games early in our relationship. Chuck really lit up when he saw me in the stands watching him, and he ended up hitting a home run! The coach later told me that it was obvious how much it meant to Chuck for me to be there because his extra energy and enthusiasm led to a great leap in his performance.

One Sunday afternoon, we went on a picnic, doing

what boys often do—passing and kicking the football around. On one of my kicks, the ball went off course and struck a pretty young lady who was deep in conversation. As the ball bounced off of her head, this woman, with whom I was faintly acquainted, displayed an amazing ability to give a "look to kill" with her eyes. We later fell madly in love and got married. Chuck forgave me for the period where I focused more time than he would have liked on "a girl."

After my marriage to Cathy, we made Chuck a part of our family life. He spent many nights at our home and went camping with us, and we attended many of his sporting, scouting, and school events. Cathy and I were blessed to have a Little Brother enrich our lives.

Granny suffered a stroke and died when Chuck was in high school. He was already so much a part of our family and our hearts that it seemed only natural to legally adopt him. It took a while, but it was finally formalized when he was twenty-two.

The twenty-six years have passed quickly. We now have two other children—Danielle, seventeen, and Matt, thirteen. They both dearly love their big brother Chuck, now thirty-five, and his wife Shannon.

Chuck is a remarkable person. He has overcome a lot of challenges in his life—including a learning disability, poverty, and abandonment by his parents— all of which might have crushed another person. After serving our country in the armed forces, he went on to graduate from college at the University of Houston.

I think my wife Cathy described Chuck the best when she said "Chuck can talk to the wall, and it will not only talk back, but it will give him money!" This persuasiveness is probably why he became the youngest national sales manager in the history of a major worldwide corporation.

Chuck's personality, drive, and willingness to work hard have served him well.

Some people think the Big Brothers Big Sisters program only helps the children it serves. I have to disagree. As for me, I've gotten more than I gave. I am truly honored and humbled to have served as Chuck's Big Brother, and I am very proud to be Chuck's father. Our relationship has developed and grown over the years, and I count Chuck as one of my closest friends. I have indeed been blessed.

By Hoagan Powell

Sisters for Life

Big Sister Pan Riley and Little Sister Lynn Nadeau

Lynn was just six years old when her mom first heard about the Big Brothers Big Sisters program in 1982. Lynn was about to start first grade, and mom wanted to give her daughter another source of guidance as she began her school experience. Mother and daughter were living in a low-income neighborhood in Hartford and barely managing to survive on state assistance. Lynn's father was occasionally around, but he was battling a long-term addiction to alcohol.

At the same time, Pan was a twenty-seven-year-old single woman living in Hartford, struggling to make a living in the world of professional theater. She had grown up in a home broken by chronic alcoholism. Pan never had the benefit of a true mentor while growing up. She vowed to make a difference for another girl and to be the mentor she never had.

At the match meeting, Lynn spent most of the time hiding behind her mom. But after Pan offered to take her to Friendly's Ice Cream, Lynn recovered from her shyness and agreed to go. The regular visits became a highlight of the week for Lynn and for Pan. Their favorite activity was playing school.

Doing well in school was easy for Lynn because she

loved to learn about new things and her mom supported her education. Unfortunately for Lynn, most of her classmates did not share her enthusiasm and dedication in the classroom. But from day one, Lynn's best friend, her Big Sister, always supported her academic ambitions.

In many ways, Pan was Lynn's best mentor. It was Pan who took Lynn to the YWCA on a regular basis until she learned how to swim. Pan was the person who helped Lynn develop a love for art, the theater, and museums. When they left the city to explore rural Connecticut, another new world was opened to Lynn.

The first challenge to their relationship came about two years after they met. Lynn's mom decided to move the family to Willimantic, a town thirty miles east of Hartford. The BBBS caseworker worried how Pan would react. Would the match be over? When asked about her intentions, Pan just laughed. "It's just thirty miles. We've already made a pact. We're sisters for life!"

Willimantic was and is a tough little town. The drug trade is a major industry in this dying mill town. In the projects where Lynn lived, the police regularly visited the neighbors—usually in the middle of the night.

But Lynn never bothered with those temptations. She stayed focused and continued to make good decisions. During high school, she had three part-time jobs and still maintained a good grade-point average. Her determination led to an early graduation from high school, and she became the first person in her immediate family to graduate from high school.

"I always knew I wanted more out of life. Pan helped me realize that advanced education was the key. She was the role model who taught me how to succeed and how to overcome family circumstances and my neighborhood."

After graduation, Lynn started a job at a small law

firm in Hartford. Nine years later, she is still there as a valued employee. In May 2003 she realized another dream by receiving an associate's degree. Of course she's not done yet. She is now attending St. Joseph's College in order to become a social worker so she can help others as she was helped during her childhood.

The themes of stability and long-term relationships can be found throughout Lynn's life. She recently became engaged to her boyfriend of ten years. Soon, Lynn will become a Big Sister to a very lucky young lady. No doubt that friendship will last twenty-one years—just like the match of Lynn and Pan.

In October 2002 the *Hartford Courant* ran a three-day front-page story about the drug problems in Willimantic. The writers dubbed Willimantic "Heroin Town." Gruesome pictures showed young women shooting-up heroin in the town park. Depressing stories were given about their lives of prostitution, sickness, and death. CBS News even came to town to interview local residents.

But Lynn has other views. "I spent half of my childhood in that town. But I had a Big Sister to guide me towards my dreams. I thank my mother for caring so much about my future that she got me a Big Sister. Good people live in Willimantic, and there are many success stories waiting to be told."

This is one success story with many more chapters to come.

By Dave Taylor

The Carver Rule

Big Brother John Carver and Little Brother Michael Burton

I have had five Little Brothers over a span of thirty-five years, starting first in Omaha in 1967 and ending in 2001, and I have been a long-time board member of the Boston chapter of Big Brothers. Needless to say, Big Brothers has played a big part in my life.

Of the five boys who passed through my life, I am still in touch with three, and we communicate regularly. There is one special relationship among them that has endured for thirty-two years.

In 1970, upon returning to Boston from Omaha, I thought I might try being a Big Brother again. I was single, age twenty-nine, and living in a "student ghetto" section of Boston. My only request upon applying was that my Little Brother live somewhere nearby where we might walk or use public transportation to see each other.

On the day I was matched with Michael Burton, he was ten years old and living in a public housing project with his family. They were the only white family in a predominately mixed racial neighborhood. School busing was the hot issue of the day, and tensions ran high.

I was dating a young lady named Carol MacDonald, whom I would later marry, starting a thirty-one-year marriage that is still going strong. We formed a threesome that often was reduced to a twosome as Michael and I went about the business of being Big and Little Brothers together. Then we would return to my apartment to find Carol in her apron with a big pile of meatloaf waiting for us. These were some of the happiest days of my life, and I'm sure that was true for Michael also.

As the pages of life kept turning quicker than ever, Michael sprouted into a skinny teenage kid with all the problems of adolescence—having acne and riotous hormones, and being mentally lazy and sports crazy.

It was obvious he was watching Carol and me pretty closely, as we were the only role models in his life. He was at our wedding, of course, and always there when we moved from place to place in the early years, lugging furniture up some narrow staircase, and diving into the pizza at day's end. In many ways Michael had managed to blend into our family as if he was everyone's nephew.

When Michael became involved with girls, we had some short sex education talks. This is when I started hammering away at the Carver Rule (passed on to me by my father) that forbids matrimony by any male under the age of thirty. Apparently he listened—as time would tell.

By now I was ready to take on Little Brother number three, Ricky Beauregard, age ten, from where I now lived in Winthrop, Massachusetts. Michael and Ricky bonded immediately, and life rolled along.

Michael was never a great student, so it came as no surprise when his first attempt at college ended in his dropping out after one term. He just wasn't ready. I was pushing him for a hitch in the Marines—as I had done right out of high school—but that didn't appeal to Michael.

At eighteen, Michael entered the real world and had an assortment of uninspiring jobs that only furthered his resolve not to live a life like this. I wangled a job for him at WGBH/ Boston, the PBS station where I worked. Manning the security desk at night gave him a chance to read books and rethink college.

At nineteen, Michael gave himself a second chance and started over at U-Mass/Boston, with a newly found maturity and resolve. The one-year break had done wonders for his ambition. Now he was on the move, ready to roll.

Carol and I were finally rolling also, as our son was born in 1979. We asked Michael to be Andrew's godfather, and that further enmeshed him in the fabric of our family.

From this point on, Michael began his steady climb up the ladder of life and is still a rising star today. He transfered all his credits to Boston University and graduated with honors. He also finagled a new job in the sales department, at WGBH, after I was long gone from there, and ultimately wound up in my former job as the national sales director.

Meanwhile, adhering closely to the Carver Rule, Michael met and married—at age thirty-two—Cate Alben, and began life for real. His first son Patrick came along five years later, and I was honored to serve as Patrick's godfather, thus completing the circle. And in yet one more twist, Michael was invited to serve on the board of directors of the same Boston chapter of Big Brothers as I did, making him the first Little Brother to serve in such a capacity.

At this writing, I am sixty-two, and Michael is forty-two. Our lives and wives and families are deeply entwined. We share Patriots season tickets together, and not a day goes by when we don't have a phone chat—usually about sports. We have no idea of why or how this all happened. It just did. And we have Big Brothers Big Sisters to thank.

By John D. Carver

Making Our History

Big Sister Sheri Benham and Little Sister Jennifer Flick

"It's interesting. Not many people in Bloomington have known me this long," says Sheri Benham, sitting in a chair on her porch, looking at Jennifer Flick. "It's been twenty years since we first met."

"Wow. Has it been that long?" says Jennifer.

Having witnessed their interactions for only an hour, I already understood that such a long history between them would not be much of a surprise to anyone. Throughout our conversation, the two sometimes forgot about my presence altogether. Sparked by a memory about the past or prompted into discussion of the present, they drifted naturally into familiar conversational territory. At times, I might as well have been a passerby overhearing a chat between two old friends and good buddies.

They met in 1983 when Sheri became Jennifer's Big Sister. Sheri was twenty-seven, and Jennifer was only eight years old.

"When I first got to her house," recalls Sheri, "one of her older sisters came out of one of the back rooms, and I thought, 'Okay, I can do this.' Then Jennifer came out and I thought, 'Oh my goodness, what am I going to do with this little girl?' We hit it off immediately though."

And despite a little shyness on Jennifer's part, it didn't take long for Sheri to figure out what to do. They went straight to the mall and shared some ice cream, a treat that became a staple of their outings together.

"I was excited," Jennifer says, explaining that her bashfulness wasn't a result of being scared. "I didn't have a father. My mother worked three jobs. And my older sisters had Big Sisters. They had several, actually, because their Big Sisters kept moving away, and then they'd get rematched. I got the best one though. I got lucky."

Other than just hanging out at Sheri's in the early years of their friendship, the two engaged in just about every activity a Big and Little Sister could—playing Frisbee, going to the YMCA, roller-skating, talking, listening to music, bowling, playing putt-putt ("*lots* of putt-putt," laughs Jennifer), going to the park, doing homework, cooking dinner, and so on. Of course, there also arose the occasional out-of-the-ordinary activity.

"Remember when I dated that guy with the private plane?" Sheri laughs.

"Oh my gosh, that was just amazing," exclaims Jennifer. "We flew all the way to Tennessee. I thought that was so neat. My mom really didn't have the money to take us places. Sheri was able to though. We even went caving once."

There also came times for more serious matters as Jennifer entered into adolescence. Talks about boys, dating, finishing school, and future plans dominated their conversations.

"Sheri had a very big impact on my life," Jennifer states firmly. "Although I wish I would have listened to her at one point."

"We had a deal, you see," Sheri hesitates. "Oh, I always cry when we talk about this." Wiping a tear from her cheek and forcing a smile, she continues, "If she graduated from high school, I'd take her to Florida. That was the deal."

"I was seventeen when I got pregnant," states Jennifer. "I was dealing with quite a bit at home then too—a lot. Then all of these grown-up decisions started hitting me: preparing for our child, buying a house. I wish I would have stayed in school. At the time, though, it was just so much."

In spite of Sheri's sadness and Jennifer's regret, both of them agreed that Jennifer's entire family has triumphed in the face of many challenges. Her husband Kevin went on to graduate and now works two jobs to support their four children. Jennifer eventually earned her GED and recently enrolled in Ivy Tech to take a full course load in the fall.

"I'm very proud of her," beams Sheri, who also is back in school, working on her master's in social work at Indiana University.

"Sheri's the one who inspired me to go back to school," says Jennifer. "I thought, if Sheri can go back with everything she has going on, then I can too. It's going to be quite a challenge with the kids and all, but I'm really excited."

As we talk, Kevin and the kids show up in their minivan, joining us on the porch. Each kid goes directly to Sheri to get a hug and then runs into the house to find something fun to do.

"Sheri is like an aunt to my kids," says Jennifer. "Very much the grandmother type."

"Well, I don't feel like I do that much," responds Sheri humbly.

"But it's a lot for me. The kids just love you. They love to come here."

"Actually, if I have a bad day," Sheri smiles, "all I

have to do is go to Jennifer's to get cheered up. I love those kids."

"Sheri does the same thing for them that she did for me."

Asked what has changed most as their friendship has grown, Sheri wonders at how wonderful it has been to see Jennifer grow as a woman. "She's very responsible and is into being a good mom, a good aunt, and a good sister. She and Kevin are great about promoting school, and I don't think that's something she got very much of when she was growing up."

When she applied to become a Big Sister twenty years ago, one of Sheri's biggest fears was that it would be too big a commitment for her—that it would take up too much of her time. It was quite the opposite, though. "How we spent our time together was up to us. We set the schedule. And now I can say it wasn't a commitment at all, but a joy. And eventually we grew into just being adult friends. I'm not a role model anymore."

"She's a good role model still, though," adds Jennifer with a loving smile.

By Tom Hargis

Forty Years and Counting!

Big Brother Lee Stauffer and Little Brother Bill Lynch

The hundredth anniversary of Big Brothers Big Sisters of America in 2004 also marks the fortieth anniversary of my family's association with this wonderful organization. It was 1964 when my older brother Jack was matched to his Big Brother, Gary Tyler. Jack was ten. I would turn eight that year; my sister Maureen was graduating from high school; my brother Mike would be a senior; and Margy, the middle child, would be a freshman in high school. My mother had been widowed for six years and was looking for work to help fill her time and finance her children's attendance in Catholic school.

Mom had done a fabulous job of raising us without a father. The older children had been influenced by the memories of our father, but she worried about Jack and me. She was concerned about our development as young men without the presence of a male figure in our lives.

Forty years ago, she turned to Big Brothers Big Sisters for help. She met with our caseworker, who became a hero to our family with the first match between my brother Jack and Gary Tyler.

On many occasions, Gary and Jack would include me in their activities, even though the match had been designed to meet Jack's needs, not mine. It was because I envied the wonderful relationship between Jack and Gary that all I asked for on my ninth birthday was a Big Brother of my own. One week after my actual birthday, I was matched with my very own Big Brother, Lee Stauffer!

First, we went to his house and met his lovely wife Gladys, who was expecting their third child. We hung a calendar to plan our future get-togethers. It was a monumental moment in our match. Before that day, I had never been shown how to properly hold or swing a hammer. It seems like such a simple thing, but we often need to be shown the simple things—the proper golf grip, how to change the oil in the car, what bait to use when ice fishing.

There were many other important lessons to learn—the importance of honesty, respect for hard work, admiring a job well done, and the rewards of a successful relationship with your spouse. It would be lessons like these that I learned over the next thirty-eight years of our match.

All that the BBBS asked was that Gary or Lee spend a couple of hours a week with Jack and me for a year or two. This year would have marked Jack and Gary's fortieth year as friends had Gary not passed away a few years ago. It will be thirty-nine years in October that Lee and I have known each other. While the match officially ended in 1974 when I reached eighteen, the friendship will last forever. We still see each other on a regular basis. Ours is a relationship more like family than that of a mentor and mentored.

While matches like those Jack and I experienced may not be the norm, they are indeed representative of many lifelong friendships that began with the Big Brothers Big Sisters program. It is not uncommon for both Bigs and Littles to become part of each other's families.

I am godfather to Lee and Gladys's youngest daughter

Dawn. She's now a young mother of three herself, and I am known as Billy to her beautiful children. The Stauffer family consists of six children; five are married with children of their own. My wife and I consider all of them nieces and nephews, and our children consider them all cousins. My brother Jack has similar relationships with Gary's family as well as with the family of one of his Little Brothers.

Many of my favorite memories of my time as a Little do not revolve around the exciting activities like trips to amusement parks or other vacations. While those were great, it was the little things I enjoyed the most—simple things like fishing or working on a car or home projects.

I especially looked forward to the occasional trips to Gladys's family's farm. Her mother and father became great substitutes for my own grandparents, although they probably were not really old enough. In the summer, I would occasionally spend a few nights at the farm and, in the winter, I learned how to ride a snowmobile there. The greatest honor I've received in the last few years was to be invited to hunt on that farm. I know this much to be true—only family is allowed to hunt there, so I must indeed be considered family. The same holds true with Lee's family.

I used to be amazed by all of the trophies Lee's father had for shooting events associated with his work at a prison. Little did I know that someday I too would work at one of those prisons and eventually I would become a shooter myself. I like to joke with people and have often said that having Lee as a Big Brother made the difference between my working in a prison and living in one!

Our mother had always hoped we would repay the program that helped us so much when we were young. My brother Jack went on to have two long-term relationships with Little Brothers of his own, and I too had a Little for a short time in the 1980s. Six years ago, I became active with the advisory committee of my local BBBS, and eventually I became a member of the board of directors.

In 1968 my mother said, “The main reason I’m so grateful to Big Brothers Gary and Lee is that they make it easier for me to finish molding the boys into men their father would have been proud of.”

While I will never know just how proud of me my father would have been, I can honestly say I am proud to have been associated with such a valuable organization as the Big Brothers Big Sisters for forty years. I am proud of my relationship with Lee and our families’ love for each other. I have never really thought about what my life might have been like without the introduction of caring volunteers like Gary and Lee, but I am sure that my brother Jack and I are richer men for having known them.

By Bill Lynch

From Six to Private First Class

Big Brother Gregory Hearing and Little Brother Andrew Entel

I was matched with my six-year-old Little Brother in 1989 in Tampa, Florida. At the time, Andrew (who now goes by Drew) was a frightened young child with low self-esteem and no confidence. Andrew needed a Big Brother to help him realize his potential.

Andrew's father walked out on him when he was four. His mother took loving care of him, but he had no siblings and no apparent buddies. He needed a Big.

In contrast, I was a twenty-seven-year-old lawyer working in a large law firm in a new and very stressful job. I worked all the time. I needed a Little boy to remind me to have some fun. We ended up being a perfect match for thirteen years.

I spent several years of my youth without a father, but I had three older brothers who helped me get through some very difficult times. I decided that, after I was through with my education, I wanted to be a Big Brother to a needy Little. Andrew fit the bill. He was intensely shy and afraid of many things.

In our first year as a match, we overcame his fear of lightning by going to the library to learn more about it and talking with a local weather forecaster. He went from being afraid to leave the house during a storm to the point that I had to drag him out of the pool if lightning was threatening.

Many people assume that having a Little Brother means that you have to make extra time in your life for him. That has not been the case for Andrew and me. I have simply included Andrew in the regular events and occurrences in my life.

Our time together was not all fun and games. For instance, if I had a lot of work to do, I would take him to work with me on Saturday morning. While I was doing my work, he would do his schoolwork or play on the computer. If I had to run errands, I included him in these mundane tasks.

Our relationship grew just by our being together. It did not matter what we did. Andrew learned about the importance of being a responsible man by watching me.

Andrew helped me grow and made me a better brother, friend, and, eventually, husband and father. In the early years of our match, he reminded me of the importance of play in our lives. We spent hours throwing footballs, baseballs, basketballs, and Frisbees. We wrestled. We giggled. We went to numerous Big Brothers Big Sisters events, ranging from sporting events to outings at the park to bowling. As he grew, our relationship grew, and we developed a lifelong bond that will not be broken by distance or other commitments.

I saw Andrew develop emotionally and intellectually. When we were first matched, he had very little interest in school. After a while, our annual goals included academic achievement as well as emotional development. Over the years, we accomplished all of our goals. Andrew was not an A student, but I believe he performed much better in school than he would have had he not had the influence of a Big Brother.

Andrew's emotional maturity level substantially improved over the years. We were able to discuss matters, like the birds and the bees, he could not broach with his mother. Instead of learning this knowledge from classmates or immature friends, he was able to sit down and discuss sensitive issues with a man.

His mother was afraid to teach him to drive. Having been the one to teach him, I now understand why! Nonetheless, we survived, and our bond grew stronger.

Andrew joined the Boy Scouts in our second match year. Over the ensuing years, he worked his way through the scouting ranks and ultimately achieved the rank of Eagle Scout. At the age of fifteen, he chose to fulfill his Eagle Scout public service project. He decided to help an inner-city, not-for-profit day care center by refurbishing its playground. He amassed over fifty volunteers who put in nearly five hundred hours of work and raised nearly $1,000 in donated materials to complete the playground restoration project. He called upon numerous other Bigs and Littles to assist as volunteers on the project.

Our "Little" moments together instilled in him a desire to help others less fortunate than he. His choice of a needy, not-for-profit agency for his community service project for his Eagle Scout badge demonstrated that commitment.

Andrew has gone from lacking self-worth and confidence to being proud of himself and feeling he can make a difference in the world. He recently enlisted in the Army, where he will support his community and his country through his military service as a private first class in the infantry.

Over the years, my relationship with Andrew has evolved from that of Big and Little to all but blood brothers. He served as a groomsman in my wedding in 1997. Since then, I have become the proud father of three young sons.

Andrew has become a big brother to my sons. I watch him playing with my oldest son and harken back to the first few years when I was matched with him. He is now giving back to my son what I gave to him.

Andrew has grown into such a great man. There is no doubt that he understands the need to keep the chain of love and support that he benefited from going. Some day, I know that Andrew will pay me the ultimate compliment, and become a Big Brother with Big Brothers Big Sisters.

By Gregory A. Hearing

Brothers for Fifty-Eight Years!

Big Brother Jim Kelly and Little Brother Pat Rickert

In 1942 Pat Rickert was a seven-year-old rough-and-tumble kid who knew his way around Minneapolis's Avenue, a rough part of the city that includes many of the city's most infamous bar halls and poolrooms. "I started going to Big Brothers because I wanted to box, play pool, and see the Little Sisters," Pat admits with a sly smile.

Pat was world-wise at a very young age. His mother was in poor health, and he describes living in an "environment that was rife with temptation for trouble." He remembers going to movies by himself when he was four or five years old. He was eight when he *quit* smoking! "I saw my refection in a store window and I didn't like what I saw," he says. Pat admits his good decisions throughout his life were always matched with positive providence. "It always seemed like somebody's been there watching over me."

Pat has no doubt that being matched to Jim Kelly in 1945 was a blessing. Jim was a twenty-five-year-old just returning from naval service in World War II. Newly married with a growing real estate career, Jim had a full life. But his commitment to community and love of children inspired him to become a Big Brother.

When they met, Jim recalls thinking Pat was "just

terrific" and is quick to point out that Pat had "one of the nicest mothers a boy could have."

Pat and Jim quickly became a part of each others' family. Jim says that the two did "just about anything Pat wanted to do." Pat remembers with vivid detail some of the little moments that shaped his life. The Little Brother's eyes grow soft and wet as he talks about the time Jim hosted a steak fry for his friends. "You see," he explains, "in those days it was popular to drive out of the city and have a wiener roast. We'd drink beer and talk smart."

One Saturday afternoon, Jim told Pat to invite his friends to a steak fry in a local park. "There we all were," Pat says, "me, my friends and their girlfriends. We drove back to his house later and this guy tells us we're going to play charades! We thought it was ridiculous, but we played." His voice grows soft as he says simply, "It was one of the best afternoons." Pat says that this "square" activity is often brought up at class reunions. His friends are still talking about the steak fry on that warm fall afternoon. They acted like kids, and it meant something to each of them.

Pat says Jim was always receptive to what he had to say. "He taught me how to talk straight and think straight. He showed me the right thing to do," he says. Pat remembers going to Our Lady of Guadalupe with Jim to pray Novenas. "He taught me about faith and how to be a good man and a good husband." Pat warms with pride as he talks about the way that Jim and his wife Lorraine's fifty-year marriage influenced the way he loves his own family. Pat and his wife, also named Pat, have now been married for forty-five years and have four adult children.

In the past fifty-eight years, Pat and Jim have marked time by shared rites of passage. Pat talks about the way Jim was there for him when he was in college. "Jim really saw me through," he says.

Jim served as pallbearer in the funerals of all Pat's immediate family members—his mother, father, and brother. He was also the best man in Pat's wedding. Jim and Lorraine were godparents to the Rickert's first son Michael, whose middle name is Kelly in honor of Jim.

After Pat grew, Jim became a Big Brother to eight additional young men. He still has relationships with some but is quick to note, "Pat was always the best" and really "set the standard for those that came after him."

Jim and Pat have unparalleled years of service on the board of directors for Big Brothers Big Sisters of the Greater Twin Cities—Jim for forty-six years and Pat for twenty-three.

Now that Pat is sixty-eight and Jim is eighty-four, their roles of Big and Little blur. Jim, growing frail, now takes Pat's arm easily as they walk. Polished even in age, Jim wears a suit to every Big Brothers Big Sisters event.

Pat visits the nursing home regularly and jokes easily with the staff about Jim's popularity. "Everyone loves him," he says. Jim smiles distantly, "If I ever need him, I know I can call him." Pat nods knowingly. He summarizes the more than half century their lives have been interwoven by saying, "We depend on each other; we always have."

By Deanna Petersen

It Started Innocently Enough

Big Brother Larry Bailey and Little Brother Steve Hicks

Trust plays a major part in any relationship—especially one between a Big Brother and his Little Brother. When it came to trusting this Big Brother to find him a date, Little Brother Steve was somewhat apprehensive, but he nervously agreed to the venture.

The first date was hastily put together. Steve and I were watching a University of Kentucky basketball game late one evening while he was home on college vacation. Feeling a little like Cupid, I suggested a call to a young, attractive coworker named Cathy. She was not quite the sports fan that Steve and I were, and the call actually woke Cathy, but she agreed to the meeting.

The first date went well despite the reluctance of my six-year-old daughter to allow Uncle Steve and his new friend some quiet time together. Another date led to countless others, and, several months later, Steve asked Cathy for her hand in marriage. At their wedding, I stood beside Steve as he had done for me years earlier. Needless to say, Steve was happy with my matchmaking skills.

Knowing each other's likes and dislikes is nothing new to us. We have been matched for over twenty-three years and have literally grown up together. It would be unfair to call our relationship an example of your typical Big Brothers Big Sisters match. We are family. We laugh together; we cry together; and we have learned that we can depend on each other through whatever curves life throws our way.

Our relationship started innocently enough. I was fresh out of high school and facing what I considered a major problem. My older brothers had left home, and most of my friends had left for college or jobs. I wanted to remain a carefree young man, but I needed someone who shared my views, and I needed a friend.

God answered my prayers in the form of a television commercial for Big Brothers Big Sisters, asking for volunteers. There was a little problem though. In 1980 volunteers had to be twenty-one. I begged and pleaded for them to let me join. After a couple of days, the agency, recognizing its needs and acknowledging my perseverance, agreed to take me.

I was matched with a six-year-old boy named Steve who lived in nearby Ashland, Kentucky. I quickly discovered that Steve was not your average run-of-the-mill boy, as his carefully worded application showed his potential and maturity.

"When I grow up I want to be a wait (weight) lifter and I want to catch a whale," Steve carefully wrote in his best penmanship on the application. "I want a big brother who likes sports . . . who will buy me ice cream . . . and likes to play."

I knew then Steve was my new best friend. Not only was he adventurous, but he also had a sense of humor and ambition. I could visualize Steve and me playing catch and eating ice cream on the open seas, searching feverishly for Moby Dick.

While we have yet to land the great whale, we have

landed a great, lasting relationship that has grown closer through the years. The emotions and memories of these years are endless and truly priceless.

As a coach for the local Little League, I knew Steve was too young to play, but I was able to sneak him in. During his first at-bat, the bases were loaded, and Steve, who could barely keep his oversized helmet from covering his eyes, strolled to the plate with his ever-present smile.

He hit a grounder. With one hand to the side and the other trying to keep his helmet from falling over his eyes, he went circling first base. A couple of poor throws later, Steve cleared the bases and touched home plate with an inside-the-park home run. I'm sure he felt like Babe Ruth as he was mugged by his teammates.

There were serious moments in our relationship, and those also helped us grow.

One day Steve asked me what Heaven and Hell would be like. I told him that I pictured Heaven as living the greatest day of your life forever and Hell would be just the opposite—living your worst days of your life and never having them end.

I could see that he was thinking about what I said. "You know what?" Steve asked. "I think the best days of my life are the days I spend with you." Needless to say, I was speechless and had tears in my eyes.

There were many special days as Steve grew. One night when Steve was in the fifth grade, I received a frantic call from his mother. She was upset and crying. I thought something happened to Steve; she quickly told me he was fine but that another problem had arisen.

"Steve wants to camp out with girls," she said sobbingly. "I can't talk with him about these things. Can you?"

I agreed, though I really had no clue how to approach

the subject with Steve. As we sat on his front porch I nervously explained to him why it was wrong to camp out with girls and proceeded to tell him about the facts of life. It was an emotional, special discussion between two good friends, but that's what friendship is all about—sharing special talks.

I am thankful a program such as Big Brothers Big Sisters exists. It has been such a rewarding experience to me. I'm often complimented and told how good I have been for Steve, but those people are missing the point. Steve has been great for me. He has helped me become the type of individual I want to be, and he has returned the love tenfold.

Who would have thought that an immature eighteen-year-old and a spunky six-year-old would hit it off so well and remain together? Today, we both teach in the public school system and are as close as ever. We are family and will be until the day one of us leaves this Earth.

By Larry Bailey

Chapter 4

On Angel's Wings

We Will Never Forget

Big Sisters Lindsay Morehouse and Sara Sparks and Little Sister Tiffany Belmond

Sara met her best friend Lindsay at boarding school in Concord, New Hampshire. "She was a year older than me, and we hit it off right away. We practically became best friends overnight, and would do everything together."

But after high school they took opposite career paths. Sara enjoyed arts and literature, while Lindsay excelled at math and finance. Lindsay graduated from Williams College with an economics degree and began working in Virginia with an investment banking firm. Sara was thrilled to have her best friend living in the same area as she finished her senior year at Georgetown University.

After Sara's college graduation, they both decided to move to New York City. Lindsay had a job as an equity research assistant, and Sara had an internship with *People* magazine. They moved into a spacious three-bedroom apartment on the Upper East Side of Manhattan with another friend.

Lindsay's mother had taught her at a very young age to help others and to give back to the community. Having heard about the Big Brothers Big Sisters program, Lindsay was very interested in becoming a mentor. In her normal convincing way, she had Sara attend a Big Brothers Big

Sisters orientation class with her. Lindsay was instantly hooked and was anxious to become a Big. Sara, on the other hand, was a little more cautious. Sara recalls, "I wanted to wait to see how Lindsay's match went first before I made a commitment."

As Sara remembered, "It was funny to see Lindsay prepare for the Big Brothers Big Sisters interview. She was always so well-prepared for everything. But this interview in particular, she acted as if she was interviewing for the most important job of her life. She was wondering if she was wearing the right clothes and hoping she wouldn't get nervous. She had her mind made up and wanted to make sure she presented herself as a good role model. Lindsay was determined not only to be a Big, but to be the very best Big."

A few weeks went by; Lindsay was happy and still bubbling about how well the interview went. She was so excited when she heard from Big Brothers Big Sisters. They wanted to set up a time when she could be introduced to her new Little Sister and complete the BBBS match. She went to work that morning, ecstatic to meet her Little Sister.

It was a normal Tuesday morning, a typical day for most New Yorkers. Lindsay made her way to work at the investment banking office of Keefe, Bruyette & Woods. Events that day would change everyone's lives forever. Lindsay's office was on the eighty-ninth floor of Tower Two at the World Trade Center, and that Tuesday morning was September 11, 2001.

That morning, Sara was trying to return to New York from visiting family in New Hampshire. She was in a car heading to Boston's Logan Airport when she heard the initial reports on the radio. By the time she arrived at the airport, all airline traffic was grounded. She wanted to get back to New York, but with all of the uncertainty and confusion and no means of transportation, she decided to stay with family and wait a while.

Sara was extremely worried about her best friend and was trying to get through to her friends, family, and coworkers to make sure Lindsay was safe. They used e-mail to communicate, and Sara recalls having over a hundred e-mails about Lindsay from other friends who worked in the towers.

Through e-mails and phone calls, Sara learned quickly that only a handful of Lindsay's coworkers left the building after the first plane hit Tower One. When the second plane hit Tower Two, it smashed into the building below the office where Lindsay worked. It would have been impossible for anyone in the upper floors to make it out alive. Unfortunately, Lindsay, along with almost all of her coworkers, never made it out of the building that day.

Sara recalls having a gut feeling. "I just knew she didn't make it out. We were so close; she was my best friend. I lost a part of me that day." Sara thought about how Lindsay was looking forward to her new Little Sister. With all the things Lindsay had accomplished, that was one goal she would never achieve.

Sara believed that the only way to move forward from the tragedy was to somehow make a positive out of it. She questioned, "How can I make a positive from an event like this?" Sara's answer came to her subconsciously when she contacted the Big Brothers Big Sisters office to inform them about the loss of Lindsay. She also told them that she wanted to take over Lindsay's match. "Lindsay would have been the best Big Sister," said Sara. "I want to fulfill the dream of my friend. She never had the chance to impact the life of a Little Sister, so I wanted to do this in Lindsay's honor."

Sara was matched to twelve-year-old Tiffany Belmond

just two months after the tragedy. Sara and Tiffany used each other to cope with the events. Sara told Tiffany stories about Lindsay, and Tiffany wrote a poem about the tragedy to help people overcome their losses and fears. They made a great team and gave speeches about Big Brothers Big Sisters and the 9/11 events. The poem Tiffany wrote was always read aloud at their speaking engagements:

We stand united both tall and true
We are together; we stick like glue.
Sara's more than a Big Sister, she's a friend
We'll be that way to the very end.
Sara and I used to feel blue
But we stand united both tall and true.

"Tiffany is a bright and beautiful girl. She lives with her grandmother and needed someone a little closer in age to be able to share her feelings with. We've done a lot of things together, but by far the thing Tiffany enjoys the most is watching movies. We must have seen at least fifty movies together in the last two years!" exclaims Sara. At her young age Tiffany has even taken some modeling and acting classes. Sara added, "I guess watching all of those movies had an impact; she wants to be an actress!"

Living in the Bronx her entire life, Tiffany never had much exposure to other cultures or lifestyles. Sara stated, "I took her on a road trip to my family's lake house in northern Vermont. It was nice seeing her getting to spend time in a very different, outdoorsy environment, and having so much fun experiencing it all! Tiffany spent four or five hours on the beach playing catch with the family's black Lab. I tried to teach her how to water-ski, and we had a few laughs after some face-first falls."

Sara also took Tiffany on her first airplane ride. Sara's family has loved getting to know Tiffany over the last couple of years, so the two of them went to visit Sara's family in Durham, North Carolina. Sara recalled, "Tiffany was so excited that when I picked her up to go to the airport, she told me she didn't get a wink of sleep the night before! Tiffany didn't really care where we were going; she just wanted to fly. She's a sweet kid, and it's always very enjoyable and worthwhile when we get together."

Recently Tiffany began dating her first boyfriend. Sara added, "It was so cute to have Tiffany share her boyfriend stories with me, but then she started asking me about my boyfriends. She felt she had to share her expert opinion and started giving me advice. The funny thing is that a lot of times her advice made more sense then what other people had told me. Adults often make things too complicated; sometimes simple answers are the best."

By Sara Sparks as told to Alan Annis

Editors' note: In keeping with Lindsay's wishes to reach out and positively affect the lives of disadvantaged youth, her parents created the Lindsay Morehouse Memorial College Scholarship fund to assist college-bound youth in the BBBS program who need financial assistance.
When the 9/11 Memorial is built at the former site of the World Trade Center, Lindsay Morehouse's name will appear as one of the 2,948 people who tragically died that day. We will never forget.

Forever, Rob

Big Brother Ken Spadafore and Little Brother Rob Neal

My match with my Big Brother Ken Spadafore started like thousands of other Big Brothers Big Sisters matches. I was a nine-year-old kid from a divorced family in need of an adult friend. But our match didn't end the way we expected it to.

After my parents divorced, my mom was left with the sole responsibility of raising three kids. She worked very hard to support us, and as a result she had virtually no time to spend with us.

I was a lonely, sad boy. I blamed myself for my parents' divorce and the turmoil that followed. My emotional state was taking its toll on my schoolwork, and it became obvious to the adults in my life that I needed some help.

Ken was the perfect Big Brother match for me. We both loved the outdoors and sports. He took me camping and fishing, and he had a young boy's fantasy—season tickets to both the Pittsburgh Pirates and the Steelers! How lucky could a guy get!

My relationship with Ken grew stronger as I grew older. When I was fourteen, my dad died. It was a really tough time for me. I called the one person I knew would help me deal with it the best I could—Ken. He stayed by my side at the funeral home and throughout the entire ordeal.

When I was first matched with Ken, I was kind of tough on him. I thought he was trying to take the place of my father, and I resented him for that. Ken was a patient guy, though, and showed me what a real friend is. He was kind, warm, reliable, and a great listener. But the best part of Ken was his sense of humor and his laugh!

Ken supported everything I did. He cheered me on in football, helped me study for my SATs, and taught me to drive.

It's kind of funny; although I originally didn't want Ken to be a father figure, that is exactly what he became. Sometimes he was tough on me like a father would be. Once he arranged for me to get a job as a dishwasher in a restaurant at which he was the chef. He wanted me to learn two things in that job—responsibility and the need to get a good education so you can get a good job. I hated the job, but I learned the lesson.

We became family. When Ken married his beautiful wife Shelly, I was a groomsman at the wedding. When I watched him get married, I knew he would be in my wedding someday.

In March 2002 we went to a game together. He was really pale. He said he wasn't feeling well, but he wasn't sure what was going on.

I left to visit some friends in Maine. A couple of weeks had passed when I received a phone call telling me that Ken had died at age forty-six of complications from a blood clot that burst in his lungs.

I was devastated. Not only had I lost the most important man in my life, my Big Brother, my dear friend, and the man I thought of as my father, but I wasn't with him when he was sick in the hospital and died.

At Ken's wake, I asked his widow Shelly if I could put

a note I had written to Ken in his casket. The tribute had a picture of my one-of-a-kind Big Brother and me in happier times and this note:

Believed in me.
Instilled values in me.
Gave me encouragement.
Became a father figure.
Reached out and changed my life.
Opened your heart.
Taught me how to drive.
Honestly gave me advice.
Earned my trust and love.
Remembered in my heart is where you will always be.
I thank God for the precious gift of your friendship. It was a privilege to have you be a part of my life and just knowing you made me a better person. For this, I will always be eternally grateful. You will always be with me in my heart and soul.
Forever, Rob.

Ken won't be at my wedding but he will always live in my heart and my soul.

By Rob Neal as told to Beth Barrett

My Son Michael

Big Brother Oscar Vergara and Little Brother Michael Yeomans

He was one week old when we got the call from the adoption service. Born in the Philippines, Michael completed our family, joining his twenty-two-month-old sister Ellie, adopted from Peru. We were living in Jakarta, Indonesia. In December 1985, when Michael was four years old, the children and I returned to Syracuse, New York. Their father remained in Jakarta and later moved to Florida.

Michael missed his father and did not get to see him very often. He began to have problems at school and at home. I knew Michael needed a male role model, so I applied to the Big Brothers Big Sisters program. I had only one criterion for a Big—someone who would be in Syracuse for a long time and be willing to commit to a long-term relationship with Michael. It was two years before they fulfilled my request.

When Michael was twelve, he was introduced to Oscar Vergara. Everything changed for Michael at that moment. It is not easy to describe my feelings the night that Oscar came to our home to meet Michael. I felt a heavy burden lift from my shoulders. I was not alone anymore, trying to raise a son and knowing that, as a mother, my efforts would fall far short of what a man could do for a boy. This was the mentor we had waited for so long, a man with high moral values, someone Michael could turn to when things got rough and talk to about girls or whatever else was bothering him.

Michael and Oscar did everything together. There was a mutual respect between them. Michael played soccer for Coach Oscar, learning about winning, losing, and being strong. Michael taught Oscar to fish, although Oscar never quite got into the worm-on-the-hook thing. They went to movies selected by Michael. Oscar would shake his head and say, "I can't believe I let him talk me into that movie!"

Oscar's joy in their relationship mirrored Michael's. I learned later that when Oscar was a teenager in Colombia, South America, his mother died as a result of a car accident with a drunk driver. After her death, Oscar became depressed, dropped out of school, and stopped playing soccer. He was clearly headed for trouble until his soccer coach took Oscar under his wing and set him on the right path. Oscar has dedicated his life to running the Big Brothers Big Sisters program in Syracuse, New York, and to serving as a Big himself, in part as a way of paying back a debt he owes to the soccer coach and mentor who saved his life in Colombia many years ago.

Michael wanted to be a chef. He would cook a special dish and invite Oscar for dinner. Michael had a great sense of humor. To see them play off one another was to see an ideal relationship and a deepening friendship. When Michael had a story about a girl he liked at school, he would briefly tell me, and then rush to the phone to call Oscar. I smiled to myself, pleased that the Big Brother program fulfilled its promise and then some—my son had a man to look up to, to share his problems with, to bond with, and to be there for him. Michael hoped one day to be a Big Brother himself. Because of Oscar's presence,

Michael was doing better with all aspects of his life.

When Michael turned fifteen, he had an epileptic seizure as he was getting off the school bus. Years of tests, medicine with varying side-effects, more seizures, and hospitalizations followed. During this time, Michael was learning to drive, had a job at Burger King, excelled in art class, took karate lessons, and enjoyed writing poetry. He was proud of his job at Burger King, teasingly asking us, "Do you want fries with that?"

The summer before Michael's senior year of high school he slipped mentally, and he was unable to control a jerking movement in his hands. He lost his job at Burger King. It broke my heart to tell Michael that he could no longer drive his car. Michael used to play soccer with incredible energy, going all out for Coach Oscar. Now he was relegated to the bench, where he sat next to Oscar and helped collect balls when the game ended.

There were months without a seizure when the "jerks," as he called them, were nonexistent. Then they would return. As the manifestation of his disease increased, his friends grew distant. Michael became depressed, insecure, afraid, and angry. He experimented with marijuana.

Michael wanted desperately to graduate from high school, to walk across the stage with his classmates, and he did it! The courage it took to earn that diploma is indescribable.

We took Michael to a specialist in New York City who told us he had a degenerative brain disease, not epilepsy. There was no cure. We didn't tell Michael. Oscar was ever present, ever constant, and always available. Oscar was included in all the reports from the doctors. How he continued to pick Michael up with a smile and a joke, never breaking down in front of him, I will never know.

In March 2001, we brought Michael to a hospice center

at Lake Katrine, New York. He had his own room, with all his special belongings—his soccer shirt, the black belt he had earned in karate for the bravery he exhibited in fighting his disease, journals for writing, art supplies, his high school diploma, photos of family and Oscar. Once a month, Oscar made the three and a half hour trip to spend a day with Michael. He would bring him his favorite food—a bacon double cheeseburger and fries, from Burger King, of course. Unable to walk now, Michael roared with laughter as Oscar ran him around the parking lot in his wheelchair. Oscar would be panting as Michael demanded, "Come on, old man, one more time!"

We lost Michael on December 1, 2002. He died peacefully, the favorite of the nurses on his unit, a character to the end, still able to find humor and to relate to his best friend, Oscar. I will be forever grateful to Big Brothers Big Sisters for making my son's short life more precious.

A memorial fund has been established in Michael's name, and each May a graduating high school mentor receives a small sum to bring that child closer to his or her dreams. Michael didn't fulfill his goal of becoming a Big Brother, but thanks to Oscar and the Big Brothers Big Sisters program, other children will go forward to fulfill their dreams.

By Marilyn Miller

Finding Victory

Big Sister Melissa Tabolsky and Little Sister Jaymil Miller

Victory in life is not about having perfect circumstances; it is about what we do with what we are given.

I will never forget my first meeting with Jaymil. She was an eager eleven-year-old living in an institutional home, and I was a college graduate excited to be a Big Sister. I had recently moved from Minneapolis to Cincinnati for a job, so with my family far away I hoped Jaymil would become my Little Sister in more than one sense.

Upon introductions, Jaymil grabbed my hand and would not let go all day. She told me her loves in life—basketball and Mickey Mouse—and her three goals: having a birthday party at Chuck E Cheese, going to Disney World, and graduating from high school. Despite the challenges in her life, she was determined to defy the odds and succeed. I promised her that when she did graduate, I would be there cheering her on.

We spent time together almost every weekend. The spunky Jaymil had a way of lifting my spirits at the end of a very stressful workweek—whether we were driving and singing with the radio, baking cookies at my apartment, or eating out. We shared our struggles, and she even gave me dating advice.

Jaymil's first dream was realized when we celebrated her twelfth birthday with Chuck E., my friends, and her overwhelming enthusiasm. Jaymil had a special appreciation for the simple things in life, and I found her zeal to be contagious. She continually helped me see my life in better perspective.

Another character trait that impacted me was Jaymil's concern for others. During our first winter together, Cincinnati was hit by a blanketing snowstorm. Jaymil had never been sledding before, so we immediately decided that would be our plan for the day. On our way to the local grocery store to buy sleds, Jaymil showed me that she had two dollars in her pocket. She was excited to have earned the money and gave me a list of all that she hoped to buy once she had saved some more.

As we exited the store with our precious cargo, she noticed a Salvation Army volunteer ringing his holiday bell. Without hesitation, Jaymil walked up and deposited her two dollars into his kettle. In the car, she explained to me that when she was little they had brought her family Christmas presents. Now, she said, she could help someone else have Christmas presents.

During this time, Jaymil was shuffled between many different foster homes and institutional centers. Her life was unstable, and she struggled with many things, including schoolwork, self-discipline, and authority. At one point she even ran away and fought to survive in a gang-infested neighborhood. My heart ached for her and the obstacles she faced on a daily basis. I tried to encourage her and give advice, but always knew that with my relatively sheltered suburban upbringing, I could not truly understand the reality she experienced.

Two years after our first meeting, Jaymil gave a thumbs

up to a handsome guy I'd fallen in love with. Marrying this man meant moving to California, so, despite my intentions, I soon added more heartache to her life. I felt guilty being yet another person coming in and out of her world. I desperately prayed for the Lord to bring her someone who would be consistent, and He graciously answered those prayers.

Shortly after Jaymil honored me by being the flower girl in my wedding in Minneapolis, she was moved to a new foster home. This became her final move. Her new foster family, where she spent the next five years, was a gift from God. Her foster mom and her foster sister became her true family. They gave her the love and stability she needed, in a safe environment.

Over the next years, Jaymil and I kept in touch and saw each other through annual visits. One perk for Jaymil was being able to visit Disneyland when she visited me in California. It wasn't Disney World, but it was close, so goal number 2 could be checked off her list. We enjoyed our time together, and I loved seeing each year how much Jaymil had grown and matured.

She was steadily making progress towards goal number 3, despite her struggles with school. Many times she considered dropping out, but she persevered, thanks to supportive teachers, her foster family, and others who believed in her dreams.

I am thankful Jaymil kept me as her Big Sister. The program offered her a new Big Sister, but she declined, telling our caseworker that she still had me. How humbling this was, knowing I could never adequately fill the role before me. This didn't matter to Jaymil with the unconditional love and loyalty she carried for our relationship.

Our final visit came in May 2003, when I cheered her

on at her graduation ceremony. Jaymil had accomplished what she set out to do, despite the many obstacles and influences in her life. It was a beautiful moment, seeing Jaymil in her glory, tremendously proud of her hard work and her determination.

Through this accomplishment, Jaymil looked forward to encouraging others in tough circumstances that all things are possible if you believe in and work toward your dreams. After the ceremony, she told me with excitement that she would be sharing her story the next month through a newsletter article and a speaking engagement at a banquet for high-risk kids.

Unfortunately, those opportunities would not be realized. One week after she walked in her cap and gown, I received a phone call in the wee hours of the morning. Jaymil had been killed in a tragic car accident that also took the lives of her best friend and her brother.

Through my heartache, I find inspiration. Jaymil succeeded despite her circumstances. She has helped me to gauge my struggles, to see my blessings more clearly, and to believe that I too can fulfill my dreams. I learned much from Jaymil in our years together, and through her death she taught me one last thing: we don't know what tomorrow will bring. I am more determined than ever to make the best of each day and to focus on what matters most.

Though her life ended much too soon, Jaymil found victory. My hope is that we all do the same.

By Melissa Tabolsky

The Magic of John's Brothers

In Memory of John Price

A very special magic was created when athletes from Holy Cross College in Worcester, Massachusetts, became Big Brothers to honor the memory of their teammate. The young men, members of the lacrosse team, and their coach were inspired by the team's former captain. John Price was an idealistic young man who volunteered as a mentor in high school. One of John's goals was to convince his teammates to become Big Brothers, but, before he could put his plan into action, he was killed in a train accident.

At his funeral, John's family and friends spoke of his experiences as a volunteer and how much volunteering meant to him. Afterwards, when lacrosse coach Mike McCaffrey and the team discussed how they could pay homage to John, the first suggestion was to follow his lead and become Big Brothers.

Every single member of the team as well as Coach McCaffrey decided to volunteer—as John's Brothers.

"It seemed like the perfect way to honor his memory," said teammate Steve Ribaudo. "We all had so much respect for John."

The team's tribute was the beginning of the magic. Big Brothers Big Sisters of Worcester County was struggling with a dilemma. The organization had proposed a new, school-based mentoring program at two inner-city schools, and they needed volunteers to fill the many requests for Big Brothers and Sisters.

John's Brothers volunteered just in time to become the first school-based mentors at Canterbury Street School in Worcester. Big Brother Steve recalled the day the Bigs and Littles first met. "I don't think they knew what to make of us," he said, "but it didn't take long to make a connection."

The team came to the school once a week. Each pair of Big and Little Brothers got together to do homework or other school projects, followed by basketball games in the gym.

A group of three Bigs and Littles stayed together for three years, until the college students graduated. "It was fun to watch the little guys become more mature," said Brian McKeon.

Many of the Littles came from single-parent homes where their moms or dads struggled to give them the attention they needed. In contrast, most of the college students grew up with plenty of support from their parents and teachers. On a one-to-one basis, as only Big Brothers can do, the young men gave their Little Brothers much-needed attention and showed them how they valued their own education.

"Simply asking the Littles every week, 'How is school?' 'Did you have any tests this week?' or 'Did you get into trouble?' set the tone," said Steve.

The magic worked both ways. Paul Washington, another lacrosse team member, was inspired by his Little Brother to change his career plans and become a teacher.

"I was an economics major, planning to work in New York City," Paul explained. "One day my Little Brother Kyle and I were talking about what each of us wanted to do when we grew up. I tried to explain my aspirations to Kyle, but I didn't do a very good job. It made me realize, if I couldn't explain to a nine-year-old why I wanted to be a businessman, maybe I didn't have the right reasons for that career goal.

"Kyle candidly told me he thought it was a dumb idea and went on to describe very eloquently why he wanted to be a teacher," Paul continued. "He told me he thought I'd make a good teacher too."

The conversation with his Little Brother "was like an epiphany," Paul said. The college student decided to add a history major to his transcript and went on to spend two summers teaching summer school. Today Paul teaches government at Strake Jesuit College Prep School in Houston, Texas.

"I am two thousand miles away from any New York City business firm, and I couldn't be happier," he said. "My time with Kyle had more of an impact on me than any other experience I had in college," Paul continued. "As I look back, what I'm most proud of is being Kyle's Big Brother."

The magic generated by the lacrosse team Bigs and their Littles spread throughout the Holy Cross campus and attracted other students who volunteered to become Big Brothers and Sisters.

A young woman who is legally blind was matched with a girl who shares the same disability. After their first visit, the Little Sister "was practically jumping up and down with enthusiasm," noted Linda Urbec, community liaison for one of the school-based mentor sites. "The two of them talked about all kinds of possibilities. Now the Little Sister has a role model, someone who can relate to her particular challenges," Linda said.

Students in the college's Deaf Studies Program were

matched with hearing disabled Littles in another school. One of them noted that being a Big Sister "was the most rewarding activity I have participated in at college. My Little Sister taught me more in a few meetings that I could learn in any classroom," she said.

Other college sportsmen in Worcester were inspired by the Holy Cross lacrosse players. Members of the Clark University and Worcester Polytechnic Institute basketball teams also became Big Brothers. In fact, the school-based program that started with 42 of John's Brothers three years ago has grown to 150 Worcester-area college students who volunteer as Big Brothers and Big Sisters.

The enthusiasm and dedication of the Bigs and their positive impact on the Littles also won over administrators at the schools where they volunteered. George Sanders, former principal of Canterbury Street School, was skeptical at first. After seeing the results—improvements in grades, school attendance, and behavior among kids who had Big Brothers or Sisters—the principal became an enthusiastic supporter. "It's been absolutely incredible," he said. "It made our school a wonderful, busy place."

The magic still inspires some of John's Brothers. Steve Ribaudo is now in graduate school in Washington, D.C., where he volunteers as a Big Brother. "I'm convinced I will maintain a relationship with the BBBS program for the rest of my life," he said.

Thinking back on the young man whom the lacrosse team honored by their volunteer efforts, Steve says his former teammate would have been proud of what they accomplished.

"John would have loved the program," he said. "And he would have wanted more teams to follow our example."

By Margaret LeRoux

Michaela's Life

Big Sister Renee Kientz and Little Sister Michaela White

When the phone rings at 2:10 in the morning, you hope it's a wrong number. Even in the fog of interrupted sleep, you know enough to fear the possibilities. My phone rang at 2:10 last Thursday morning.

Without my glasses I found the toggle of the bedside lamp, squinted at the Caller ID, and saw a familiar number. It registered the home of my little sister Michaela White, the girl with whom I was matched by Big Brothers Big Sisters almost ten years ago.

I picked up the receiver, knowing something was wrong.

Sobbing, a girl's voice choked out what sounded like "They're dead, they're dead!" Between gasps, she was trying to tell me something terrible.

I said, "Baby, who's dead?" Again the words were hard to understand, more wailed than spoken.

"There was an accident. They were both killed."

Then, more calmly, she said there had been a terrible car crash. As she talked, a sick feeling squeezed my chest. This didn't sound like Michaela. The voice, the inflection sounded like her older sister. I had to will myself to say the words out loud.

"Is this Mandisa?"

Yes.

"Mandisa, are you telling me that Michaela is dead?"

Yes.

And then we both sobbed for our little sister, stunned and aching with pain I cannot describe. I am crying now. As much as I hurt, I cannot imagine how Michaela's mother feels. She lost two of her three children, her oldest and her youngest, about 8:30 last Wednesday night. Michaela was riding with her older brother, Maurice, twenty-five and the father of two young children, when the accident happened. For their mom, Kimberly White, who has multiple sclerosis and who lost her job with the Housing Authority last year, it is the latest and most devastating blow imaginable.

What do you say in an obituary for a seventeen-year-old girl? She hadn't found her first love yet, hadn't had children. She didn't have a driver's license, or a job, not even a glimmer yet of what she would make her life's work, though God knows I nudged her toward medical school.

Michaela A. White, born May 23, 1985, died on September 25, 2002. A senior at Gulf Shores Academy. Pretty good grades, though she could easily have made better. Recently chosen for the cheerleader squad. Sneezed in bright sunlight, liked shoes and sleeping, in that order. Rolled her eyes at my husband's jokes but adored him and the bear hugs he greeted her with.

Smart, wickedly funny. Intolerant of fools. Biracial, she got annoyed with people who asked her, "What are you, white or black?" It was, she said, a stupid question.

Michaela never met her father, had a fond but long-distance relationship with her grandparents, whom she never met in person. And yes, she felt an emptiness, though she didn't talk about it more than a few times in the ten years I knew her.

The lack of extended family around her was one reason Michaela's mother signed her up for Big Brothers Big Sisters. A single parent whose time and finances were stretched painfully thin, she wanted her little girl to have new experiences and other influences in her life.

Michaela and I met on a cool spring day in 1993. She was almost eight and tiny, sitting on a chair in her mother's apartment. The Big Brothers Big Sisters caseworker introduced us, and that was that. We were sisters.

In 1997 I wrote about our relationship in a story for the *Houston Chronicle*, about what a great kid she was and how I worried what hormones and teen pressures would do to her. I worried that the drugs and too-early sex that derail so many young lives would derail hers. That at age twelve she'd already been to more funerals and held more babies than I had. That she'd taught me a lot of things, some silly, some sweet, profound, and life-changing.

I said she'd learned from me, too. Big things, like even a poor kid can go to college and become a doctor or teacher or reporter. Small things, like how to use a napkin in a restaurant or how checking accounts worked. Small lessons, I wrote, sometimes really are stepping-stones to the big ones.

I took her to Mardi Gras and to Sea World, and, during her first plane ride, showed her what clouds looked like from the other side.

Michaela would have been a good teacher. Was a good teacher.

A natural with kids, she was often pressed into babysitting service after Mandisa's first daughter was born. She alternately complained about the imposition and bragged about how smart Daejonnae was. She read to her, played Spanish tapes and Barney videos; she beamed when her feisty little niece, so much like her, shadowed her steps and repeated her words. It pleased her that the little girl, who called her Aunt Kaykee, pouted and cried when she left her behind.

Thanks to her, Daejonnae knew her alphabet and numbers, how to stand up to a bully, and how to crack a joke long before she headed off to kindergarten this year. I know that Michaela had much more to teach her, like how to use a napkin in a restaurant or what clouds look like from the other side.

By Renee Kientz

Editors' note: Renee Kientz is a reporter with the Houston Chronicle. *This story originally appeared in the* Chronicle *on October 2, 2003.*

I Wouldn't Trade a Second

Big Brother Paul Oberg and Little Brother Nathan Baker

Listening to the car radio doesn't often turn into a life-changing event. More often than not, it just leads to changing the station. In my case, however, a simple radio ad led to a lifelong relationship I will never, ever forget.

Flash back to 1978. I was driving home from work, much as I did nearly every weeknight, when I heard a public service radio ad for Big Brothers of Rhode Island. At that point in my life, I had limited contact with kids. As I listened, the ad reached me. Why not become a Big Brother? After all, I had plenty to offer a kid who needed guidance and advice.

After I went through the standard approval process, the director said they had a match for me. His name was Nathan Baker, but there was a caveat: nine-year-old Nathan had a serious medical condition. His kidneys hadn't worked properly since he was a year old. Four hours at a stretch, little Nathan had to suffer through dialysis treatments.

Undaunted, I decided to accept the match.

When Nathan and I first met, we figured we'd go for Chinese food, a favorite for both of us. At that dinner, we also discovered several other similarities. Our birthdays were one day apart, and we both used our middle names as our first names. Cool stuff, we thought. It looked liked our match was getting off on the right foot.

To that point, Nate's life had been extremely tough. He had undergone a kidney transplant when he was four, but the kidney had to be removed when he was nine. His parents had divorced early in Nate's life, so it was Nate, his mom Betty, and his sister Natalie. Times were hard for Nate's family financially. His mom tried to better their lives by attending college and trying to earn a psychology degree. It wasn't easy raising two kids alone under those conditions.

Because of his illness, Nate would never grow beyond four feet, eleven inches. He tired easily and couldn't play like the rest of the kids.

I knew that being a Big Brother would have its challenges, but this was going to be extra tough. Even so, I dove in headfirst. I wanted to be Nate's best friend outside the family, and I wanted him to confide in me.

It didn't take long for us to click. Our Saturday outings included ballgames, car shows, the circus—you name it. We went sailing. We even visited the White House, a trip that gave Nate his first airplane ride and first night in a hotel. Even with his condition, we managed. I carried Nate on my shoulders at times, and we found a dialysis center in Washington, D.C. From the Smithsonian to the Tomb of the Unknown Soldier, we saw it all.

While I helped Nate in those years, he returned the favor when he had the chance. As I went through a painful divorce, Nate was there for me. In fact, Nate made my life bearable during one of the most trying periods.

Of course, on the flip side, when a new woman, Betsey, came into my life, she had to pass the "Nate test" (which she did with flying colors). At thirteen, Nate served as my best man when I married Betsey in 1982. I remember telling him that day that no matter what, he would always have a special place in our family. I wanted him to know he would never be alone.

In 1987 something wonderful happened in Nate's life. He met a special girl, Melissa, at Pawtucket High School. And, of course, Nate's first date with Melissa included Betsey and me; we all went out for a great dinner. Naturally, Nate had plenty of questions about relationships, and I answered them the best I could.

Perhaps my proudest moment for Nate came when he graduated from high school. After the ceremony, Nate, Betsey, Melissa, Nate's mom Betty, and I celebrated at dinner. It was a wonderful party!

Nate's condition took a turn for the worse in 1990. Dialysis wasn't working, so he had to switch to an even more invasive, longer procedure that required six hours on five nights a week as he slept. It worked at first, and Nate enrolled in Rhode Island College.

A year later Nate and Melissa became engaged—a very happy event for all of us. But that was a turning point in Nate's life in other ways. He began to suffer severe pain and had to be hospitalized frequently. I was there with him many nights (the nurses referred to me as Nate's uncle). As if Nate wasn't suffering enough, his mom, who had moved to Kentucky, died in 1992 after suffering a stroke.

Out of nowhere, Nate and I started discussing the idea of becoming spokesmen for Big Brothers, helping the local organization in its recruiting efforts. Nate believed that our fourteen years together would be an inspiration to others who might be on the fence about volunteering.

He was, of course, right. But he never got to realize that dream. In October 1992 Nate was again hospitalized with severe pain. I stayed with him for a few hours, and after he was stabilized and starting to improve, I figured it was okay to take a one-day business trip to Houston. At 4

A.M., my hotel phone rang. It was Betsey, telling me that Nate had taken a turn for the worse. Two hours later he died, with Melissa near his side.

My plane ride back to New England will always be remembered as one of the worst of my life. When I got home, my last act as Nate's Big Brother was to arrange his funeral.

Today, nearly twelve years later, I look back with nothing but great memories. I have no doubt that my time with Nate made his life better. Of course, the same holds true for me. He made my life better as well.

Thinking about Nate, I have never met anyone with so much courage and strength. When I first met Nate, he was a nine year old who wanted to die. When I last talked with him, he was a young man of twenty-three who wanted to live and who wanted to get out on the speaking circuit in order to convince others of the value of being a Big Brother.

Despite the pain, despite the grief, I wouldn't trade one second of my time with Nate for anything. Today, I am a father of two boys, and Nate's legacy lives on in the way I love and care for them. Thanks, Nate, for all you have given me.

By Paul Oberg as told to Tom Starner

Big, Little, for Life

Big Brother John Kador and Little Brother J.J. Heflin

Although the Big-Little relationship formally ends when the Little reaches eighteen, I thought of J.J. as a son until he was twenty-six, the age I was when we met, the age he was when he died. He wasn't expected to live that long.

"Cystic fibrosis! You're going to match me with a Little Brother who's sick. A kid who has a fatal disease, for heaven's sake." The caseworker just looked at me.

This wasn't the deal I signed up for. I wanted another match like my first, with a smiling, athletic golden boy named Ted. We played Frisbee, hiked in the woods, went bike riding, and connected on the basis of our common interests in being outdoors and active. It was a perfect match as far as I was concerned, and it ended as I thought perfect matches should: with hugs and tears and appreciation for how we gave each other a hand. When Ted and his mom moved away, I told the folks at BBBS National Capital Area that I was ready for another match.

My breathing became labored as the caseworker described what he had in mind for me. "I can't blame you if you feel this is too much for you to take on," he said. "He's a pretty sick boy sometimes. But he needs someone.

I have a feeling about you. Will you at least meet him? His name is J.J."

I resisted at first. I resent cute nicknames that threaten my fears. I'm not good with sick people. He was too ill to do the stuff I loved. J.J. was too young. I was grasping for any reason I could live with for turning my back on this adventure for which I felt so unprepared.

As I researched the facts about cystic fibrosis (CF), my apprehension only increased. CF is a genetic condition that causes the lungs to fill with mucous until the sufferer literally drowns. In the late 1970s very few CF kids lived past seventeen. I was looking into a great abyss. I was totally unprepared to meet the challenge of being a Big Brother to J.J.

My caseworker agreed with me. I *was* totally unprepared. "You just happen to be the best person available," he said, confidently. "This kid needs you. Just meet him."

I met him. John Joseph Heflin—everyone called him J.J.—was ten years old in 1977 when we first met. He lived not far from me in a small bungalow in Silver Spring, Maryland, with his mother and older sister. His father, divorced, now lived out of state and rarely contacted him. J.J. was small for his age. Most CF kids are. He had light brown hair, a very pale complexion as if he didn't spend much time outside—which he didn't—and, incongruously, a musical voicc that was a rcgistcr lowcr than his slight frame suggested.

His mother demonstrated the daily treatments J.J. had to take to fight off the suffocating effects of CF. Every few months, J.J. checked into Georgetown Hospital for procedures to further clear his weakening lungs.

Over the next five years, we saw each other at least once a week, sometimes more. We did the usual stuff:

bowling, movies, video games, libraries, concerts, dinners at our house. Anna Beth, my wife of four years, welcomed him into our family. In his healthy periods, we explored the cultural treasures of Washington, D.C. He spent at least two months of each year in the hospital, where I visited him frequently and got to know the other CF kids on the ward. I grieved with him as, one by one, his friends died. When he got out, we celebrated by sharing a banana split with Oreo cookie topping.

I also pushed him to be more physical: hiking, playing catch, Frisbee, swimming. As he entered his mid-teens, J.J. seemed to thrive, and he told me that he liked his life for the first time in his life. I smiled, but inside I dreaded the future. The facts were unavoidable. Almost every kid with CF at the time died by age eighteen. J.J. accepted this reality with an ease I found incomprehensible. In this, as in other matters of life and death, he would be my teacher.

Life goes on. J.J. grew up. My career took me away from Maryland. Our own children came. For his part, J.J. finished high school and got a job and then a girlfriend. He even married. The formal part of our relationship ended, but as it sometimes happens, our bond transcended both time and distance. Our visits, though fewer, were just as sweet, and when J.J. held my own son in his arms, I was fulfilled.

By 1991, when he was twenty-four, J.J. had outlived all of his CF contemporaries and was trespassing on the end. Only the grace of God and extraordinary medical care were keeping him alive. He was in and out of hospitals, sometimes staying for months at a time. And then, as they always do, his ruined lungs failed. All the activities that those of us with lungs in the pink take for granted—walking up the stairs, opening a can of Pepsi, breathing—were one by one denied to him by the relentless onslaught of CF.

There was almost no life left in my Little Brother when J.J. was approved for a bilateral lung transplant. He was airlifted to St. Louis for the very difficult operation. God guided the hands of the skilled surgeons at Barnes Hospital who removed J.J.'s ruined lungs for a new set donated by a young woman who died in an automobile accident.

It was a miracle. I got J.J. back as the life that had ebbed out of him now returned in triumph. Through much of 1992 and 1993 we were Big and Little again. We rejoiced together as we explored the bounty of the Midwest. My children, now nine and five, got to know this remarkable young man.

After fifteen months of health, J.J.'s body rebelled, his immune system ruining the new lungs even as CF ruined the old.

Although another set of lungs was available, J.J. told me that he had enough of hospitals, drugs that burn, and invasive treatments. J.J. had no more fight left in his ravaged body. It was time to accept the awesome fury of CF. There was no bitterness in his voice. It was his decision to accept the fact his life would end. Not only would he decline another set of lungs, but he would also stop taking the medications that slowed his deluded immune system from devouring the borrowed lungs currently in his chest. He knew that in a matter of days he would be dead.

As the words came out of his ravaged chest, I too accepted his decision, no longer able to hide from the reality he had accepted even before our first meeting sixteen years earlier. Though we had been practicing this good-bye for more than decade, the farewell tore at me. I admired the relaxed way he made his decision. It was August 10, 1993.

J.J. died on August 19. A few days later the last letter he wrote in this life arrived in my mailbox:

"I wanted to thank you for all that great times we've

had. All the things you have shown me and taught me. I feel that I've been a finer person for having known you. You had a big influence on me. Take care of your beautiful family. I love you, J.J."

Here's the response he'll never get: "J.J., I've done my level best to take care of my family. I know that my children have a better, smarter, more loving father for knowing you and all the things you have shown me and taught me. You had a big influence on me. I love you, John."

By John Kador

Chapter 5

The Magic Continues

Four Generations and Room for More

Big Brother Ed Rapport and Little Brothers Michael Blumenthal, Ken Soule, and Matthew Block

Most families have traditions that are passed down from generation to generation. It doesn't matter if the family is related by blood or by choice. Everyone from the youngest to the oldest knows the stories of the traditions that make the building blocks of that family's loving memories.

In Big Brothers Big Sisters, those memories can begin in ways that no one could have predicted more than half a century ago.

In 1952 Ed Rapport, a young advertising executive, watched the movie *Room for One More* about a husband and wife who took troubled youngsters into their home and raised them with their own children. The movie touched Ed so much that he decided he had to help a child.

Nine-year-old Michael Blumenthal had lived the last six years of his life in children's homes. Although the staff members were wonderful, Mike needed an adult who would give him the one-on-one time that they were not able to provide. He was put on the waiting list for a Big Brother and anxiously awaited the day when some man would volunteer.

Ed Rapport recalls that day fifty-two years ago when

he drove up to the cottage in the Bellfaire Jewish Children's Home in Shaker Heights, Ohio, to meet his new Little Brother Mike. He expected his shiny convertible to impress this little boy. Instead, Mike told Ed that he didn't like convertibles; he was obviously quite *un*impressed with the car.

After taking a spin around town with the top down and having dinner, Ed drove Mike back to the BJC Home. Mike's cottage mates came running out to see the great-looking car. Suddenly Mike was beaming with pride as he showed off his newly learned skill of taking the top down.

Mike and Ed started a friendship that day that blossomed into a family. Ed says, "I don't recall any specific event that made me realize Mike was learning to trust me. Our relationship was a gradual merging of personalities. I knew Mike liked me. He showed it in many simple ways. I remember a Sunday walk in the park, when Mike suddenly reached up to take my hand. When we'd visit relatives and friends, Mike would sit very close to me."

Just as he had seen in the movie that inspired him to volunteer, Ed brought Mike into his family. They would often go to the farm for tractor rides and to play with the animals. "My family embraced Mike, and Mike embraced my family," Ed recalls. Young Mike would call Ed to make sure he would see him that Sunday. Ed always followed through and let him know there was an adult who wasn't paid staff like most of the adults he had known and who loved him simply for who he was.

Mike credits Ed, who voluntarily entered his life as his friend and role model, for making him the successful man he became.

After graduating from Louisiana State University, Mike moved to Atlanta and then to St. Louis, where he decided it was his turn to help another young boy. He was matched with Ken Soule.

Ken's father had died just before his fourth birthday. His mother was suddenly left with two young boys to raise. Ken remembers, "She did a great job keeping us busy, but male role models were missing from our lives. By the time I was eight, I had more energy than a nuclear reactor and the attention span of a goldfish. Fortunately, my mother was smart enough to look for an outlet. She enrolled me in Big Brothers."

Mike and Ken had two common interests that kept their relationship thriving—sports and pizza. "Sundays soon became *our* day to go to sporting events, movies, the gym, eat pizza, or just hang out," recalls Ken. "I remember getting the fishing bug, so, one Sunday Mike took me to a stocked, pay-by-the-pound trout lake. Well, they don't let you throw back any of your catch at those places, and it's impossible not to catch a fish, so I think Mike must have gone home with twenty pounds of trout that day! Years later, I really got a laugh remembering this when I took Mike's young sons, Marty and Eric, into the Colorado Mountains on one of their first fishing trips."

In 1982 Mike went into his own land development business in Denver. Although Ken was in Nashville attending Vanderbilt University, they kept in touch. Ken would visit for ski vacations during college, and one summer Mike hired him to care for his two sons. "In a way, Ken is like a big brother to my sons," Mike said.

When Ken graduated from college in 1984, he moved to Denver to be with his "family." "Though not blood," Ken emphasizes, "they are my chosen family."

Although Mike had originally been unimpressed with Ed's convertible when he saw it in 1952, interestingly, when Ken moved to Denver and needed a car for a short-term loan, he borrowed Mike's 1975 Mercedes 450 SL convertible!

Mike did a favor for his Little Brother Ken in 1984 that many biological brothers have done. He introduced him to his wife Christine. They now have four children, and Mike's and Ken's families spend holidays together, just like any other family.

The convertible theme in Mike's life arose again in 1990 when he decided once more to volunteer as a Big Brother. He drove to his new Little Brother Matthew Block's home. Matt, his mother, and the BBBS caseworker were waiting by the window for Mike's arrival. As he pulled his convertible to the curb and parked, seven-year-old Matt excitedly said, "Wow, sweet car!"

Now here was a Little Brother who was indeed impressed by a convertible! Mike took Matt out for a pizza and a ride in his car as their first match activity. Matt's Mom, Wendy, received a phone call from her son while he was out. He called from Mike's cell phone to excitedly report that he had a "totally cool" Big Brother!

Mike and Matt have played a lot of sports, attended sporting events, had cookouts, and hung out together over the last thirteen years. Mike was at Matt's side during the many milestones that turn a boy into a man—including his bar mitzvah, getting his driver's license, and his high school graduation.

Matt says, "Mike is one of the most compassionate people I have ever met. He has always treated me as if I were his own son. He shows me respect, dignity, and teaches me life lessons. The times I spend with Mike are priceless in my eyes . . . Priceless memories that will assist me when I get older. Our relationship is nothing less than amazing."

Today, Matt is a junior at Coe College in Iowa. He is interning with the Cedar Rapids BBBS agency while he goes to school, raising money for their annual Bowl for Kids Sake fundraiser. When he is finished with college, he plans to add yet another generation to this story when he is matched with his own Little Brother.

Matt wants to give back to another little boy what he received from Mike, who was only giving back to Ken and Matt what he received from Ed. Ed is now eighty-five years old. He gets Father's Day cards from Mike's Little Brother Ken in thanks for making Mike the generous man who showed him the man he could become.

Ed started this family fifty-two years ago with the simple intent of helping one boy. Little did he know that he was to become the patriarch of a loving family of four generations of brothers. In this family everyone, from the youngest to the oldest, knows the stories of the traditions that make their loving memories—consistency, trust, mutual respect, and friendship, mixed with sports, pizza, and the ever-present convertibles.

By Beth Barrett with Stephanie Block and Chris Craig

What's Age Got to Do With It?

Big Sister Marie Kish and Little Sister Courtney Hunkins

A summer day, a trip to McDonalds, and a coloring book meld into a wonderful, glorious afternoon for a seven year old. Surprisingly, mine was spent with a virtual stranger—a sixty-four-year-old woman who was to become my Big Sister. Who would have thought that one afternoon would lead to a lifetime of memories?

Yes, Marie and I were matched with quite a bit of an age difference, but her heart had the room and I had the time to make my way into that heart. Marie gave me opportunities to see another side of the world. She showed me what it was like to be a mature young lady, and I showed her what it was like to be silly. The age difference was never a factor between the two of us. As a matter of fact, I sent Marie an invitation to my thirteenth birthday sleepover party.

Marie had been a Big Sister before me, and that girl grew out of the program as we all eventually do. It is our hearts that always stay.

The opportunities I have had with Marie are unbelievable. I became a part of her family and even called her mother Gramma Nunn. When Marie and I were first matched, we visited Gramma Nunn every other Sunday for lunch. This was my absolute favorite outing. Gramma Nunn passed away when I was eleven, and through Marie's own grief, she helped me with mine.

I was able to confide in, trust, and love Marie unconditionally. We would spend hours playing board games and laughing together. Sometimes, we would make macaroni and cheese and watch each other eat. Those are the days that are as fresh as yesterday in my memory.

Once, as we left a restaurant on one of our many afternoon outings, a drug bust was occurring across the street. This was a whole new learning experience for me. Marie led me, at thirteen, down the parking lot to watch. I was impressed. She explained what was happening and kept a reassuring hand on my shoulder at all times. Marie and I made memories only sisters can make.

Marie gave me self-confidence. She has been my copilot in life for the last fifteen years. I am now in my senior year of college and getting married. She is going to be at my wedding, sitting in the front pew along with my mother, rooting me on.

I was very lucky to become a Little Sister in the BBBS program. Originally, my mother went there intending to find my brother a male role model, not knowing she would also bring home a best friend for her oldest daughter. While arranging a match for my brother, the director of the agency told my mom that she had the perfect match for me. In the end there was no mistake in the word *perfect.*

Had it not been for Marie's guidance, understanding, and support, who knows where I would be? Now, at twenty-three years old, I can honestly say that Marie is one of the best things to have happened to me. I wouldn't change a thing about our sister bond. Marie has taught me what it means to love and to be loved. She has taught me to be proud in all of my endeavors and hold my head high in times of trouble. Marie has given me courage and helped make me the woman I am today.

Because of Marie, and the other BBBS volunteers I saw open their hearts, I too have volunteered as a Big Sister. My heart has the room to love a child toward a better future. The magic of this program is so fantastic; it has to be shared!

By Courtney Hunkins

The Compassion Cycle

Big Brother Anthony Pearson and Little Brothers Clifton Sherrod and Audwin Barlow

One day I asked my Big Brother Anthony Pearson, "What compelled you to be my Big Brother?" He paused for a few moments and slowly responded, "I read your family's story in the newspaper and felt compassion for your situation." My widowed mother was left to raise me and my seven sisters alone. This was the hand we were dealt. Despite its grim start, my story is not a sad one. In fact, my unfortunate reality led me to Anthony Pearson, my Big Brother, and the true understanding of compassion.

The BBBS program helped me become the individual I am today. I know intimately the impact this program has on the mentor and the mentored. I've been fortunate to experience both sides.

Being the youngest of a family of eight and the only male in my household, I was in desperate need of male guidance. My mother raised me to be obedient and courteous, but she could not teach me how to be a man. So she enrolled me in the BBBS program in hopes of giving me an opportunity to share my feelings and inner thoughts with a responsible male. Never in my wildest imagination did I think this program would result in a lifetime friendship.

Looking back, when I was a child my Big Brother

meant the world to me. There were times I had done things I had no business doing. When my Big Brother was told about my misbehavior, he would say, "You're not bad. God doesn't make people bad. You just do things that you should not do." Well, I did my share of "things that you should not do." But he was there to guide me through the worst and the best of times.

Anthony exposed me to many things. He enrolled me in the Boy Scouts and took me to cultural events. Over the next ten years, we shared many special moments together. In 1984 he took me to my first sporting event and on my very first vacation to Disney World and Epcot Center.

Anthony never let me down, and I did my best not to let him down. There were times when I thought I had let him down, but he was always patient with me and explained thoroughly my wrongdoing with a smile. That's the compassion I experienced in his presence.

Anthony was an angel sent from above to guide me. I could never repay Anthony. Or could I?

In 1996 I moved to Washington, D.C., embarking on a career in the housing industry, settling into a new apartment, and enjoying the single life. What more could a twenty-six year old ask for?

Nonetheless, I felt a void. I could not understand what was missing until, late one night while channel surfing, I came across a show that caused a flood of memories. It was *The Courtship of Eddie's Father*. Anthony and I used to watch that show and sing the opening song about the love of a father and son together. That song epitomized the way Anthony and I felt about each other. Listening to that song again, I felt compelled to follow in Anthony's footsteps and offer my friendship to a boy who needed me.

Within a week, I called the local BBBS agency to

enroll. I was so nervous when I was told I had been matched that I missed the bus to my first meeting with my Little Brother at the local Boys and Girls Club!

From the moment I first met seven-year-old Audwin Barlow, Jr., I knew it was a good match. I felt compassion for Audwin's background and challenges. Audwin lives with his grandmother. He never met his mother, and his father was in another state. Those are tough issues for a child to handle. I sometimes questioned whether I was ready for this responsibility. Did I have what it takes to be a Big? But I knew I did. I had to be a model of consistency for Audwin.

The first few summer months were filled with fun and excitement. I knew my Little Brother was intelligent, but when the school term started I realized he needed guidance in school. Audwin was so much like me at that age. The first few months in third grade were challenging for him. I called almost every night to check on his schoolwork, and I occasionally visited his school, just as Anthony had done for me nineteen years earlier. At the end of the year, Audwin passed to the fourth grade.

Over the years, Audwin has brought the best out in me, too. When I first met Audwin, I smoked cigarettes. How could I tell him not to smoke when I was smoking? That weighed heavily on my conscience and heart, so I stopped smoking. I have not touched a cigarette in over five years, thanks to my Little Brother.

After more than five years with Audwin, things are still the same. I am still involved in his schooling and helping him achieve the stardom to which he is destined.

One day on a bus ride, I asked the now adolescent Audwin, "What do you want to be when you grow up?" To my surprise he said, "A Big Brother." "Why?" I asked. He answered, "I want to help others that are not as fortunate as me." I was so touched. He smiled at me when I told him, "Have compassion for others and you will succeed."

In 2003 I was honored as the Big Brother of the Year in the Washington, D.C., area. When I called my Big Brother Anthony, who is now a minister, to tell him about the award, he was as proud of me as my father would have been.

Anthony came to the awards banquet and met my Little Brother Audwin. They looked at one another, shook hands, and smiled. That was a very touching moment for me.

Even though the award was for me that evening, the speech I gave was dedicated to my Big Brother, my Little Brother, my mother, Audwin's grandmother, our caseworker, and the BBBS program. This program has proven to be a magical experience for me, my Little Brother, and my Big Brother. The cycle of friendship and compassion continues.

By Clifton Sherrod III

Giving Back

Big Sister Alice Zinoble and Little Sister Jennifer Perez

My experience with Big Brothers Big Sisters has had a big impact on my life in more ways than one. From a young girl in need of help to a grown woman wanting to help, my role in the program has come full circle.

When I was nine, my mother, trying to protect her children, left my alcoholic father, walking out the door with nothing but my brother and me. Getting settled on our own was very difficult, and I was very lonely. My mom said I threw hostile tantrums when I didn't get my way, and I was what you might call a bratty, antisocial kid.

My mother knew that I could benefit from having a friend, someone who could listen and be supportive, someone who could help me navigate the difficulties I was facing at that time, and, most importantly for a kid, someone with whom I could go out and do fun things! My mom called and enrolled me in Big Brothers Big Sisters.

I will never forget the day I met my Big Sister Alice. It was just after my tenth birthday. Being the klutzy kid that I was, I had broken my foot and was wearing a cast. When the Big Brothers Big Sisters social worker pulled up to my house with my new Big Sister, I was so excited that I ran through the house on my crutches, screaming, "They're here! They're here!" I hobbled out of the house and onto the street to meet them. That day we sat in the living room and got to know each other. I found out we had many similar interests—horseback riding, ballet, and reading, just to name a few.

Over the years we were matched, I enjoyed numerous outings with Alice, all memorable in their own way. There were adventurous days spent on horseback and even skiing during a family trip. Likewise, I enjoyed casual days spent at the movies, eating at restaurants, and educational outings to the museums and library.

She made me feel like I was part of her family, and I often just spent the day visiting at her parents' house. I had come from a less than perfect family environment, and Alice's family provided positive examples and role models.

The highlight of my involvement in her life and family came the day I walked down the aisle as part of her wedding party. Even after she married and moved to the next county, we still spent time together. Alice and her new husband came down every month and spent the day with my little brother and me.

As a child, I was never able to express to Alice how much she positively impacted my life. She wasn't an authority figure like my mother, but I always listened to her. She was patient and kind, and she never missed an opportunity to teach me about values. In fact, over the years we were together, Alice taught me many things from how to use silverware at the dinner table to how to properly introduce myself in a social setting.

Over time, I became less concerned with myself and more interested in other people. I began volunteering in high school and, through that experience, learned that I wanted to teach kids. Eventually, I went to college to study education. I always told myself, "Once my life settles down,

I will volunteer to be a Big Sister."

After finishing my master's degree in special education and completing my first year teaching exceptional students, I was ready to volunteer. I called Big Brothers Big Sisters and finally came back to the organization that did so much for me as a child.

The caseworker had a ten-year-old girl she wanted me to meet. This sounded perfect since I had been teaching ten year olds for nearly two years. But there was more. My caseworker asked if I was willing to be matched with a child with special needs.

Although her special needs were not visible, my Little Sister had been diagnosed with sickle cell anemia, a chronic and often painfully debilitating illness. Her previous match did not last, and my social worker was hoping that this time it would be different.

It has now been over three years since I met Lynnette. She was a stiffly shy, soft-spoken little girl. In the beginning, it was difficult to get her input on our outings or to get her to socialize with others. On one occasion, her shyness prevented her from asking for the materials she needed for a craft project she wanted to do. She stood back, waited, and watched the other children delightfully participate in the activity until she found what she needed.

Through our activities and outings together over the years, I have seen Lynnette become more confident in her social skills, more assured in her decision making, and more assertive in pursuing the things she wants. Recently, she gracefully—and without hesitation—participated in an interview to be aired on a local television show.

Our time spent together has varied depending on what has been going on in the community and her life as well as the interests she has expressed. We have enjoyed new experiences together such as skating, visiting a farm, baking homemade brownies, and flying giant kites.

I helped her when she was at risk of repeating sixth grade by tutoring her every weekend and helping her with school projects.

When she has been hospitalized due to her illness, I have spent time in her hospital room, reading and talking to her to help her pass the time as pleasantly as possible.

Being a Big Sister has shown me a different side of the match experience. When Lynnette's family moved to the opposite end of the county, I realized how time-consuming it was to drive the long distance to and from a Little's home—as it had been for Alice.

Times of stress and tribulations in Lynnette's family also have had their effect on me (just as my trials and tribulations must have affected Alice), but they have also made me more assured of my original decision to volunteer, and they have given me the motivation to continue.

Through Big Brothers Big Sisters, Alice helped me become a competent, confident, and caring adult, and I hope to have that same effect on Lynnette. Lynnette dreams of one day being a pediatrician, a profession in which she can help others. I'm going to be there, by her side, watching her reach her dreams.

By Jennifer Perez

To Be Continued

Big Sister Mary Pitzen and Little Sister Dawn Huibregtse

In 1983, on the recommendation of my second-grade teacher (a Big Sister herself), my mother decided to enroll me in the Big Brothers Big Sisters program in my home town of Sheboygan Falls, Wisconsin. Hesitant at first, thinking that the program was for problem or maladjusted children, my mother was quickly assured by my teacher, as well as by the BBBS caseworker with whom she initially met, that the program was for all children of single-parent families.

My father had died of heart complications the prior year, leaving my mother to care for my sisters and me; we were then ages six, three, and one. While my father's death was unexpected, we were fortunate to be financially stable and to have the support of many friends and family. Due to my mother's strength and protection from any real tumult in our lives and my young age at the time of my father's death, I was a relatively average, well-adjusted second grader.

I was introduced to my Big Sister Mary, then twenty-six, a few days before my eighth birthday. To me, she was young, fun, and someone from whom I received undivided attention—something that my mom wasn't always able to give me amidst trying to manage three young children.

We would get together three or four times a month for a few hours, and our weekly activities included things like baking cookies at her apartment, taking walks to the park, and playing games or cards. Over the years, she introduced me to her friends and family members, came to my school events and piano recitals, and introduced me to new hobbies, including camping, painting, and bowling. She broadened my horizons by taking me to professional sporting events and to museums. We even saw *The Phantom of the Opera* during my senior year of high school—my first real theater experience! These are opportunities that I would not have had outside of our relationship.

My involvement with Mary continued through high school, though on a more limited basis as our schedules filled up—mine with high school activities, hers with increased work and other responsibilities—and our relationship continues today.

Looking back, probably one of the most profound ways in which Mary affected my life was in her role as professional mentor to me. Mary was single and a college graduate, and she obtained positions with increasing responsibility within her company. She showed me the importance of working hard and the success that doing so can bring, exposed me to different possibilities within the business world, and encouraged me to strive for what I wanted to do. I even had the opportunity to observe her firsthand when I worked for her company in a summer job during college. To this day, I consider her both a personal and professional mentor in my life.

Clearly, Big Brothers Big Sisters has had a tremendous impact on my life. In fact, the impact was so significant that, upon graduating from college and moving to Naperville, Illinois, in 1998, one of the first things I did upon arrival was call the local office and find out what I had to do to become a Big Sister.

I was matched with my Little Sister Megan in October 1998. She was eleven years old, did well in school, participated in various extracurricular activities, and appeared to be a relatively well-adjusted sixth grader. Immediately it was evident that there were many parallels in our lives. Her father, too, had passed away at a young age, and she lived with her mother and younger brothers.

Over the years, our activities have mirrored Mary's and my activities, and our relationship has taken a similar form. It has been a rewarding experience for me to be on the other side of the match and to experience the joy that comes from giving of myself to mentor someone in whom I see so much of myself.

At sixteen, Megan is a poised young woman with clear college goals. Just yesterday, on our way home from a large group activity with other Bigs and Littles, a fellow Big asked her if she intended to become a Big Sister in order to "keep the chain going." Her response was a resounding yes! As a result, this story is to be continued.

By Dawn Huibregtse

Art by Little Sister Brittany Gordon

You Can Have All of This

Big Brother Dave Geise and Little Brother Joe Morales

After graduating from Notre Dame University, Dave Geise moved to Austin, Texas, and was getting his masters degree at the University of Texas when he decided to become a Big Brother. He didn't know much about Big Brothers Big Sisters but liked the idea of a one-to-one relationship with a child.

Meanwhile, Joe Morales was being raised in a single-parent household with his younger sister. His dad left home when Joe was eight years old and didn't stay in touch much after that.

In 1974, with no male figure in his life, Joe's mom signed him up for the BBBS program. "Mom had the foresight to get a positive male role model in my life. Looking back, my grades were slipping, I was not listening to my mom, and I was hanging with the wrong crowd," Joe said.

At the time they were matched, Joe was twelve years old and Dave was twenty-three. The two gradually warmed up to each other. Dave included Joe in his family, and Joe helped Dave build part of his patio. Dave taught Joe how to water-ski, which required a lot of patience on Dave's part, but it's something they laugh about today.

Joe also vividly remembers that, once a month on a Sunday, Dave and his wife Sarah would invite Joe to dinner at their house. Dave said, "It was good for Joe to see us as a family." Joe remembers a particular occasion when Dave brought him to his house. He said, "Man, Dave, you've got a great house and a wife and a dog!" Dave responded, "Joe, you can have all of this—it's easy. Just remember three things: One: Get your education. Two: Whatever you decide to do, be the best. And three: Stay out of trouble."

Now, at age forty-one, Joe lives less than five miles from Dave's old house. He's been married for seventeen years and has a daughter, a three-bedroom house with a two-car garage, and a dog! "He showed me that I could have this," said Joe about Dave. He laughingly said, "Man, Dave, my house is actually a little nicer than yours was."

One turning point in Joe's life was his freshman year in high school. He received his first F, was skipping school, and became a juvenile delinquent. In the midst of vandalizing a house, Joe said a chill came over him, and he thought, "If Dave knew what I was doing right now, he probably wouldn't want to be my Big Brother anymore." Joe said he was scared. He said to his buddies, "I'm out; I can't do this anymore." "My friends called me names and threatened to hurt me, but I didn't care."

"I decided to go back to school," said Joe, and that's what he did. He went back to school, and his grades improved.

"One day, about three years later, I was reading the newspaper and saw an astonishing story. Out of the six guys I used to hang around with, three were arrested because, while they were high on drugs, they had kidnapped a young girl and raped and killed her." At the age of seventeen, they were charged as adults and sentenced to twenty-five years in prison.

"When I read it in the newspaper, I knew it could have been me. Had it not been for BBBS and the positive influence of Dave, I don't know where I'd be today. I thank God my mom had the foresight to get me involved with a positive male role model."

What the two remember is having fun every week together. They water-skied and played chess. Dave and Joe were matched for six years. Their match officially ended when Joe turned eighteen in 1980. Twenty-plus years later, they still stay in touch and are good friends.

Joe graduated from high school and started attending classes at Austin Community College. Later, he applied for and got a job at IBM, where Dave worked as an engineer. Joe said, "I was so excited to tell Dave that I was working for IBM and that we were working there at the same time."

In 1991 Joe graduated from the University of Texas. "It was one of the toughest things I've ever done," said Joe. "I was married, working forty hours per week on IBM's assembly line on the night shift from 10 P.M. to 7 A.M., and going to school during the day." Joe invited three people to his graduation: his mom, his wife, and his Big Brother Dave. Joe said, "They were the only people I invited because they were the ones who supported me and helped make it possible."

Joe went on to become a Big Brother himself for eleven years to a Little Brother named, of all things, David. Joe comments, "If it weren't for Dave, I wouldn't have become a Big Brother." About Dave, Joe said, "Not only did Dave touch me, he touched my Little Brother. I used to tell my Little Brother the same things Dave told me about staying in school and being the best at what you do." Joe remembers when his Little Brother David said, "Joe, you have a great house." Joe responded the same way his Big Brother did,

"You can have all this—it's easy."

Dave has "seen Joe's life come together—getting married, graduating. That is when I realized it was an extremely worthwhile thing to do. It's hard to make a difference in a lot of people's lives, but Big Brothers Big Sisters lets you make a difference in one person's life, and then they will pass that difference on to others."

Joe sees BBBS as opening the doors to a child who would not otherwise know what was beyond the walls. "There's a whole other world out there for them," Joe says.

After spending many years in the technology industry, Joe now sells cars for Austin Infiniti. Last year he was the salesman of the year, and he is on pace to do it again this year. He *is* the best at what he does. Joe also served on the board of directors of Big Brothers Big Sisters for several years and volunteers to share his story whenever he is able.

"It all started when my mom signed me up for BBBS. What could have been the worst years of my life without a dad turned out to be the best," said Joe.

In March Dave became a Big Brother again to a new Little Brother. Another lucky boy is learning he too can have a dream life by following three simple rules.

By Julie McAllister with Jennifer Grimsley

From Little to Big

Big Brother William Johnson and Little Brothers James Gaillard and Durrell Brockingham

Two weeks after my ninth birthday, my mother, Anna Marie Gaillard, her best friend, Carol, Carol's sister, and I went on vacation. En route to Georgia, a car traveling in the opposite direction crossed the center line and ran head-on into our vehicle. My mother and Carol were both killed.

Carol's sister miraculously received only a cut on her foot. I had two broken legs and was in traction for six months in a South Carolina hospital before being shipped home by ambulance in a body cast.

Shortly after my return to Philadelphia, a gentleman from our church, William "Chunky" Johnson, approached my grandmother, who was now my guardian, about becoming my Big Brother. My grandmother happily complied. She thought this would be great for me, since my father was not around much anymore.

Chunky, as he was fondly called by everyone, was a stout man. He was also an incredible man who was always smiling. I don't think he ever complained about anything in his entire life. He was a single schoolteacher who sang in the choir. He used to lead the song "Well, I keep so busy praising my Jesus, I ain't got time to die!" I loved to hear him sing.

He inspired me to join the Academy Boys Choir, with whom I traveled throughout the United States and abroad. As a member I had the opportunity to meet President Jimmy Carter.

Chunky and his family were well respected in the church. His father was a prominent businessman, his mother was a homemaker, and Chunky and his brother and sister all had college degrees.

I felt very fortunate to be his Little Brother because he showed me a world I had not seen. His parents had been married forever; they lived in a big house, and his father drove a brand new Cadillac.

I recall with delight my very first Christmas with Chunky. The Jaycees had given Big Brothers Big Sisters gift certificates for the Littles to use to buy gifts for their friends and families. Chunky took me to John Wanamaker's, an immense department store. It was so exciting! I remember the huge crowd, the big organ, and the famous light show. And the best part was that I had my own money to spend for the very first time!

On Christmas Day, Chunky arrived at my house, and we exchanged gifts. He took me to his house to have Christmas dinner with his family. I remember all the people and all the love. This was the first of many Christmases we spent together.

As I got older, Chunky taught me to drive. Aptly, as my role model, he helped me pack and drove me to college.

Chunky was a part of my whole life growing up. Among many other things that Chunky taught me was how to be a gentleman. He taught me to always open the door and pull the chair out for a woman. "Always treat, never Dutch treat. If you are walking down the street with a woman, you should always walk by the curb," he said. We teach our young men to get a good education and a good job and to have a family, but so many times we fail to teach them to be gentlemen.

Chunky died approximately ten years ago of a massive heart attack. He had just married. Amazingly, he had been part of my life for twenty years.

After Chunky's death, I worked with his widow to set up a scholarship at the school where he had taught for over twenty years. It was befitting after helping so many people, young and old, that he have a scholarship named in his honor.

I always said that I would become a Big Brother because of the tremendous impact Chunky had on my life. I, like Chunky, went on to college, sang in the church choir, and was a youth mentor. But, after college, there was my job and my daughter, Ashley Janell. Then I went to paralegal school and on to business school, and started my own millinery business, James & James. I had always been involved with young people but never took the step to become a Big Brother.

While I was a teen mentor at my church, a mother asked if I would be a Big Brother to her son. I applied and was accepted into the program. In the meantime, that family moved back to North Carolina.

I asked to be matched with another Little Brother and was matched with Durrell Brockingham. Had it not been for my church, Durrell and I may have never met. I think of it as divine intervention.

I remember my first meeting with Durrell. His grandmother, Mrs. Greenfield, told me how she had raised Durrell since he was a baby because his mother had drug problems and had been in and out of jail. She was currently incarcerated. Durrell and I were matched through Amachi Big Brothers Big Sisters, a special program to connect children of current and former prisoners with Big Brothers or Big Sisters recruited though congregations. *Amachi* is a West African word that means "who knows but what God has brought us through this child."

I told Mrs. Greenfield I wanted to make sure Durrell was well rounded and that he had a strong religious, educational, and social background. I wanted to take him to teen Bible study, libraries, museums, and sporting events and do everything in my power to make sure that he went to college, including getting scholarships. I told her that, when the time was right, I would teach Durrell about sex and how to prevent pregnancy and sexually transmitted diseases. She was thrilled. It seemed as though we were old friends who just hadn't seen each other in a while.

Then I met Durrell. After chatting for a few minutes, I could tell how intelligent he was. I felt proud about becoming a part of this bright young man's life.

When we first began going out, it was a little awkward. It seemed as though we were trying to make conversation. I would usually pick Durrell up on Fridays; we would get something to eat and then go to Bible study. We chatted about school, his grandmother, his mother, sports, and things in general. When Durrell told me that he had never met his father, it became even more important for me to be there for him.

Before you knew it, a bond was forged. We do everything together—going to see the Sixers and the Harlem Globetrotters, going to Great Adventure, or just hanging out. Durrell has become a very important part of my life. I recently told him how much I miss him when we don't get a chance to go on our Friday outings.

The first time I realized the impact I had on Durrell's life was a Christmas morning when he telephoned me. I asked him what was going on and reminded him that I would be over later to give him his Christmas present. He said he just wanted to call and wish me merry Christmas. The fact a child would take time out of his busy Christmas morning just to call and say "Merry Christmas" almost brought tears to my eyes.

Because of my experience as a paralegal, Durrell has aspirations of going on to college and studying law. More importantly, Durrell considers me to be his best friend. Out of all the friends that Durrell has in school, in his neighborhood, and at church, he considers me to be his best friend.

Life isn't about social recognition or monetary gifts; it's about a phone call on Christmas morning or being called a young person's best friend.

My hope is that Durrell will go on to become a Big Brother. My motto is, "If every adult were to mentor a young person, the world would be a better and much stronger place to live." Chunky taught me that.

By James A. Gaillard

Making a Difference

Big Brother Dale Kelly and Little Brothers Tracy Dieterich and Justin Vecchio

There is a famous saying that perfectly describes what it is like to be a Big Brother or a Big Sister: "Give a person a fish, and you will feed them for a day. Teach a person to fish, and you will feed them for a lifetime."

When people ask me why I decided to become a Big Brother volunteer, I always like to tell them about the person who inspired me.

This man, Dale Kelly, became a Big Brother thirty years ago when he was matched with a nine-year-old boy from an underprivileged family. The Little Brother never knew his father, and his entire family lived in a one-bedroom, one-bath apartment while the mother worked three jobs. Kelly (as his friends call him) was a successful business owner who was just starting a family of his own, but he was willing to be a part of this boy's life. The two of them would get together for a few hours each week, and eventually they spent some weekends hunting and fishing.

Kelly offered a listening ear and an encouraging word, and as their friendship developed, the boy's grades began to improve in school. Yes, just having someone special around who cares can really make a difference. Later, the Little Brother joined the Boy Scouts, became an Eagle

Scout, and was the only person in his family to graduate from college. His Big Brother had a significant influence on this young man at such a critical time in his life.

Today, that Little Brother is thirty-nine years old. He is now a vice president at a large company and sits on the board of directors for Big Brothers Big Sisters of Dallas. Kelly is proud because he knows that he played a major part in his Little Brother's development. He was a mentor and role model and has been there to watch and help this at-risk child mature into a successful adult. Thirty years later, they have developed a deep, lifelong friendship, and they still meet for dinner, talk several times each month, and even spend holidays together.

The real reason I enjoy telling this story is because I was, and still am, Kelly's Little Brother!

I still thank Kelly all the time for being such a special person and sharing his friendship with me. About two years ago, our experience with Big Brothers Big Sisters expanded to three generations. I became a Big Brother too (and Kelly became a "Grand-Big Brother") when I was matched with my Little Brother Justin, who is now thirteen years old.

Justin and I have quickly become good friends, and we usually see each other several times each month. He and I enjoy all kinds of different activities from attending professional sporting events to working in the yard—and sometimes just going to get a haircut or eating dinner and talking. Justin is a great kid who comes from a good family, and he always makes me laugh. He has already shown major improvement in school, and I know Justin has a bright future ahead of him! The first time I met him, Justin looked up at me with his big brown eyes, and I saw *myself* when I was about his age. Wow! It was definitely a magical moment.

I'm very proud to be Justin's Big Brother, and I hope

to make a difference in his life during the next thirty years. There is no doubt in my mind that I would not be here today without having been introduced to Kelly and the Big Brothers Big Sisters program. Now it is my turn to share the magic!

By Tracy Dieterich

Art by Little Brother Andrew Walter

Little Brother and a Sister Too

Big Brother Tom Smith and Little Brother Lal Chand

I grew up in a family with a twin sister, a brother, a mom, and a dad. My brother was five years older and most of the time couldn't be bothered with me. He had his own life, and I just didn't fit into it during our growing-up years. My dad was a busy man and had no time to play with his children. His days were long and filled with business deals that offered his family a comfortable lifestyle and future security. He believed he was doing the very best for his wife and children, but he left us wanting his attention and time.

The happiest days of my youth were spent in Boy Scouts. I loved camping, earning badges, exploring new places, and meeting new people. My scout leaders were men who happily devoted their time to scouting; and for some boys, it was the only time they had a chance for a one-on-one relationship with a father image. These men taught us life lessons, and I respected and admired them very much. I knew that someday I would take an active part in helping boys, too.

In 1969, when I was in my mid-twenties, I left Pennsylvania. My career had sent me to San Francisco for a new job assignment, and I was excited about starting a new life in California. I met my wife Stephanie a year later, and we were married in 1971. I was having a great life, but I wanted to spend some of my weekend time helping a youth organization.

It had always bothered me that I had missed out on spending quality time with my father and older brother. I knew that when I became a dad I would do things differently. It was a priority for me to have a hands-on relationship, so when Big Brothers offered me the opportunity to spend time with a young boy who did not have a dad in his life, I jumped at the chance.

I had been a Big Brother to two other boys before I was matched for the third time with Lal in 1973. The third match was the charm! This little guy held the magic that one feels when two pairs of eyes meet for the first time and the room lights up! Lal had just turned seven and had been waiting for a Big Brother.

He came from a family of four children—three boys and a girl. His brothers were twelve and ten, and little sister Priscilla was five. Lal's mother wanted her boys to have a male influence in their lives, so she went to Big Brothers to give her sons this opportunity. Lal's two older brothers already had Big Brothers, and now it was his turn.

Right from the start Lal and I knew we had a special match up, and the two of us had a great time getting together each week. Very soon after I started picking Lal up, it became obvious that Priscilla felt very left out. Since she and Lal were closest in age, they had always been best friends and playmates. Now that I was in the picture, Lal had someone else to do things with.

Whenever I came to pick him up, Priscilla would position herself on the front steps, holding her dress by the hem and swaying back and forth, sweetly saying, "Hi, Tom, where are you going today?" It was clear to me that she wanted to come along, too. After all, why did her brothers get to go on adventures while she was stuck at home? She asked if she could come along, and I always deferred to Lal. He nearly always said okay.

We had such great times, and it wasn't long before Stephanie and I were going places and doing things with the children and other members of their family. We went to BBBS Christmas parties and annual picnics, pumpkin picking, snow trips, camping trips, car trips. We cut out Valentines, made green shakes for St. Patrick's Day, colored Easter eggs, wrapped gifts, cooked, played games, and shared dreams.

This kind of activity continued long after our children were born. In a way, Lal and Priscilla became big brother and sister to our son and daughter. They were a big help to us; and there were times when our children would rather discuss things with them than with us, especially when they reached their teens.

My relationship with Lal and Priscilla grew into something much more than I ever expected, and I prize the years and all the special moments we have been able to share. It has meant the world to me to have these fine young people in my life. We have loved and respected each other for over thirty years now and are proud to consider ourselves a close extended family.

There is no way to express the gratitude I feel for this surprise enrichment. I started out wanting to make a difference in a young person's life; and as it turned out, I have been given a feeling of pride and worth that no words can describe.

Some say Priscilla was lucky that she had the advantage of having a Big Brother, since normally little girls could not have Big Brothers, only Big Sisters. And as true as that may be, I was lucky too. She was a wonderful plus and has endeared herself to me and my family in so many ways.

She is a mother now to five-year old Madison, who calls me Grandpa. It just feels so natural, and I love it!

Lal and I have had many wonderful occasions over the years when it was just the two of us. We relish the times that we can get away and be together to share our thoughts. We have made a difference in each other's lives, and we are grateful for the wonderful bond we share.

Lal has grown to be strong and independent, and I am so very proud of the man he has become. He felt that his positive experience with Big Brothers had such an impact on his life that he became a Big Brother. Now he is enjoying the experience of being the adult and sharing his time and knowledge with a special boy. Immense pride wells up inside me when I realize that I have made such a difference in Lal's life that he wants to have the same effect on someone else's life, too. Our relationship has come full circle. What a feeling!

Without BBBS, the bond I have with Lal and Priscilla would not have been. What a wonderful difference your organization can make in the lives it touches. Thank you for an experience that has enriched all our lives and brought my family and me so much happiness.

By Tom Smith

The Sky's the Limit

Big Brother Jerald Hertzog and Little Brother Albert Walonick, MD

In 1933 Albert Walonick stood before a judge in his hometown of Minneapolis, Minnesota. Only his widowed mother was with him. The very stern judge looked down at the young boy and shook his head. "Albert, this is the fourth time in two months you have come before me for mischief. I have no other alternative than to offer your mother a choice. Either you go to reform school or join this new program in town they call Big Brothers. Which will it be?"

Not knowing what Big Brothers was, but knowing that reform school would mean that Al would be taken away from her, his mother readily agreed to the Big Brothers program.

Life had been difficult for the two of them. Mrs. Walonick worked long, hard hours in a factory ever since her husband died of a ruptured appendix. Her husband, a fur trader who had emigrated from Russia, feared he would die if he went to the hospital when he became ill. Untreated, he passed away, leaving her to take care of her two-year-old son and herself with little money.

Al never thought that they were poor. After all, they ate dinner out three nights each week. Monday night was the Salvation Army, Wednesday night was the Catholic Church supper, and his favorite was Friday night at the Temple with food, services, and then cookies or a special treat. Al was left alone most of the time while his mother worked. He had a bright, curious mind, and he got into more trouble with older boys than most youngsters his age. Now it had come to this. He would be forced to see a stranger every week and listen to him talk about being a good boy.

He was matched with Jerald Hertzog and right away Al thought he might actually like this guy. Jerald was young and had kids of his own, so he understood that boys were not always perfect gentlemen. He opened up a new world to Al–the public library. Every Tuesday night he would pick Al up after school, and the two of them would go to the library to talk and read books. Al brought his homework, and together they studied advanced subjects. What Al did not know for years was that his Big Brother went to the library one other night each week to keep ahead of Al in his math and other subjects.

Jerald sold shoes at a department store. Even though he had two children of his own, he always felt that it was his duty to help another child. That lucky child was Al. Over the years the relationship grew, and Jerald realized what a gifted boy he was mentoring. Even though it was the Depression and he had his own children to buy gifts for, Jerold always found the money to give Al a special gift. The year Al got his first bicycle he thought a miracle had happened.

Al graduated with honors from high school and was immediately drafted to serve in World War II. His Big Brother went to the draft board and convinced them to put Al in a special program that would allow him to go to college and then become an officer in the Navy. Al finished his bachelor of science degree in three years and became a Navy officer. He was promoted to captain on a minesweeper after the captain of the ship died shortly after Al got his station. When the war was over, he received his discharge papers.

He intended to go home, go back to school, and study to become an engineer. Much to his surprise, he found out that his mother and Big Brother had already enrolled him in the University of Minnesota School of Medicine. When the school asked why Al was not applying himself, they responded, "Don't you know there is a war going on?"

Again his Big Brother knew best. Al became a medical doctor, working fourteen years in family practice, and then he went back for an eight-year residency in urology at the University of Minnesota. He had a private practice in Minneapolis for twenty years.

During this time he found another love—flying a small airplane. Al bought a plane, and every spare moment he was flying. He began doing volunteer work for Angel Flight in Minnesota, and when he retired to Florida he immediately began flying for Angel Flight there.

Now that he was retired and had some free time, he knew it was time to pay back all the love and attention he had received from his Big Brother. Al formed the Kids Flight program with the Big Brothers Big Sisters program in Fort Myers, Florida. Every other weekend Al took children and their Bigs or their parents up in his airplane to a Florida destination, landed the plane, bought them lunch, and then flew back. During the flight it was common for Al to let the Little take the plane controls.

Al used this time to talk to the children about dreams and setting high goals. He told them his life story and analogized the plane ride as the ability all of us have to fly as high as our dreams carry us. He let them see that they could achieve whatever they set their minds to, if they stayed focused and worked hard.

He also became a Big Brother. Al took a boy with mental health issues who was difficult to handle. With Al the boy was like all of the other children at our events. Al had that way about him. He made you believe in yourself. He made you thankful for each beautiful day, and he made you believe in the future.

Al often called himself the world's oldest Little Brother. Even though he attained great academic and professional success, Al's greatest achievement was living a full life—full of fun, and full of sharing his immense love with everyone.

Al left this earth in May 2003. The hundreds of children who soared through the sky with him in his plane continue to grow and achieve their own success. The cards and letters sent to Al's wife Charlotte are testimony of his profound impact on their lives.

Like a pebble dropped in a pond, one man, Jerald Hertzog, started a ripple more than seventy years ago. Who knows what effect Al's influence will have as that ripple grows wider and wider. Only the sky is the limit as the magic of this program lives on.

By Judith Saint-Sommer

Chapter 6

Dream Weavers

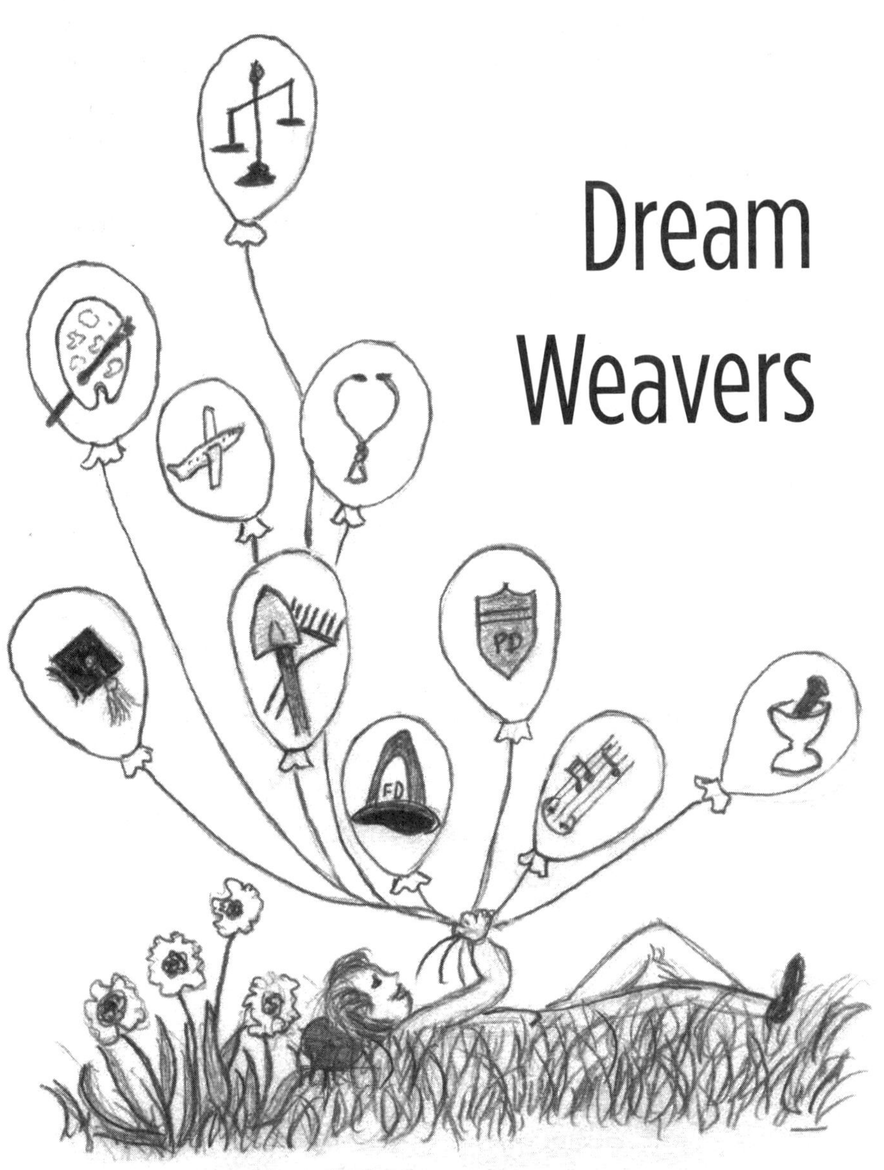

Big Benefits

Big Brother Rick Rosu-Myles and Little Brother Nathan Hunt

I originally got involved with Greater Portland Big Brothers and Big Sisters because I had a very fortunate upbringing and felt that it was time for me to give something back to the community. What I did not anticipate was how much I would get out of becoming a Big Brother.

I was matched with Nathan when he was ten years old. He was close to being a fifth-grade dropout. Nathan lived in one of the most difficult environments that I had ever even read about, much less been part of. Quite regularly he was sent home from school, and he had been diagnosed as being severely depressed (at nine years old!). If I explained his circumstances, one would understand, but Nathan would not appreciate my sharing those details. He is a very proud young man. I often question, though, whether I would have been able to overcome many of the obstacles he has.

The first time I met Nathan was hilarious. He was so excited that he couldn't sit still for a minute. He wanted to skip all of the formalities and race right into our match. He kept interrupting our caseworker and asking me random questions. "What should we do first?" "Do you like riding bikes?" "Why do you have funny hair?" It felt like a great match from the start.

One of the first things that amazed me about Nathan was how, despite being constantly faced with negative situations, you couldn't take the "boy" out of him. He always greeted me with such enthusiasm that it would immediately put me in a great mood. Nathan always liked to do things outside, even in January when it was subzero here in Maine. Part of the reason was that Nathan's house was constantly filled with cigarette smoke—so much so that he developed respiratory problems.

One winter I took Nathan skiing for the first time. We had an absolute blast the entire day. He was the loudest and happiest kid on that mountain. On the ride home he told me, "Today was the best day I ever had." It put me on cloud nine.

Another moment I remember was when the Big Brothers office got Celtics tickets for a group of us. We loaded a bus and went to Boston. I was very excited for Nathan to see the game and the sports complex, but, in the end, what he was most excited about from the experience was that he visited three states in one day. He had never been out of Portland except with me, and he had never left the state of Maine. He was absolutely amazed that we drove through three states in one day.

One of the things that has always been great about spending time with Nathan was that he is incredibly appreciative of the little things that many of us take for granted. His enthusiasm is a constant reminder that it is really the simple things that matter. Most of the time we do fun, outgoing things together, but some of the best moments have been just hanging out and talking with Nathan. He has gone through so much that he is very open—especially with me. There isn't a topic that we haven't covered, and he is comfortable trusting me with anything. I think this is partially because he knows that I do not judge him, but also because, except for his younger brother, I have been the most consistent figure in his life.

About five years ago, Nathan was removed from his home by the Department of Human Services following a very traumatic event, and he was placed in a foster home. It was a very difficult period, and Nathan and I almost lost touch. I have to credit our caseworker for working very hard to ensure I could remain in Nathan's life. This was an especially important time for Nathan, as he was uprooted from everything he knew, and I was the only familiar person. When I saw him during this period, I could see his relief that at least one thing hadn't changed, and he knew that I would stay in his life.

Nathan, like every child, has the potential to do whatever he wants in life. Until my experience with Nathan, I thought this was just a cliché. As a Big Brother, the most important thing that I believe I am doing is showing him that he has other options and encouraging him to pursue them. Nathan's environment was extremely negative, and he had no one—other than me—who was a positive influence on him.

I remember taking Nathan to a basketball game at Boston University where I had played. He asked me, "So, why did you go to college?" It was very evident that no one had ever explained that he had options other than dropping out of high school. When I showed him the BU campus and he sat in on some classes, Nathan saw a world he did not know existed.

Last year, Nathan made the honor roll at school. Now he is planning where he will go to college next year. He will be the first person in his family to attend college. Even more important to me, he is now a happy, well-balanced young man who is liked and admired by his many friends and teachers.

Recently, Nathan and I went to see a movie, and, halfway through, he elbowed me and said, "Oh, I forgot to tell you. I have signed up to be a mentor at my school." He told me that he recognized how great it was to have a mentor in his life, and he was really excited to be a mentor himself. I have no doubt that he will be a fantastic influence on someone.

I have gained so much from being a part of Nathan's life. I laugh at myself now when I think that I got involved because I wanted to "give something back."

By Rick Rosu-Myles

My Road to the NFL

Big Brother Terry Cusack and Little Brother Ben Nowland

When my dad died accidentally in 1989, I was as stunned as any nine-year-old kid who unexpectedly lost his dad could be. We lived in Point Vedra Beach, Florida, and, since kids that age typically aren't used to losing a parent, I retreated into myself. My mom, a native of Scotland, found it very difficult to convince me to do the fun things boys my age should be doing.

Even with a loving mom to care for me, I needed more. As great as she is, she worked long hours, and I often had to go to the neighbor's house after school.

Of course, being a loving parent, my mom searched for a way to get me out of my shell. She gave Big Brothers Big Sisters a try, signing up for the Jacksonville program. It proved to be the right answer for me. Having a Big Brother gave me another positive influence in my life.

Soon after my mom signed up for the Big Brothers Big Sisters program, I met Terry Cusack, my Big Brother. Terry is a big, hulking guy, probably 6-2, 245 pounds. I was a big kid as well, so we had that in common. We hit it off right away. He loved sports, and so did I. But our personalities were as different as night and day. I was shy and withdrawn, while Terry was outgoing and gregarious—

the kind of guy who makes a great first impression.

When he signed on to become a Big Brother, Terry will tell you, he was just looking to touch a boy's life. He certainly didn't know that his experience would help me reach such a high level of success.

At first, Terry and I shared the typical "get to know you" Big Brother experiences—dinners out, ballgames, and concerts. Before long, I began to open up, and Terry was responsible for my positive changes. He told me that, when we went out for dinner, I had a hard time looking the waitress in the eye when I ordered. I was that shy.

My mom would invite Terry over to the house for dinner to help us get comfortable with each other. I remember Terry being hilarious, a "get-after it" type of person. It was just what I needed. Right from the beginning, Terry was always supportive, trying to get me out of my shell.

With my dad gone, I no longer had someone who would play sports with me and let me climb trees and go camping. I didn't have anyone to answer questions that guys would ask. It was good to get a Big Brother who was funny and who would take me places to get my mind off things. A trip to Adventure Landing to play laser tag is one memorable experience. But Terry also had a strong moral code, and he gave me the confidence to be myself and emerge from my shell.

At first, I took it slow, but the bond between Terry and me began to grow stronger. In time, it blossomed into a great relationship. We became part of each other's family.

As Terry will tell you, he was a wild guy, but at the same time, he was responsible and successful. I needed a little of that too.

When I was thirteen, Terry and his long-time girlfriend decided to marry. It was so exciting to serve as groomsman.

The day was great, and I felt as if my own brother were walking down the aisle.

With the good news of Terry's wedding came some bad news also. Within a year, Terry landed a new job several hours away in Atlanta. Our official match ended, but the relationship endured. I was really disappointed when I heard the news that Terry was leaving, but I was excited for him too. It was a great job opportunity, so I couldn't blame him.

Today, Terry is a father of two boys. He honored me by naming his oldest son Benjamin. I was surprised and touched. Imagine a twenty-three-year-old having a child named after him; it's an amazing honor.

Even though Terry moved away, we maintained our friendship. He never abandoned me. We kept in touch, and during middle school and high school, I often traveled to Atlanta to spend time with Terry and his family.

Terry encouraged me to get more involved in sports, since I had grown into a pretty good football player in high school. He especially urged me to stick with football. When it came time for college, I had a couple of scholarship offers to smaller schools. Terry urged me to be patient because he believed something better would happen. Well, it did. The University of Auburn offered me an athletic scholarship; my dream had come true.

I remember how proud I was after our freshman season, and how I wanted to share that feeling with Terry. Even though the team had not made it to a bowl game that first year, I had played varsity on a limited basis as a freshman—not an easy thing to do on the college level.

When the season ended, I gift wrapped one of my game jerseys and gave it to Terry. Later, when we captured a Southeastern Conference championship, I gave Terry a ring identical to the one each Auburn team member received.

He was especially touched when he read the note, which, I am not ashamed to admit, was signed, “I love you, Ben.” My entire Big Brother experience with Terry has been awesome.

In my senior year I was selected as an All-Southeastern Conference player, and I graduated from Auburn in 2002 with a degree in industrial design. In November 2003, Terry, my mom, and I were wildly excited when I signed a free-agent NFL contract with the Washington Redskins.

Having Terry in my life has made me a better person, a more confident person. He wouldn’t let me get away with doing things halfway. He has always supported me in everything I’ve done, and I can’t imagine what my life would have been like without him in it. Terry’s my brother—and will be for the rest of our lives.

By Ben Nowland as told to Tom Starner

Thank You for My Scholarship

Big Brother Kurt Inderbitzin and Little Brother Brian Lopez

Brian won one of the two $20,000 scholarships that Arby's awards each year to Little Brothers and Little Sisters. This was his acceptance speech.

There are two things that petrify me; dancing and public speaking. So I apologize in advance—not because you're going to have to watch me dance, but because the only way I'll survive giving this speech is if I don't look up from this paper not even once. If I do, I'll see all of you staring at me, which will freeze me up faster than you can say Arby's roast beef, and that will be the end of my little talk.

That all said, I want to tell you about two things: what it's meant for me to be in the Big Brothers program and what the Arby's Big Brothers Big Sisters Scholarship Award will mean to me in my life. Let's start with my being in the Big Brothers Big Sisters program and what I've learned from it.

One way I've benefited from having a Big Brother may sound materialistic, but is nevertheless crucial to my having had opportunities I never would otherwise have had. I'm talking about my Big Brother's intimate knowledge of America and how its systems and government work. A few examples of this is that my Big Brother knew which high schools and colleges were really good; how to get me health care, dental care, braces, and even admission to summer camp, all for free. He even showed me how to play the negotiation game with colleges to get the best financial aid package possible.

These are all things my mother may have known how to do in her native country, Guatemala, but that she simply didn't know how to do here. While all these materialistic benefits have been important, they pale in comparison to the leadership and mentoring my Big Brother has given me.

As you may have figured out by now, I'm a tad bit shy—not only in public speaking but also in trying new things. But now I can honestly say that, after twelve years of my Big Brother's not-so-subtle urgings, I'm more outgoing. If it weren't for him, I would still be eating only vanilla ice cream instead of Rocky Road, which is a million times better. I would still refuse to ride on roller coasters, whereas I now sit in the front seat of the so-called scariest roller coasters on earth with hands in the air and loving it.

More importantly, I wouldn't have done several extraordinary and life-altering things—like raising $2,200 for AIDS research and bike riding five hundred incredible miles in the Hawaii AIDS ride; like applying to world-class colleges such as Berkeley and Swarthmore and then getting accepted.

If I have given you the impression that my Big Brother is merely a mentor to me, I have misinformed you. My Big Brother became my friend, somebody to hang out with, somebody to go to the movies with, somebody to play basketball with, somebody I have learned to trust and who I intend to keep in my life forever.

The truth is, without my Big Brother's guidance, I

wouldn't be going to college, and I wouldn't have such an incredibly bright and hopeful future ahead of me. But even with all his help and support, I don't think I could get where I want to go without receiving the Arby's Big Brothers Big Sisters Scholarship Award. You see, I come from a very poor family. It's just my mom and me, and we simply have never had the money to send me to college.

Swarthmore, the school I've decided to attend, has provided me with some financial aid, and my own summer jobs and work-study programs will add to that aid. Still, there's been a part of me that dreaded going to such a terrific and, frankly, wealthy college because my high school, a private one that I also attended on scholarship, is also wealthy, and that wealth sometimes made me feel like an outsider.

It is hard to fit in when your classmates all drive BMWs, take ski trips, and wear expensive clothes, and you're dropped off at school in your mom's ten-year-old Pontiac, and you can't afford any luxuries.

At Swarthmore, I have the opportunity to take full advantage of everything college has to offer. I have the chance to really fit in. I'll be able to take trips home at Christmas and spring break to see my mom and Big Brother. I'll be able to study abroad, to have a computer, and to go out occasionally with friends and have a pizza, or, better yet, an Arby's roast beef sandwich. The truth is, without this scholarship, I really don't know how I would have pulled off going to Swarthmore at all, while with it I have the extraordinary opportunity to go to a world-class institution as just one of the gang. I thank Arby's, Big Brothers Big Sisters, and my Big Brother Kurt for all of this.

By Brian Lopez

Camping, S'mores, and GT Mustangs

Big Sister Bobbie Gumtau and Little Sister Cindy Glover

Camping, s'mores, and GT Mustangs were all things I shared for the first time with my Big Sister Bobbie Gumtau. Many a sunny afternoon was spent with sun on our faces and wind in our hair as we cruised the town in her red convertible GT Mustang. Boy, did we think we were cool!

I was matched with Bobbie when I was ten. Although we graduated from the Big Brothers Big Sisters program upon my high school graduation, Bobbie continued to influence my life for years to come. Bobbie was a truly amazing role model and an indescribable friend.

Once, when I was thirteen and sicker than ever could be explained, Bobbie somehow convinced my mom to let us go to Oregon! We were gone for two weeks and, *wow*, what a transformation! My mom barely recognized me when we returned. I had gained weight, had color in my cheeks, and had found my smile again! Looking at the pictures, I am amazed at the transformation. Bobbie knew just what I needed.

While in Oregon, Bobbie took me to a candy store. I had never imagined that the world had stores totally dedicated to candy. I was bursting with excitement! By the time we left, I was toting eight pounds of variously flavored saltwater taffy. Maybe that is what cured me!

When my mom couldn't travel to my drill team competitions, Bobbie was there. She watched my drill team perform at countless football games and was loved by all the girls. Scanning the stands, I always found her smiling face, providing the comfort and support I needed. Afterwards, she would always say, "Great job, Honey!"

Bobbie, along with her husband Richard, provided boundless influence in my life. Richard helped me get through trigonometry, while Bobbie and my mom helped me get through boys and broken hearts. Bobbie and Richard even included my younger brother in many of our outings.

Bobbie also introduced me to what has become one of my true passions, working with people with disabilities. Bobbie and Richard invited me to attend a swim party they hosted for some people from the Mental Health Mental Retardation Center. That party introduced me to a world of warm, loving, and generous people. Subsequently, Bobbie and I attended many functions together and shared in the joy of helping this special community.

At one time, I was asked to share my experience of having a Big Sister and how it had changed my life. I likened the change in me to a turtle. Bobbie, Richard, and my mom all worked together to pull me out of my shell. Bobbie listened when needed, coached as required, disciplined when appropriate, and loved me always. She accepted me unconditionally—such a rare trait. Through the love, patience, and support of Bobbie and Richard, I developed a vision of the person I could be.

Sadly, we lost Bobbie two years ago. My heart is still broken. This is not the way it is supposed to end. I still had things to say and to do with Bobbie. I still had so much of my life to share with her.

While growing up, I knew that I wanted my kids to look to Bobbie as another family member. Now all that remains are stories. They won't be able to share her personally, but her love will certainly be passed on.

I walk by people who wear her favorite perfume, and it makes me pause. I thank my Creator for the blessed time I could call her my Big Sister and, more importantly, my friend.

The sight of red convertible GT Mustangs always brings a giggle; her picture, a smile. All I can say is thanks to Bobbie and Big Brothers Big Sisters. You made such a difference!

By Cindy Glover

My Reading Teacher

Big Brother Scott Dressel and Little Brother John Johnson

I have learned that one man can make a difference in this world. I've seen it with my own eyes and benefited from it.

The man who made a difference in my life is Scott Dressel. Scott and I met in the summer of 1995 when I was just twelve. When we first met, I thought Scott was too old. He was forty-five. I soon discovered that Scott's stability and commitment to me made him different from other people I had known.

Before I met Scott, I didn't have anyone to look up to. I didn't like school. It was only December, and I had already been absent over thirty times. I didn't have many friends, and I kept to myself. I lived alone with my mother. She was smart enough to see that I was starting to slide down the wrong path and enrolled me in the Big Brothers Big Sisters program.

Scott and I began by learning a little bit about one another. We shared our family backgrounds, educational backgrounds, and the things we liked to do. As time went on, we shared new things with each other. We started setting goals together.

I remember Scott teaching me about many things all at

once. Everywhere we went together, he was a teacher. I wish I could remember every little thing that Scott told me and showed me!

I do, however, remember his reaction when he found out I could not read or write. We made a plan. Scott and I met twice a week—on Monday and Wednesday. We ran a mile together to the public library to get a book. With the book in hand, we ran back to Scott's apartment and ate dinner. Then we read the library book. We worked until I could understand how the sounds of the letters came together to make words. Scott introduced me to a tutor and had me tested at a speech and hearing clinic. They found I had a learning disability.

Knowing that I liked football, Scott promised that he would send me to the University of Missouri summer football camp if I didn't skip school anymore. I made it; I won the bet! And I think Scott was happy to pay off. Amazingly, the more I worked on my reading and went to school, the better my grades got. After attending the camp, I made the junior high football team and, later, the high school team.

I never had to make a decision about whether I could trust Scott. I learned to live by this rule: "It is not about whether you can trust a person but whether that person keeps your trust over time." Scott has consistently proven that he is trustworthy; whenever we scheduled a meeting, he was there.

The only person in my family I talk to about my goals is my mother. While my mother believes in me, I think sometimes she doubts I'll accomplish my goals. Scott, on the other hand, always thinks I can do whatever I set my mind to. Sometimes I do not know how much effort it takes to reach a goal. Scott taught me to break the goals down into steps. I did not know this growing up, and I had failed in reaching some of my goals before Scott taught me this key to success.

Even after I grew too old for the Big Brothers program and graduated from high school, Scott continued to mentor me. After my first semester of college, I was put on academic probation. Scott recommended I take some time off from college to give me time to mature and get my life in order. Scott and his wife Mary helped me look for a job. When I first started working, I was living with my mother. After I had saved two paychecks, I had enough money to get my own apartment. I have been living on my own for a year now, and I'm ready to go back to college and take one class at a time.

I have so many memories of my life with Scott. When I was thirteen, I had a job at a pet store. I did not have any transportation, so Scott bought me a bike for my birthday! We climbed the Grand Canyon together. That was the first time I had been outside Missouri. After that, I thought I could do anything. Throughout my teen years, Scott has been there for me with advice and support.

Now I am a young man, and Scott is not only my best friend but also a father figure. I never had a father when I was growing up. If I had not improved through Scott's help, I might have dropped out of school. Only God knows what type of man I would have become. Both my mom and Scott had hope for my future—but it was Scott who made it happen.

Scott showed his commitment to me by taking time out of his life to show me the right way to do things. Because Scott did not give up on me, I did not give up on myself. Many people thought I would never learn to read or write—but look at me now! Because of Scott's commitment to me and my own hard work, I know how to read, and I write well enough to tell my story.

As I mature, I think more about what success means to me. To Scott, it means having a place you can call home, the ability to reach personal goals, and a college degree. To my mom, success means having money in the bank to buy what you need and having a high school diploma. To me, success means having a good job so I can afford things I love.

We all agree, though, that living a successful life means living life to the fullest. This means having enough money to do what you want to do. Otherwise, you will be limited. My life is not all about money, but I want to have enough money, education, and inner strength to have a better future.

As usual, Scott was right about my taking time off from college and giving myself time to mature. I am a better person now because I know myself a lot better than I did a year ago. I have to thank Scott, his wife Mary, my mother, and the Big Brothers Big Sisters program. Without that organization, I would never have met Scott. So thanks, BBBS, for giving me a lifelong friend. He has made a huge difference in my life, and I know now that I have a chance to succeed!

By John Johnson

What a Lucky Girl

Big Sister Tracy Noctor and Little Sister Jami Jensen

As a painfully shy eight-year-old growing up in Butte, Montana in the late 1980s, I didn't have many of the things other kids had—like a two-parent family. But I did have something any child would be thrilled to have—a fantastic, caring Big Sister who has played a pivotal role in helping me become the successful twenty-four-year-old woman I am today.

When my Big Sister Tracy Noctor came into my life in 1987, I was one of four sisters from a single-parent home after my dad left us. My mom was doing her best to raise four kids alone, but we still had to depend on public assistance to survive while mom attended college to try to make a better life for us. I was so shy at the time that the folks from the local Head Start program at first thought I couldn't speak.

In 1987 Tracy, a new mail carrier with the U.S. Postal Service, saw firsthand how her younger cousin Corey had been helped by having a Big Brother. She was amazed by all the fun things Corey was able to do and the interesting places he had visited because of the nurturing relationship he shared with his Big Brother.

Tracy read a story on Big Brothers Big Sisters in the

Butte Sunday paper. During the same period, she served on a jury in a child abuse case, and it touched her. She decided to do something about it. She signed on to become a Big Sister.

For Tracy it was a major decision to walk through the doors of the Butte Big Brothers Big Sisters office. She was very nervous as she underwent the agency's exhaustive interview process. But she has told me many times that, despite her initial fears, it was the "absolute best" decision she had ever made.

Early on, I was extremely nervous that Tracy wouldn't like me. It was hard for me to open up to anyone, but Tracy was patient and kind. From the start, I could tell she always made a special effort to connect and to learn to do the things I wanted to do. Instantly, she made me feel special.

Tracy also made a tremendous effort to include my family in our activities. When one of my sisters' Big Sister matches didn't turn out, she helped as much as she could. Even Tracy's family, wonderful people, offered their support and help.

Looking back, I feel that single parents are very vulnerable—and their kids even more so. People make judgments and offer all this information about how to do one thing or another, but Tracy never interfered. She was really a big sister to me—not someone who had all the answers. She would listen patiently and was never judgmental.

In our ten-year match, we shared many great experiences. We skied, visited amusement parks, took my mom and one of my sisters to Disneyland, went camping and boating, sampled restaurants, and saw movies together. We celebrated our first anniversary together by getting our ears pierced.

We had a brief bump in our relationship when I was in

fifth grade. My mom got a good job that required a move to Helena, about forty-five miles from Butte. It didn't matter to Tracy. Helena wasn't a particularly friendly place for me, but Tracy called every week and came up every month. Technically, we were still matched.

When I was a teenager in Helena, I became moody and difficult to get along with. I was, frankly, at a point when I really needed Tracy most. She gave me space and stuck with me even when I was tough to handle. Throughout it all, in typical Tracy style, she was never judgmental or preachy. Her unconditional, positive regard was extremely helpful for me those days.

As I moved through high school, with Tracy's encouragement, I started to improve academically. In my senior year, I panicked when I realized that, even if I could get into college, I couldn't afford to go. I was sure I would be stuck in Montana forever.

But things worked out, and I got a partial scholarship to St. Mary's University in Kansas. Tracy urged me to follow my dreams and offered me financial and moral support.

When I graduated magna cum laude from St. Mary's, Tracy was, as you can imagine, extremely proud. Tracy said the fact that she had never obtained a college education made her want to help me achieve that goal.

When I was accepted in the masters program for social work at Washington University in St. Louis, Tracy was there to help again. Both she and my mom came with me on my first day of both undergraduate and graduate school. In fact, in my senior year, Tracy surprised me when she and my mom came for parents weekend, and she came to all three of my graduations.

She did so much for me. Whatever I needed, Tracy was there for me. Without Tracy serving as a friend and role model, I would never have gotten where I am today. She's been the difference for me—especially in later years when I went to college.

In truth, we both think of each other as real sisters, and there's no doubt we will be close, lifelong friends.

I'm happy to say that I'm not the only person who has benefited from Tracy's loving kindness. Tracy is currently sharing her life with her third Little Sister. What a lucky girl she is!

By Jami Jensen as told to Tom Starner

A Hand Up

Big Brother Cliff Fanning and Little Brother Kevass Harding

On a hot summer day in June 1977, I was ten years old, and my brother, cousin, and I had ridden our bikes to the neighborhood swimming pool. I was trying to liberate a candy bar from the vending machine without paying when the pool manager caught me. Rather than kick us out, he sat down, bought us candy bars, and talked to us.

This was the first time I could ever remember talking to an older male who wasn't an uncle. I'd never lived with my dad and had rarely even talked to him. I asked Cliff, the manager, lots of questions, and we talked for two or three hours. I learned he was a football player who had recently graduated from college and he was also a lifeguard. It was so cool to talk to him!

Later, as we peddled the eight blocks back to my grandmother's house, my pant leg got stuck in my bike chain. As I struggled to get free, a brown Monte Carlo pulled up. I couldn't believe it when Cliff stepped out of the car. As he was freeing me from the bike, he asked if I had any older brothers. I told him I didn't, but that my mom had put me on a waiting list at Big Brothers Big Sisters. My mom provided a wonderful home for us, working two or three jobs to do it, but she realized I was at the age where I needed some male direction.

A few weeks later, we were told I had been assigned a Big Brother. The caseworker brought my new Big Brother to our house to meet me. It was Cliff! I couldn't believe it! I started to cry. Cliff had requested me as his Little Brother, but didn't know my last name. BBBS located me because of my unusual first name.

Cliff and I were well-matched extroverts. We loved spending time together talking. One of my fondest memories is when Cliff played on the alumni football team in a game against the Wichita State varsity team that fall. I was the water boy, standing right next to the coach and hanging out in the locker room. I even had my jersey signed.

Because Cliff was a football player, I wanted to be a football player. Because he made good grades, I wanted to make good grades. Because he graduated from college, I wanted to. We went everywhere together, and it became a special ritual for us to go to action-adventure movies together, such as *Star Wars* or *Top Gun*, whenever they came out.

Cliff helped me with my homework and introduced me to church. Cliff picked me up on Sunday mornings and took me to church and Bible study. I'd always thought church was for sissies, but having a grown man and a football player take me to church changed my mind.

When we moved to West Virginia the summer before I started ninth grade, I felt like my heart was ripped out. But Cliff and I stayed in touch, and I spent summers with him. Those were the most wonderful times! I dreaded August because it meant I would have to leave him.

Fortunately, we moved back to Wichita when I was a junior, and I graduated from Southeast High School in 1986. Cliff helped me get my first job and taught me to drive. Amazingly, he didn't even raise his voice when I almost ran into a car while driving his brand-new dark blue Camaro.

Because of Cliff's training and guidance, I was able to get a college scholarship to play football at the University of Texas at El Paso. There's no way I could have afforded to go to college without a scholarship. There were nine kids in my mother's family, but I was the first to graduate from college.

I majored in criminal justice and became a police officer, intending to go into the FBI after a few years. I also wanted to help kids like Cliff had helped me, so I became active with the youth at church. This experience stimulated a new interest in me.

Rather than pursuing the FBI, I decided to attend seminary and graduated with honors in 1999. I loved theology and discovered my passion in life. While still at seminary, I was assigned to the Dellrose United Methodist Church in Wichita. The membership when I became pastor was only 25; now it's 550. This fall I am beginning work on my doctorate at United Theological Seminary in Dayton, Ohio. My dissertation will be about church growth and administration in an urban setting based on the work at my church.

While working with youth at Bible study and tutoring kids at the recreation center where Cliff was director, I was amazed to discover that some of the children couldn't read. How could this be? We live in one of the wealthiest countries in the world, and our kids can't read! Cliff and I talked about what could be done, and he urged me to get involved to help solve the problem.

I decided to run for an at-large vacancy on the Wichita school board last year. Traditionally, African Americans only ran for the District 1 seat, but I lived in District 5 and that position wasn't up for election. So I tried for the at-large seat even though I knew it was a long shot. I campaigned, meeting people across the city, and talked to every Rotary group I could find. It was quite an honor when I won, and I tip my hat to Wichita for having faith in me.

When I was married in 1994, it seemed only natural for Cliff, the man who has always been there for me, to be my best man. We still play basketball together and go to movies and football games, and our two kids call him Uncle Cliff.

Cliff taught me to seek God first, and I want to pass that lesson on to other children. We've started an after-school program at the church as a way to mentor them. We have a counseling center, and someday I hope we can offer scholarships. A few years ago, Cliff changed his membership and joined my church. Every Sunday, he's there listening attentively to what I say. He's my mentor, and I'm my Big Brother's pastor. It's an amazing relationship.

Cliff Fanning taught me what it meant to be honest, to have integrity, to be truthful, and to love people regardless of whether they're black or white. I still walk with that. I am so grateful for him. He's definitely been my guardian angel, a wealth of compassion, knowledge, and love.

He taught me to give a hand up, not a handout. Like that day more than twenty-five years ago when he stopped to help me with my bicycle, he gave me a hand up, and I've been riding ever since.

By Kevass J. Harding

My Guide in Life

Big Sister Patricia Wolf and Little Sister Ruth Ponce

At age fourteen, when I was first matched with my Big Sister, my self-esteem was low. I felt misunderstood by everyone. It was hard to be positive when I was surrounded by negativity from family members and peers.

At school I was told, "You're ugly," "You'll just be another statistic who never does anything with their life," and other horrible, mean things. But the hardest thing I ever heard came from a teacher who told me, "You will never amount to anything."

I guess I saw no point in proving him wrong. I ran away from home. I was suspended from school several times. My mother had to attend numerous parent–teacher conferences, and I had to go into counseling. I was clearly on a path of self-destruction.

Actually, I was probably just a normal teenager who needed a real friend to help her realize her potential. Big Brothers Big Sisters of Los Angeles helped me find that friend in Patricia Wakely Wolf, who has been my best friend, the believer I needed, and my guide in life for more than six years.

In October 1997 Patricia and I met for the first time at Santa Monica Pier. She also came to my house and talked with my mom and older sisters. They agreed that having another Big Sister would help me discuss issues I was uncomfortable talking to them about.

It was the first time Patricia had been a Big Sister. She decided to do something good in the community after she met a guy at work who was a Big Brother. She watched a video that discussed kids who needed help, and she came back for a training session. Patricia told me that because she had experienced her own troubled teenage years, she wanted to give someone the guidance that she didn't get at that point in her life. She knew she could help someone, and, it turned out, I was the lucky someone.

As soon as we met, I knew Patricia would be perfect to discuss feelings and problems with, the things a teenager can't always talk about with family. It was the first time that both of us had been involved in anything like this. We hit it off right away.

In our first meeting we walked around the Pier, ate shrimp, and talked about our mutual interests. Mainly we talked about me. We found common ground, things like movies and shopping, and we realized we shared a lot of things and emotions.

Patricia was single and in her early forties. Her father had died when she was ten, so she could relate to not having a father around while growing up.

Today, we still have a strong relationship. Patricia helped me find my way. She helped me with my decision to go to college. She also helped me figure out what I really wanted out of life. In fact, without Patricia, I don't think I would have attended college. She expected it from me. It was something she wanted me to do, but along the way I figured out it was something I also wanted to do.

From the start, Patricia was very open. No issues were off limits. And no matter what, she never judged me. She would often give me advice about the obstacles of life, and I always listened because it was great advice.

Our friendship has survived the good and bad times. Patricia changed my life by simply listening. She took an active role in my life and always opened her arms when I needed a hug. Patricia helped me make college decisions during my senior year in high school and helped me find a way to afford the best college for my major.

As I think back, there are many things we did together that were never part of my life before our match—simple things like baking a bunny cake at Easter and buying a Christmas tree, for example. Patricia even taught me how to swim. We've been everywhere together.

I've always considered Patricia more a mentor than a Big Sister. But no matter what I call her, I expect we will remain friends for rest of our lives. She's part of my family now. No doubt about it, we're both hooked.

Patricia's desire to make a difference has rubbed off on me as well. I currently serve as a peer educator with the It's Up to Me program through Big Brothers Big Sisters of Los Angeles, helping young teenagers understand their bodies as well as their responsibility for their actions.

I am so thankful to the Big Brothers Big Sisters organization for matching me with Patricia and contributing to my pursuit of a higher education. They provided light for me where I only saw darkness. For that, I will always be grateful.

By Ruth Ponce with Tom Starner

Someone Like Jeff

Big Brother Jeff Wheaton and Little Brother Vince Reese

Every Big Brothers Big Sisters agency has a Little it will never forget and a Big it wishes it could duplicate. For Big Brothers Big Sisters of Sangamon County, the Little is Vince Reese and the Big is Jeff Wheaton. They have the kind of relationship we hope every Big and Little get to experience. When our agency talks about "Little Moments . . . Big Magic," we're talking about Vince and Jeff.

In the years since they were matched, Vince has appointed himself our spokesman, often writing appeals and sharing his story at speaking engagements. This duty is a perfect fit for him. I have never met a teenager with more poise, grace, and sincerity. To hear him speak about his match with Jeff is to know the impact of this program.

When Vince finishes speaking, people are usually lining up to shake his hand, offer him a job, or hug him. Here is their magical story:

"September 16, 1993, is one of those days that I will never forget. That is the day I met my Big Brother Jeff. I was so nervous. I was on the waiting list for about sixteen months, but I guess you could say the wait was worth it," recalls Vince. At the match introduction, eight-year-old Vince ran to greet Jeff on the porch, and they talked as if they had known each other forever.

Over the following years, their relationship grew. In the beginning, they would go out to eat and to Jeff's house, where they would work on projects, all the while learning more about each other.

Vince says, "Jeff is just fun to be around. When I was younger, I thought he knew how to do everything. I was always doing projects with him, and he taught me tons of things, like how to build a deck and how to lay a concrete pathway. He has made me more responsible and willing to work hard for what I want and need in life."

As much fun as they had together, there were some rough times as well. Vince's father was in prison for the first part of his life, and only in the last five years has he begun to spend time with Vince. Starting high school was especially hard for Vince, and he actually had to transfer schools to improve the situation.

To help Vince adjust to high school, Jeff encouraged him to try out for the wrestling team. Vince excelled at wrestling, and it soon became one of his passions. He was so good that he obtained wrestling scholarships to college.

In these and other trying times, Vince turned to Jeff. "Jeff has been there for me when no one else has been there for me—even when I could not go to my family for help. I am very proud of him for taking the time to change a young man's life. I also want to thank him for being there for me."

Eventually, Vince wanted more independence from his family. As soon as he was old enough, Vince talked with Jeff about how he could get a job and earn his own money. He found an after-school job, which he held for two years, often working more than twenty hours a week.

Once again, Vince exceeded Jeff's expectations. He maintained his grades in high school, accumulated enough credits to graduate early, was the star of the wrestling team, and was eventually promoted to manager at his after-school job.

Once Vince started making his own money, Jeff helped Vince open a savings account. Vince saved some of the money, but he also helped his mom pay bills for the house, even though he was not living there at the time—which speaks volumes about the kind of young man Vince is.

During Vince's senior year of high school, he often talked to Jeff about his future. He had earned wrestling scholarships for college, but he was also interested in joining the Marine Corps. Jeff helped Vince make one of the most important decisions of his life.

In May 2003, when Vince graduated from high school, Vince and Jeff shared an achievement that made both very proud. Then, in August they shared one of their most bittersweet moments. Vince had enlisted in the Marine Corps and was off to California for basic training.

According to Vince, "Jeff's positive influence and encouragement have led me to make good choices. He has shown me the track of success and helped me stay on that track. I know for certain that, without my Big Brother pushing me in the right direction, I would not be where I am today."

Wherever Vince goes in life, he will pass along what was given to him. He has experienced the power of what a caring adult can bring into the life of a child.

"Big Brothers Big Sisters has helped me in so many ways. I was introduced to someone who has turned out to be my best friend. My hope is that every child could have someone in their life—someone like Jeff."

That is our hope too, Vince.

By Jackie Watson

Art by Little Sister Lupita Calderone

The Rest of the World

Big Sister Debi Vance and Little Sister Jennie Mustafa-Julock

When I was fourteen, I had big dreams. I wanted to be a doctor, an astronaut, a teacher, or anything that would take me out of the cramped trailer park home that I shared with my mother, sister, grandmother, aunt, and cousins. Given my circumstances, none of my dreams seemed attainable. Little did I realize then how meeting my Big Sister would impact my life by introducing me to the rest of the world.

My Big Sister Debi and I were matched in April 1989. At our first meeting I told her I wanted to be a fighter pilot, partly because I desperately wanted to impress her and partly because I had recently seen *Top Gun*. The next day she took me to an air show. Debi often says it was then she realized I was not an average kid. We bonded immediately and embarked on a lifelong sisterhood.

My most precious memories with Debi are the simple, everyday activities that we did together. Sometimes she would simply invite me to run errands with her. While running between the dry cleaner and the carwash and taking her dog for walks, we talked about everything under the sun. She made me a part of her everyday life; she always made me feel safe and appreciated. Since I often felt lost in the shuffle at home, it was an amazing gift to have an adult's undivided attention. I quickly felt that I could confide my deepest thoughts to her.

Debi supported me through my high school angst, instilling valuable lessons along the way. I made the junior varsity basketball team, but I mostly warmed the bench. Debi encouraged me to finish out the season, teaching me the value and pride in fulfilling commitments. She attended nearly all of my home games and was the team's loudest cheerleader.

Her loyalty and commitment taught me that I did not always have to be the best at something to be successful. She inspired me to persevere and believe in myself and showed me that getting pregnant and dropping out of high school did not have to be my destiny. I had the right to discover my own path and do whatever I wanted.

It was in restaurants and dressing rooms that we gabbed and giggled about the challenges of puberty, including sex, drugs, violence, and first loves. In addition to this regular dose of quality time, Debi sought to expose me to a variety of new experiences and adventures. We took road trips to the beach and Disney World, and she brought me to countless art and music festivals, concerts, movies, plays, and sporting events. I sometimes resisted the less-than-cool activities, but Debi gently encouraged me to continually try new things. In time, I began to open my mind and stretch my comfort zone. Only as an adult can I truly appreciate the value of these experiences.

One occasion stands out as a pivotal event in my life. Our plan was to eat at my favorite restaurant, but first, Debi said, we were attending a poetry reading. As a teenager, I must admit I was only interested in dinner. However, the poetry reading proved to be a turning point for me, one that even Debi did not anticipate. That evening,

I heard Maya Angelou read her moving poetry and speak candidly about her life and personal struggles. At that moment I stopped feeling sorry for myself; I decided that if Maya Angelou could make her dreams come true, then so could I! I began to look toward my future and made positive changes in my life. I applied myself in school and vowed to graduate on time. When I graduated from high school, Debi's gift to me was an autographed copy of *I Know Why the Caged Bird Sings,* personalized by Maya Angelou herself. This book remains one of my most cherished possessions. I often refer to it in times of doubt or change to regain the perspective I need to take the next step.

Like many recent high school graduates, I was lost after graduation, trying to find myself. Graduating high school was such an accomplishment for me that I never planned the next step. I attended community college for a few years, dropping as many classes as I completed. While our match was long-since officially over, Debi and I continued our friendship. This was probably a frustrating time for Debi, but she continued to patiently encourage me.

At age twenty, my life drastically changed when my mother died suddenly of cancer. I was devastated; I thought my world had ended. As always, Debi was there for me, providing a safe place to cry and grieve. As I emerged from my grief, I realized that life was precious and I wanted to make the most of mine! With Debi's love and support, I mustered the courage to transfer to Flagler College and seriously pursue my studies.

Throughout my undergraduate career, Debi's support never wavered, even as her own life began to change. I was honored to stand up in Debi's wedding as she married an incredible man, William. My place in her life was never compromised by the marriage. Together, Debi and William invited me warmly into their new family. I continued to return "home" from school and celebrate vacations and holidays in their home throughout my college years.

Since then, Debi and I have shared in many of my own life-altering events. She attended my college graduation, again as the loudest cheerleader. She helped me prepare as I relocated to Washington, D.C., to pursue my career and graduate studies at American University. Two years later, she surpassed her own cheering abilities as I walked across the stage and received a masters degree in public administration.

The following week, Debi and William hosted the rehearsal dinner for one of the most memorable events of my life, my wedding. The next afternoon, they walked me down the aisle. During this emotional time, they did not try to replace my parents, yet it was natural for them to fill this role.

Throughout everything, Debi's guidance and support remained one of the only constants in my life. I credit my open mind, love for life, and desire to never stop learning to her. She was my Magellan; she taught me how to navigate the narrow straits of my life as she showed me the rest of the world. Part compass and part rudder, she allowed me to discover myself and find a lifelong best friend and sister.

By Jennie Mustafa-Julock

Chapter 7

A Little Inspiration

The Costume Party

Big Brother Mitch Sibley-Jett and Little Brother Jeremiah Wasson

In 1990 I was a second lieutenant in the Air Force, moving to a new assignment in Lubbock, Texas. I had been a Big Brother for two years while I was stationed in Florida, and it was such a good experience that I wanted to try it again.

I was really nervous before the match meeting with my Little Brother Jeremiah. When I met him, I could tell he was as nervous as I was; but in a strange way, that made it easier. We had something in common already. He was smart, a bit shy, but very funny, and soon we were laughing together, and I felt my nervousness dissipating. Jeremiah also possessed a keen sense of observation about people and the world that I have come to appreciate. We went out behind his house and played on his playground for a while. I thought, "He's a great kid; we're going to have a great time together!"

And so we did. For the next two years, Jeremiah and I spent many weekends doing a dizzying array of activities: wrestling matches, monster truck races, fairs, movies, restaurants, taking things apart (often), putting things together (less often), taking road trips, hanging around, fighting each other in epic squirt gun battles, watching old bad movies together, and even trying our hand at learning how to cook. When Jeremiah was around, we just always seemed to be having fun.

Most Saturdays we spent part of the day in pursuit of silliness, fun, and frivolity. One of our favorite activities was to go to Toys R Us to search its halls for a new squirt gun or a kite to fly for the afternoon. The kites never lasted much more than a day before the ferocious west Texas winds tore them up. Other times, we would blast each other with squirt guns, silently grateful for the cool water on our skin in the middle of summer. When our squirt guns were empty or our kites damaged, or we were just plain exhausted, we'd head over to our favorite restaurant, Taco Bell, to gorge on chimichangas or burritos. What a great day!

One of our best memories was the Big Brothers Big Sisters costume party with a famous couples theme. This challenged Jeremiah and me, and so after discussing it for a while, we decided to go as a very odd couple indeed: King Kong and the Empire State Building!

I'm not even sure who thought of it, but since we both loved old horror movies, it seemed like a good idea. Jeremiah wanted to be King Kong (I think he liked the idea of climbing all over me and pounding me!), and so by default, I became the Empire State Building.

But now, how to create this famous pair? The ape costume was easy; we went out and rented one. The harder part was designing the Empire State building costume. After obtaining a large refrigerator box, we spent the better part of a weekend cutting, drawing, and modifying the box so not only did it look like the Empire State Building, but it would also fit me. We created coat hangar antennas, fabricated a conical top section, and drew what seemed to be thousands of little windows on all four sides!

The party itself was great fun, and seeing other Bigs and Littles dress up with such creativity was inspiring and great fun. At the end of the evening, to our great surprise (and slight embarrassment), we won the costume contest! We couldn't believe it. Later that same year, Jeremiah also won Little of the Year! I was so happy for him. I knew all along what a neat young man he was; now everybody knew it!

In 1992 I was reassigned to England. While it was a good assignment for me and my family, I knew it would be hard to leave Jeremiah. I would miss him terribly. In 1994 I arranged for Jeremiah to come to England to spend a week with my family and me. We had such fun together! He was the same sweet, good-natured young man that I knew, and I was so pleased to see him.

For a time, our lives took divergent paths. I lived in England for two more years; my family grew; and Jeremiah left home after high school to attend college. He later joined the Marine Corps Reserve. I took an early retirement from the Air Force in 1995 and later moved to Connecticut, where I live today.

In 2000, at a time in my life when I was feeling low because I had just lost my job, Jeremiah called me out of the blue! I was overjoyed to hear from him. He said he was now living in Atlanta, had a nice girlfriend, and was studying art. Wow! He certainly wasn't that eleven year old any longer—my Little Brother had grown up!

On the phone, Jeremiah said so many nice things about me and the things we did together. But I was the one who was blessed by him. That's the thing with mentoring; as you give, you receive at the same time without even knowing it. I have a feeling this graceful mutuality is the way all relationships are supposed to be. In my case, I believe I got the better end of the bargain, and I know that

Jeremiah feels the same way.

In early 2003 Jeremiah was called up to active duty and later went to Iraq. He returned later on in the year, thankfully unharmed. While he was there, Allied forces captured Saddam Hussein. Though it was not reported as such, I believe that my Little Brother Jeremiah captured Saddam Hussein. I think he saved that old King Kong outfit, and using the training from endless squirt gun battles on the dusty plains of west Texas, he single-handedly captured the dictator. The look on Hussein's face as a giant ape armed with an M-16 came up to capture him would have been priceless! Because Jeremiah is a very humble man, I know he would never take credit for anything like this. He's just too modest. In truthfulness I cannot confirm this story, but I believe it is true.

Fourteen years have come and gone, and we are still Big and Little Brothers. I hope he never stops referring to me as his Big Brother, and I hope I always have a place in his life. Jeremiah has undergone a remarkable transformation from sweet young man to Marine Corps veteran—but he'll always be my special Little Brother.

Since 2001 I have worked at Nutmeg Big Brothers Big Sisters making matches like the one I was part of. I hope that these matches are as enriching, joyful, and magical as the one that Jeremiah and I enjoy.

By Mitch Sibley-Jett

My Buddy

Big Brother Bill Scott and Little Brother Johnny Brown

There are several different kinds of Big Brothers Big Sisters programs. One is a school-based program where volunteers, often employees of corporations, meet with grade-school children for one hour a week. Some of these school-based matches are called Buddies instead of the more common Big Brothers or Big Sisters.

In December 1992 Bill Scott, a district manager for ALLTEL, met his Little Buddy, Johnny Brown, a second grader at Roan School in Georgia. As a Big Buddy, Bill visited his Little Buddy Johnny once each week for the remaining six months of that school year. At the end of second grade, Johnny moved away, and Bill had no further contact with him.

Ten years later, as his high school graduation approached, Johnny had a special request for his mother. He asked her to help him find an old friend whom he wanted to send a note to. His mother delivered the note along with a graduation invitation to an office building in the hope that Johnny's friend hadn't changed jobs. The note said:

"Dear Mr. Scott,

"Hi, this is Johnny Brown. You were my Buddy when

I was in 2nd grade. I would like to thank you for who you made me today. From your bringing me books to read, I'm a better person now and I thank you. I include my graduation invitation with this and I hope you are able to be there. But I would like to say from the bottom of my heart, Thank you.

"Sincerely,

"Johnny Brown"

The note was delivered to Bill Scott at his office, and he attended Johnny's graduation. The joy on Johnny's face when he saw his old friend watch him graduate lit up the room.

Who would think you could do so much in one lunch hour a week?

By Beth Barrett

The Christmas Glow

Big Sister Beverly Maher and Little Sister Amy McDade

When I heard BBBSA was looking for stories to include in the Centennial Celebration, I thought, "Wow, what a great idea! I would love to submit a story." Then, almost as quickly, I thought, "Where do I begin? I have been matched with my Big Sister Beverly for almost nineteen years. How do I fit nineteen years of experiences into a *short* anything?

I still remember the day I was interviewed to become a Little Sister. My case manager came to our house to interview my siblings and me to enroll us in the program. She came into my room and actually sat on the carpet to talk to me. She asked me questions about what I liked to do and what I would like to do with a Big Sister. I remember thinking, "Wow! This lady is talking to me while sitting on my floor! She sure doesn't seem like the grown-ups I know."

After the necessary processes were completed, Bev and I were matched up.

As I think back on our activities, mostly I recall just hanging out at her house. We didn't go to extravagant places like Six Flags or concerts, and yet we had some of the best times!

One Christmas when I was about ten years old, Bev and her family bought a live Christmas tree to decorate. This tree was *huge*! It was at least fifteen feet tall. I don't know how the monstrous pine got inside, but it did, and it took up two stories. Bev, her sons, and I decorated the tree with all the trimmings—tinsel, ornaments, lights, even real candy canes!

After it was decorated, Bev's three-year-old son Adam, her seven-year-old niece Beth, and I all decided it would be fun to camp out under the tree. We grabbed all the blankets and pillows our arms could carry and spread out under the branches. The branches were so big you could almost sit up under them without hitting your head.

To this day, I still remember the smell of that live Christmas tree, the glow of the lights, and the candy canes. I think we all but emptied that tree of those candy canes by morning. Bev and I still laugh about how she heard the sound of candy wrappers and giggling all night long!

It truly was the little moments that were magic. Bev worked in the bakery of a small-town grocery store. She worked after hours when the grocery had closed, and sometimes she would take me with her. We entered through the service door, and I thought that was really something special. After all, only workers could enter through the back entrance. While Bev decorated the cakes, I sat on the table with my legs dangling off the side—eating spoonfuls of icing. Once she finished a color and moved on to another, Bev would let me eat the rest of the icing. With all that sugar, I was in absolute heaven!

Another great memory occurred just a few years ago. Bev and I went to see a movie for my birthday. We had gotten our tickets and snacks prior to the movie, and we still had a little time before the picture actually started. So we decided to check out the arcade section. Since neither of us was a video game connoisseur, we decided to explore the photo booth—the kind where you sit on a bench and select your background. We decided to live on the edge and go with the *Bride of Chucky* scene. Of course, we had no idea what this would look like. So we popped our quarters in and snapped the picture. We ended up with this crazy photo of our faces superimposed over Bride of Frankenstein hair with Marge Simpson-style gray highlights. I still carry the pictures in my purse and pull them out for a good laugh!

These are just a few of the countless memories I have. Bev has been there for so much of my life. She's been a shoulder to cry on when some boy has broken my heart. She's been there for school plays, and she watched me graduate from high school and college. And I know that, when I marry, she will be there front and center to share that moment as well.

Bev is more than a Big Sister and a friend. She is a part of my life I can't imagine not having. Not only has she been a role model, but she has always believed in me. She helped me become the person I am today.

I still see Bev; we hang out on a weekly basis. It's just that, now, instead of her picking me up, I can swing past and pick *her* up for an outing.

Currently, I work at Big Brothers Big Sisters of Southwestern Illinois. I enjoy the sense of purpose and pride I have working for the agency I was part of as a Little Sister. Someday I know I will have the privilege of perpetuating the sense of magic that I experienced!

By Amy McDade

Hawaii's First

Big Brother Henry Sumida and Little Brother Dennis Brown

Sometimes the circumstances of a child's birth and the economic status of the family determine the child's destiny because children often mirror the adults around them.

Dennis Brown was born into circumstances that didn't raise great expectations for his future. His father, a Caucasian, was in the military, and his mother was from Japan. When he was four his parents divorced, and his mother moved her children from Missouri to Hawaii because she felt it would be a better cultural environment for her half-Asian children. But they struggled financially and emotionally, living in low-income housing projects. Dennis missed his father and acted out his anger and grief on his mother and in school.

A boy like this doesn't usually go on to earn bachelor's and master's degrees in sociology and urban planning and become the CEO and president of the Honolulu office of the largest and oldest mentoring association in America.

What kind of influence would cause a boy to break free from the social and economic circumstances he was born into? In Dennis Brown's case, his name was Henry Sumida. Henry, a civil engineer, volunteered to be the first Big Brother in Hawaii over forty years ago when he was matched with Little Brother Dennis.

Initially, ten-year-old Dennis was difficult. “I was rebellious and hard to get to know,” Dennis says. “I wasn’t too keen about having a Big Brother and, like most kids who lose their fathers, I was resentful of anyone trying to take his place.”

Henry and Dennis were matched based on similar personality types and interests, though, and those similarities soon won over Dennis’s hesitancy. Both of them were quiet people who enjoyed doing things on their own instead of group activities.

Henry opened up new worlds to a boy from the projects. He taught him to play tennis and to bowl. They built model airplanes together, and went to the movies and to amusement parks.

Even more important than the activities was the emotional connection. They always ended their outings with ice cream or dessert at a restaurant. “That’s where we would have our conversations,” Dennis recalls. “Henry was such a good listener. I was very withdrawn, angry at the world, and felt that I was the victim of divorce. But here was someone who voluntarily listened to me vent about what I didn’t like. I hated school, but Henry never lectured. He offered me advice and encouragement without being an authority figure. He was more of a friend, which is what I really needed then.

“Henry was instrumental in showing me I had a future. We toured the University of Hawaii campus and he inspired me to believe that I too could go to college. Henry was an impressive guy to me. He had his own successful engineering business and I looked up to him.

“I knew my mom couldn’t afford to send me to college, but Henry explained how he had joined the Air Force and gone to college courtesy of the GI Bill. With that model in mind, I also joined the Air Force, and used the GI Bill to finance my college tuition. I probably wouldn't have known that joining the military could be my road to a college education, graduate school and a great career were it not for Henry and his influence in my life.

"I was officially only matched with Henry for one year and ten months. I had become so well adjusted that there were other boys who needed Henry's mentoring more than I did. But we kept in touch, and Henry was always there for Christmas and my birthday. He came to my high school graduation, and we corresponded through letters throughout my four years in the military.

"While I was in the military, it dawned on me how much influence my Big Brother and the program had on my life. Even in high school, I leaned toward wanting to work in the human services field. Because I had so many people helping me along the way, growing up in public housing and in a single-parent family, I gravitated toward social services. I wanted to be involved with helping people. As a kid I didn't realize what an impact the program was having on me; I just enjoyed the outings and the friendship. It is only when you get a little older that you realize those little moments have had a life-altering effect on you."

Today, forty years after he was matched as Hawaii's first Little Brother, Dennis Brown is once again involved with the agency that matched him with Henry. He is now the CEO and president of that agency. I guess you could say he is still first in Hawaii's Big Brothers Big Sisters program!

By Beth Barrett

Some quotes were previously printed in the Honolulu Star Bulletin, on September 25, 2003, and the Honolulu News on March 3, 2003.

It Takes a Village

Big Sister Marsha Ammerman Nee and Little Sister Amber Harshburger

They say that the third time is the charm. Amber, my little sister, had two Big Sisters before me, and it appeared that we were finally the perfect combination. Amber was fifteen when we were matched in the summer of 1998. She loved hanging out with me, playing sports, and talking about her life.

Amber did not have many role models or mentors in her past. I own my own business and am the executive director of a four-star golf resort. As a result, I have an extended source of business associates and friends.

That first year with Amber was a learning experience for both of us. My husband and I went to her soccer games, helped with homework, and welcomed her into our lives. She spent holidays with our family, learned to properly set a table, and often helped me with my business. She traveled with me to meet our daughter in Coral Springs, Florida. Amber is a very pretty, intelligent young woman who just needed a support system to enhance and reinforce the fulfillment of her goals and dreams for success.

Amber and I took children from the neighborhood to nursing homes at Christmas time to sing carols. Afterward, we would share hot chocolate and cookies at my house.

Then, we would hurry to meet Santa at a local business to give him our wish lists. Amber felt that she was too old to give Santa a list, but, upon my insistence, she wrote her requests and sealed them in the Good Old Saint Nick letter. Santa, with his infinite wisdom, kept her note, which included her desire for a job when she was sixteen and her dreams of getting a car and going to college. Santa, actually the business owner, told her to come back to his pharmacy when she turned sixteen.

At sixteen, Amber and I worked to create a top-notch resume for her. Her year's experience working with me in my business—learning to shake hands, smile, and hold conversations with members of the business community—gave her confidence to start applying for jobs. We made a pact; she could work part-time if she kept her grades at a B level or above, and she would still play sports.

Amber revisited Mr. Thompson, alias Santa, and applied for a job as a clerk. A few days later, she received a call informing her that she got the job. Mr. Thompson called me the same day to let me know that he had kept her letter to Santa because he had been touched by it. This was the beginning of a new life for Amber.

Hillary Clinton quoted an African proverb, "It takes a village to raise a child." The wonderful employees of Thompson Pharmacy and I became that village for Amber. A business leader and friend, Mr. Thompson, Sr., had once been my mentor, and now he became Amber's.

Amber believes that many of the employees opened up their hearts and loved her as much as my family and Amber's own family loved her. One of the women at the drugstore gave her a gown for her senior prom, while others traded hours with Amber so she could play in her soccer games. One of the pharmacists had her babysit his children, and the owner and his son again adjusted Amber's work schedule to make it all happen. Many shared their experiences of life and provided useful advice to my Little Sister.

The community helped in many ways. When her car broke down, a local car dealer fixed it at no charge. My girlfriends pitched in and helped in very special ways. The employees at the pharmacy guided Amber in her professional development. The two Mr. Thompsons, Bill Sr. and Bill Jr., believed in her ability and promoted her within two years to a pharmacy tech position. Amber felt that Bill Sr. was like her grandfather, and Bill Jr. was her brother. Another pharmacist, Brent Ronan, was the father figure. My family graciously accepted Amber as an intricate part of our household. Amber had become a key part of a large expanded family.

Amber graduated from high school two years later. A year later she announced that she would be attending the University of Pittsburgh at Johnstown.

This year Amber and I were honored at a Big Brothers Big Sisters event. Amber spoke to the group, expressing heartfelt thanks to her extended family. She gave special recognition to Karen, the director of BBBS, Mr. Thompson, Sr., and me. It was exciting to see this great young woman doing so well. It was wonderful to have her share her appreciation and understanding of all that went into her growing up in our supportive village. I used the opportunity to thank everyone there and to tell them why my involvement with the BBBS program was so important. I wrote a letter to Mr. Thompson that began, "Yes, Amber, there is a Santa Claus."

A few weeks ago, I threw a party for Amber before she left for college, and our circle of friends all came out to wish her well. Perhaps not surprisingly, Amber has decided to become a pharmacist.

The village saw her needs and forged the path leading to Amber's future. The small pebble had an impact on the pond of Amber's life.

And Amber's pebble had an impact on my life. Thank you, Amber, for sharing your life with me; you kept me young at heart and gave me the chance to see life through your journey. I love you, and I'm so very proud of you!

By Marsha Ammerman Nee

1968

Big Sister Trudy DeCanio and Little Sister Gwen Andrade

1968 is filled with a lot of memories for me, many of them sad. It was the year that Martin Luther King, Jr., was assassinated, rendering a devastating blow to the black community. It was also the year that my mother and father split up, which wasn't necessarily bad, since they never got along, but the split placed the burden on my mother of supporting us all on her own. There were many more sad memories that year, but I will spare you and move on to a couple of my happier memories of 1968.

I had my sixth birthday party that year, and we had a great time dancing to *James Brown's Live at the Apollo* album. Mama signed me up for a new program for little girls, Big Sisters of Rhode Island. When we learned that I had been matched with a Rhode Island School of Design (RISD) student, Mama and I were both a little hesitant about going forward, because RISD represented a whole different culture for us: late 1960s, art students, hippies, flower power, free love, etc. Surprisingly, Mama decided to at least meet the young woman, and we did. This was the best thing that happened to me in 1968, and as I look back, it was the first of many happy memories that year and beyond.

My big sister was Trudy DeCanio, a nineteen-year-old German-Italian RISD sophomore from Cresskill, New Jersey, a small suburb with no black residents. When we met, Mama and I loved her immediately. She exuded an energy aura that made me feel calm, relaxed, and happy. For the next three years, until she graduated, Trudy and I spent one day together every weekend between September and June. Those times were some of the best of my life. We went to the movies and visited the famous RISD Art Museum often, especially to see my favorite Egyptian exhibit with the mummy sarcophagus. I never got enough of that room! Other days we had lunch at the RISD cafeteria, made brownies in the dormitory kitchen, and listened to music. I had Trudy listening to James Brown and the Jackson Five, and she got me into the Beatles and the Rolling Stones. In addition, I met and hung out with a lot of her friends, most of whom were RISD students, and of course there were the Big Sisters agency activities, like the Halloween party for which Trudy made me a butterfly costume out her sheets!

In addition to the many benefits having a Big Sister brought me, Mama was blessed with a well-deserved respite every weekend.

Over thirty-five years later, Trudy and I are still friends. After she graduated, we stayed in touch by phone, letters, and cards for birthdays and holidays, and I've visited her several times over the past twenty years. I was recently appointed to the board of Big Sisters of Rhode Island, the first Little to serve on the board; and Trudy, who now lives in Philadelphia, came up for the Recognition Dinner at which my appointment was announced. It was the first time my two children had met her, but they greeted her in unison: "*Hi, Auntie Trudy*!"

I believe that I am the well-rounded, socially adept

individual I am today at least in part because of my relationship with Trudy. She expanded my horizons in so many different ways. Naturally, my Mama deserves most of the credit, but Trudy greatly influenced me. 1968, when we met, was a turbulent time, both societally and personally, and I was an angry little black girl. My relationship with Trudy helped me realize that Mama's statement, "You can't paint people with a broad brush," was true. You have to get know people on an individual basis before you judge them. In 1968 I learned that a middle-class German-Italian woman from an all-white suburb could have a lifelong relationship that includes learning and teaching, respect, understanding, and love with a working-class African American girl from the inner city.

Over the years, I've stumbled and made some mistakes, which I strongly feel were just downright stupid. While Mama and I were always close and I had other folks I could talk to, Trudy has always been the one person I know I can call and tell any news without being judged or given unwanted advice. She just listens and follows my lead as to how much discussion needs to ensue. She is the keeper of many of my life secrets and is always full of encouragement for me. She is my sister of the heart, and I love her tremendously!

By Gwendolyn Andrade

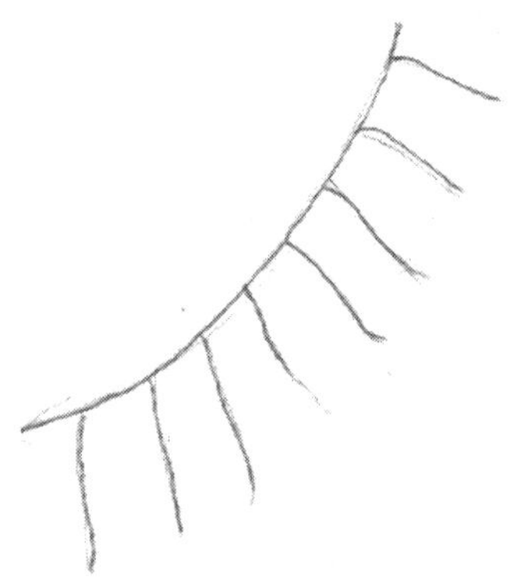

Chapter 8

The Family's Perspective

A Mother's Point of View

Big Brother Ken Tomozawa and Little Brother David Rogers

I always thought of myself as a very average person. I lived and grew up in a small town in Indiana and had family and friends who loved and supported me. After school, I struck out to seek my fortune in the big city. Along the way I was blessed to meet the love of my life. We got married and had three beautiful children, a house, a dog, and a station wagon with a pop-up camper. We were living the American dream.

Then one day our lives were shattered. My husband, best friend, and father of my three young children was diagnosed with cancer. After fourteen agonizing months, he lost his battle. I will never forget going home, sitting on the landing of the stairs, and watching as a neighbor dropped off the kids. How was I going to tell four-year-old Michael, six-year-old David, and seven-year-old Angi that their hero was gone? That he would never be there for the wrestling games and the bike rides? That he wouldn't coach soccer or baseball and wouldn't see them grow up? As we sat on the stairs, Michael asked, through his tears, "Who is going to take care of us now that Daddy is gone?" I assured him that I would. But that confidence was only surface deep. Nothing had prepared me for being a single parent.

A friend and neighbor was a volunteer for Big Brothers Big Sisters and suggested that I call their office and enroll my boys in their program. I never thought of that as being something we would ever need. I thought it was for other people. Well, we were now those other people.

I called the office and a BBBS staff member, Larry, came out to interview us. As he interviewed David, he asked what he wanted in a Big Brother. David said, "I want him to be big and white." Larry looked at me, and I just shrugged. So he asked David why, and David said, "Because my dad was big and white." My only qualification was that I wanted his Big Brother to be a man with good Christian values.

David was put on the waiting list, and we finally got a call from Larry saying he had found the perfect match for David. I was so excited and asked, "Who is he?" Larry took a deep breath and said, "Well, he's not exactly big." OK, I thought. We don't really care about that. "And he's not exactly white." Well, that wasn't a problem. "And he's not exactly a Christian." At that point I finally had to say, "Well Larry, just who have you got for us?" And he answered, "A short Japanese Buddhist, but I think he and David will be great together."

And, of course, Kentaro Tomozawa—Ken—and my son David were a perfect match.

I look back to that time: how impressionable David was and how good Ken was with him. He would talk to him about girls and sports and things that just didn't make as much sense coming from a mother's viewpoint. When Ken was dating Kathy, his girlfriend, he treated her so gently and nicely. All the time, my son was watching. And I knew that he was learning how to be respectful to women. That's something difficult to teach unless you're a male role model.

Ken's only concern throughout the match was that someday David would be bigger than him. Their match officially lasted ten years. And, yes, David topped out at 6'5", compared to Ken's 5'8". But to this day, they are still close and keep in touch with each other.

The following year, my son Michael was matched. He remembers his Big Brother Tom as "just one of the guys." Looking back, Michael says, "I remember the first night I met Tom, and he came with me to basketball practice. We were going to scrimmage around. I didn't know Tom really well. At that age, you're pretty sensitive and embarrass easily. I just knew that I was going to be embarrassed as we began the game because there was Tom, this little white guy, out on the floor. I knew he couldn't get the ball in that basket." But Michael came home that night full of enthusiasm, running through the house and shouting, "Mom, it was so cool, Tom could dunk, he could hit three-pointers, he could do it all!"

Today, Michael says of his Big Brother, "I just think I would have been in a heck of a lot more trouble if I hadn't had a Big Brother. He kept me on track."

I watched as these men became friends with my boys and was thankful for the wonderful role models they were. If all my boys had as role models were the athletes, musicians, and movie stars that they were so fond of, I would have been in trouble. But we were lucky: through Big Brothers Big Sisters, my sons were surrounded by men who set wonderful examples.

My boys watched their Big Brothers very closely. These were men who valued their educations, were responsible to their employers and communities, dated nice young women, got married, and started families—and did it all in the right order. David and Michael knew them as friends who loved them unconditionally, who coached their baseball teams, who came to their birthday parties, who shared special talents, and who stood by them in the good times and the bad.

At one point I started dating a wonderful widowed gentleman. We fell in love, and he loved my children. Normally, a father influence in a family would have ended my sons' matches, but Big Brothers Big Sisters staff recognized that this would be a difficult transition for my sons and kept their matches intact. The first year of our blended family was tough, but gradually things improved. My children were adjusting to their new father. Life was good again.

One evening we were all heading out the door to the high school football game for a fun family outing. Suddenly, in front of us all, my husband of eighteen months, my children's new father, died of a massive heart attack. It was unbelievable! How could this happen to us again? How could we survive this hurt and pain one more time?

Once again my family was gathered in a crowded room at a funeral home. As I greeted those who were paying respects, I wondered where my children were and how they were doing. I couldn't get away to comfort them. But I looked up, and through the many faces in the room, I saw both of my sons standing in a corner, their Big Brothers on either side of them like bookends of strength. Tears came to my eyes, and I was so grateful right at that minute that my two sons had these young men in their lives.

Their Big Brothers were constant companions throughout the difficult weeks and months to follow. I am so grateful to those wonderful young men for their love and attention. I'm not sure that I or my children could have made it without them.

By Yvonne Rogers

Twenty-Five Years

Big Brother Rick DeBruhl and Little Brother Brent Beath

Cars, soda, and rock slides are rather insignificant when taken out of context, but for my son Brent and his Big Brother Rick they represent meaningful experiences of a friendship now celebrating its twenty-fifth year.

I'll never forget the look on my son's face when his Big Brother came to our door for the first time in 1979. Brent rounded the corner when I called to let him know his Big Brother had arrived, and his jaw dropped in complete amazement. "Hey, you're the guy on TV that does sports!" Of course, Rick got a kick out his reaction, and I was completely caught off guard. Because I had been so concerned about the safety issues of a stranger taking my son out of my protective arms, I had completely overlooked the fact that this particular Big Brother was also a television anchor for the local NBC affiliate.

Of course, the match was off to a great start! I think I learned the most along the way while the boys were off sharing sodas, crashing model airplanes, covering court cases for the news, watching professional auto races, and experiencing many of life's firsts, like professional baseball games and snowstorms!

As a very, probably overly, protective mother, my

purpose in life was to raise Brent in a safe and loving home. Brent's father left us when Brent was just two and a half years old, and I wanted nothing more than to bring him happiness while protecting him from further heartache.

Intuitively, I knew I was doing the right thing by helping put a much-needed male role model into Brent's life, but my anxieties nonetheless made it challenging for me to let go. I was admittedly cautious, nervous, and downright skeptical about letting Brent out the door on a number of occasions.

One day in particular stands out in my mind. Rick planned a hiking trip to take Brent out of the oppressive summer heat of Phoenix, Arizona, into the beautiful desert mountain terrain. Brent was overjoyed as he explained his expectations of the trip to me. My natural maternal response was to simply arm him with several helpful safety hints.

As it turned out, the trip ended quickly. Rick could not convince Brent to set one foot out of his car upon reaching the trail's starting point. It seems my helpful hints resounded in Brent's young mind to the point of immobilizing him with complete fear: "Have fun honey, *but* remember, with every step watch out for rock slides, scorpions, rattlesnakes, and centipedes!"

That story best illustrates my personal journey in the Big Brothers Big Sisters program. For this mother, letting go of my son and allowing him the special opportunity to learn and grow through the rich and diverse experiences that only a male confidant could provide was the most precious gift. Rick shared his hobbies, his family, and his wisdom with Brent. That alone allowed the curious and rambunctious nine-year-old boy to experience the external world with a mentor who has since molded him into the well-adjusted, social, and confident thirty-four year old he is today.

Brent is the first to admit that Rick's influence allowed him to take more risks. "If it hadn't been for Rick, I wouldn't have tried many new things, including track and other sports. I've liked the journey we've taken together, but also the journey we've taken separately. We've learned from one another, as Rick is the 'work with a purpose' master planner, and I'm definitely more of a free-flowing kind of guy. It's been great to blend our personalities and enjoy such a deep friendship."

In 1986 Rick was nominated as the Big Brother of the Year for the local agency. Brent spent hours in front of the mirror rehearsing his speech for the special awards dinner. He wanted to say something that would convey his deep appreciation to Rick and his family for all they had shared.

As Rick took the stand to accept his award, the composed television anchor broke into tears and literally could not speak. Brent's speech immediately went out the window, and he too wept. The moment was priceless as we honored their genuine intimacy with silent understanding. Rick's candor taught my son that being kindhearted and gentle in spirit were indeed natural and positive emotions for men.

Now as Rick and Brent experience life man to man, Rick better appreciates the lessons learned as his own two sons go off to college and he now depends on Brent to keep a close eye on them in California. The tables have turned, and through the generous gift of being Brent's friend and mentor, Rick gained a special insight into what it has meant to raise wonderful boys.

My life has been filled with the normal uncertainties experienced by all concerned parents, but at the end of each day I know I did my absolute best to raise my son. I also know I could not have done it without the Big Brothers Big Sisters organization and the love and selfless dedication of Rick and Patty DeBruhl.

Rick is still a prominent television anchor with KPNX/ Channel 12, the Phoenix NBC affiliate. He's a local TV star, but more importantly to Brent and me, he'll always be a star in our family!

By Carole Beath as told to Denice Riffey

Thank You, Mark Griffin

Big Brother Mark Griffin and Little Brother Mike Vest

I am a lucky woman. I have been blessed with my warm, loving husband Mike. It is doubtful, though, that my wonderful husband would be who he is today without the influence of his Big Brother Mark Griffin and Mark's family.

This story is a tribute to the Big Brothers Big Sisters Organization of Birmingham and to Mark and the entire Griffin family, who made such an incredible difference in my husband's life. I hope to give them a glimpse of the ripple effect one man had on so many other lives.

Mark took the initial challenge of becoming a Big Brother to a little boy who was on a downward spiral. Even though Mike had a loving mother, he had no father in his life. His mother had to work many hours just to support him and his brother, which left them with too much free time. At nine years of age, Mike was already experimenting with drugs and alcohol.

Desperate to find a better male influence for Mike, his mother called Big Brothers Big Sisters. Under Mark's guidance, Mike chose an entirely different path for his life. He stopped using drugs and alcohol, attended church, excelled in sports, became a leader in the Fellowship of

Christian Athletes, graduated from high school, attended Samford University on a football scholarship, and earned a college degree.

During Mike's most formative years, the Griffins embraced him as if he were their own. They took him on family vacations, paid for his mission trips, helped him financially, and provided discipline when he needed it. They opened their home to him and his friends, giving them a place to hang out and play basketball. They attended all of his sporting events and became his personal cheering section.

Mark took him to football games and church. Most importantly, the Griffins introduced him to Christ, and his life was changed forever. His most cherished memories are family holiday gatherings at Bert and Mary's home and tagging along on dates with Mark and Louise.

After college, Mike moved to Nashville to pursue a singing career and then to Dallas to headline at Cowboys-Red River. His true calling, though, was to work with kids in a Christian environment. He accepted a position with Legacy Christian Academy in Frisco, Texas, as a coach and teacher.

Thanks to Mark and his family, Mike kept his promise and is now a Big Brother to over five hundred students and athletes. In addition to coaching football, basketball, and baseball, he speaks to youth groups about the effects of alcohol and drugs on families. He also teaches Sunday school, attends youth camp as a counselor in the summer, sings at charity events, and volunteers at sports camps.

Mike is an outstanding and loving husband and father to his two stepchildren and his two-year-old son. He is devoted to his mother and his nine-year-old nephew T.J. I've never known a man with such love and respect for his family. He truly appreciates how hard his mother worked to provide for him and his brother, and he is grateful that she made that call to Big Brothers Big Sisters so many years ago.

Thank you to Bert and Mary Griffin for raising a son with the kind of heart that Mark has. He took on a challenge, and he has stuck with it for many years. He chose to make his role as a Big Brother a long-time commitment, and his entire family took on the challenge. I only wish there were more men like Mark—men who would be willing to invest the time it takes to make a difference in a boy. There are so many boys who need the influence of a man in their lives.

Perhaps the greatest tribute we can give you is naming our son Griffin after the family that made such a difference in our lives. We only hope to instill in Griffin the heart of his namesake and the knowledge that the ripple effect expands to touch many more lives in the years to come.

Mark Griffin molded my husband into a loving successful man, and as one of the many beneficiaries of his love, I extend my deepest gratitude.

By Diana Vest

Art by Little Brother Shawn Farmer

From Mother to Son

Big Brother Bill Davis and Little Brother Jason Powell

Each of you knows me. I am your aunt, neighbor, business colleague, and friend. I am one of the many people you meet each day in your activities.

I am a mother who, with the death of my children's father, found myself with a twelve-year-old daughter and a five-year-old son to nurture as a single parent. Living far from any immediate family members, I relied heavily on close friends as a support system. With the death of my son's godfather, however, I felt the urgency of ensuring that he had an individual relationship with a male figure. I learned about the Big Brothers Big Sisters program from a colleague.

How do you articulate what your hopes are for your six-year-old son? I did not desire a father figure for my son. I needed a kind-hearted Big who could be sensitive to a little boy's loss of his father and understand the importance of discussing all those things little boys talk about with a guy. My son loved sports, so I needed a man who enjoyed sports himself and would be enthusiastic and toss the baseball around, but also attend some of his games and cheer him on. I needed a male who would not be afraid to give active guidance about humility, thankfulness, and what it takes to be a caring, responsible individual. I wanted someone who would stress the importance of good grades and set an example about being part of a family.

Large expectations! Jason and I waited over a year for Big Brothers Big Sisters to fill the order with Bill Davis. Suffice it to say, this man today holds in his hands the spirit of my family. He started with my hopes for what a little six-year-old boy could become as a man. I will let Jason tell you about their relationship:

My father's death was the most difficult period in my life. I cried a lot, struggled in school, and felt different from the other kids who all seemed to have their fathers around. My mom was an excellent parent who was always there for me, but she recognized that there was a void of a male presence in my life.

At the age of eight, I was matched with my Big Brother, Bill Davis. I was a little bit nervous before we met, but Bill and I formed an instant bond because we were extremely well matched, and he began to bring out the skills that I possessed. Bill and I share a love for sports, movies, dogs, and many other things. I still want two German shepherds like Bill's old dogs, Maxwell and Elsa.

I am often asked what types of things Bill and I did together. The answer is that we did the typical guy things, like see lots of movies and attend each others' sporting events. The memories of what Bill and I did together have faded, and in their place are the realities of what Bill did for me in my development as a young person.

I loved playing baseball as a kid, but my hitting was suspect at best, and I rarely saw the playing field. Bill gave me some advice, which I still take to heart. He encouraged me to volunteer to play catcher, the position no kid wants to play because it's tough and unglamorous. Bill explained that if I loved baseball, I should do whatever it takes to play. He said that if I was a team player and did what others wouldn't, there would always be a spot for me. I was the sturdy catcher in baseball, the rebounding forward in basketball, and the relentless lineman in football. By excelling in the roles no one else wanted, I became the ultimate teammate who always got to play.

Even though I had not been a star football player in high school, Bill told me he thought I had what it took to walk on to a college football team. After my first year at the University of Colorado, I decided to give it a try. Most people thought it was unrealistic to try to walk on to a college team. I made the team, though, and was an offensive tackle on the Colorado Buffaloes football team from 1997 until 2000. After my last season, I had the privilege of giving Bill a football autographed by the entire team.

In November 2003 I was presented with a unique opportunity to work on John Kerry's presidential campaign in Waterloo, Iowa. Although it was a once-in-a-lifetime experience with the potential for great rewards, I questioned my decision to take this job because of the sacrifices it involved. At the time, John Kerry was behind in the polls, and most people doubted his chances of winning the nomination. In addition, the pay was minimal, and I would be forced to leave a lot behind in order to work on the campaign. In spite of these factors, I decided to join the campaign staff. While many people questioned my decision, Bill wanted to ensure that I would have the best possible experience. He gave me his old electronic organizer and advised me to keep track of all the contacts I made. This is just another example of how Bill encouraged and supported me in pursuits that sometimes involved having faith and taking chances.

After many long weeks of work, the Kerry campaign was still struggling. Finally, one week before the Iowa caucuses, his campaign gained momentum and support. We shocked the nation and won the Iowa caucuses. I was fortunate to be offered the opportunity to continue on the campaign in Phoenix, Arizona. David Lujon, a campaign supporter, offered me and another staffer a place to stay. I discovered that he was a Big Brother who was on his second match with a Little Brother. The night before the primary, we had a rally with more than two thousand people in Phoenix, which David and his Little Brother, Danny, attended. I was able to introduce Danny to John Kerry. It was rewarding to see that David had been as positive an influence on Danny's life as Bill had been on mine.

Even though the road for many Littles is tough, we are given the opportunity to overcome our setbacks and realize our dreams. I doubt these pursuits or many of my other accomplishments would have been possible without Bill. To this day, eighteen years after our match, Bill remains an integral part of my life. I turn to Bill for professional advice and guidance. We still see an occasional movie, and I am proud to see his two wonderful kids, Tyler and Elizabeth, grow and develop.

While I wonder how my life would be different if my father was still alive today, I count my blessings daily for having Bill in my life. I am proud to be a former Little Brother and hope to live up to the standards Bill set as a Big Brother.

By Mary Powell and Jason Powell

Roger's Story

Big Brother Jeff Poor and Little Brother Roger White

Roger was a welcomed child, born into a family with a mother, a father, and three older sisters. He was a healthy, happy child, mild-tempered, intelligent, and very congenial. His mother was a stay-at-home mom who spent many hours nurturing him, of course with the help of his three sisters. His dad was his best friend. Roger loved learning new things, like where the stars came from, how wide the ocean was, and how a computer works.

Like many children, Roger began his social life at age three when he attended preschool. He was a curious child, always asking questions, and his desire to learn new things was insatiable. He advanced through two years of preschool and was excitedly looking forward to kindergarten.

But, just ten days after Roger's fifth birthday, all that changed. Roger's dad, tired of family life, left his wife and children with no financial support. While Roger's mother was educated, she had never worked outside the home to help support the family.

Suddenly there was no money for piano lessons, sports, movies, birthday parties, and all of the other childhood activities that Roger was used to. The little savings the family had was quickly used up to cover living expenses.

Roger and his family were forced to give up their spacious home in a lovely area of Salt Lake City and move into low-income, barely affordable housing. With no income, the family had to count on the state's welfare system for support until Roger's mother could find work.

Once Roger's mother found employment, she was less available to help Roger adjust to these traumatic changes in his life. He and his older sisters came home from school daily to an empty house and had to fend for themselves until their mother got home. Although Roger's mother was able to find work, the pay was not sufficient to meet all of the family's financial needs.

Roger's mother decided that if she were ever going to earn sufficient money to support her children, she would need additional education. That meant working all day and spending many nights and weekends at school. This left Roger and his sisters home alone even more.

Roger did not adjust well to these changes in his life. He became a very angry child who constantly talked of suicide. His academic performance declined, and he had angry outbursts at school, where he would throw things and spew out long strings of profanity. His behavior often resulted in his removal from the classroom.

At home he became very withdrawn or quarreled with his sisters. I know how incredibly difficult Roger was during this time because Roger is my son!

It didn't seem to matter what I tried—therapy, Scouting, a soccer team—nothing worked to get Roger back on track. I realized that Roger felt very alone with no male role model.

Roger's life seemed to be overrun with women. He lived in a house full of women and girls; his school and church teachers were all female; his therapist was female; and even his Cub Scout leader was a woman!

Roger needed help, and he needed a man in his life. I needed help in a big way. That's when I contacted Big Brothers Big Sisters. But there were not enough volunteers for Roger to be matched with a Big Brother right away.

In the meantime, Roger's problems escalated. He began to stutter and refused to talk to his therapist, and his outbursts at school, and suicide threats became more frequent.

Then, two days before Roger's twelfth birthday, he was matched with his Big Brother Jeff.

The first thing Jeff did was take Roger out for ice cream so they could get acquainted. Roger was still a very angry child, and he didn't make things easy for Jeff. As Jeff attempted conversation and suggested things they might be able to do together, such as biking or hiking, Roger sat silently defiant. Finally Jeff suggested, "Maybe I could help you with your homework." Roger angrily retorted, "I don't need help with my homework. I already know more than half of everything there is to know in this world."

Amazingly, Jeff wasn't discouraged, and he would not give up. As their friendship developed, they went Rollerblading and biking together. Roger and Jeff usually got together one night a week and for a few hours on Saturday or Sunday. Within six weeks, I got a call from Roger's teacher at school. She was elated at the dramatic change in Roger's behavior. His violent outbursts became almost nonexistent. He began participating in class. At home he was less reclusive. All of these changes came about less than two months after Jeff became his Big Brother.

As Roger progressed through elementary school, middle school, and finally high school, he became a straight-A student. Jeff frequently helped Roger with his homework, not because he needed the help, but because he needed a friend. When he took the SATs he scored in the ninety-eighth percentile. By the time he graduated from high school, with a class ranking of 9 out of 375 students, he had already completed sixty-five college credit hours. Roger is now an electrical engineering student at the University of Utah, which he entered with a full-tuition honors-at-entrance scholarship.

It's been many years since Jeff became Roger's Big Brother but he is still Roger's best friend. Although the Big Brothers match officially ended after Roger's high school graduation, Roger and Jeff still hang out, as good friends do. They go biking and camping, watch Utah Jazz games, and work on projects like putting up a basketball hoop at home and repairing bike tires.

Does the Big Brothers Big Sisters mentoring program work? It did for my son. I am eternally grateful that the wonderful young man Roger was born to be is back in our lives, thanks to the influence of his Big Brother Jeff.

By Susan White

My Officer and a Gentleman

Big Brother W. Larry Ross and Little Brother Micah Garside White

Until his fifth year, my son Micah was a cheerful, highly active child. Then his father left us. When Micah called, his father hung up on him. Micah's self-esteem spiraled downward. He asked me, "If I were a better boy, would Daddy love me again?" We struggled for years afterward in a single-parent household.

I remarried when Micah was nine. We formed a new family, and Micah began calling David, his new stepfather, Dad. But my new husband was killed in an auto accident on our second wedding anniversary. As Micah and I sat in shock in the hospital waiting room, I knew I needed help raising this twice-devastated child.

In March 1993, after I contacted Big Brothers Big Sisters of Ventura County, Larry Ross came into our lives. Larry called me before his first meeting with Micah and asked me how I envisioned Micah's relationship with a Big Brother would work. I told him Micah would need extra courage to learn to trust another adult male.

As soon as I saw Micah and Larry together, I knew Micah had found the right role model. This quiet, caring man could see through the walls Micah had built up to hide his sensitive nature. And he would give my son the encouragement and support to reach for the stars. There could not have been better match for my son.

Mentoring a child is the sum of many small actions. Larry smiled his way through first-year band concerts that can be painful experiences. He cheered at sporting events until he was hoarse. They celebrated after every game, win or lose, with an outing for ice cream. Larry encouraged Micah in school and supervised school projects when Micah's ideas exceeded his talents with power tools. Micah and Larry traveled to New York City for a performance of *Cats* arranged for Little Brothers and Sisters with an interest in music and dance. Larry was able to give my son a fuller life experience than I could have as a single parent.

Micah is not very eloquent in expressing his emotions. He found a different way to demonstrate his feelings at a BBBS volunteer appreciation night. Many of the Littles created artwork or wrote poems. Micah did the one thing he knew best: he choreographed and performed a dance dedicated to Larry. He danced to the song "The Wind Beneath My Wings" in honor of Larry's teaching him to soar. His performance was blurred by our tears. We learned that Micah has eloquent feet.

With Larry's assistance, Micah applied for a scholarship to a private college-prep high school. In addition to assisting us in the application process, Larry held mock interviews to add extra polish to my shy son. Micah was accepted and, with Larry's encouragement, excelled in academics, sports, and performing arts. Larry was in attendance at swim meets and school plays. He was also there to help guide Micah through the bumps and lumps of high school life, ensuring safe passage through his vital teen years.

Micah was awarded the Arby's Big Brothers Big Sisters Scholarship. Micah, Larry, and I traveled to Chicago for the award ceremonies. I don't know who was smiling more that weekend, my son or his proud mentor.

Winning the Arby's Big Brothers Big Sisters Scholarship allowed Micah to attend Harvey Mudd College. On graduation weekend, Micah was the student speaker at the luncheon. It was thrilling to see my son's poise and self-confidence at the podium. The fearful child had become a wonderful young man with the help of his mentor and lifelong friend. Later that day, Larry and I cheered with tears in our eyes as Micah crossed the stage to receive his diploma.

Micah has chosen a career in the U.S. Army. The Army is offering Micah the opportunity to become an officer and a gentleman, but I will be forever grateful that it was Larry who first taught my son how to be a gentleman.

By Marie Garside

Chapter 9

Leaving A Legacy

Little Brother Ed

Big Brother Fielding Childress and Little Brother Ed Harrison

A few years ago I called the Big Brothers Big Sisters agency in St Louis, Missouri, from my home in Wyoming. I introduced myself as Little Brother Ed, and I asked them if they could help me find the family of my Big Brother Fielding Childress. I wanted to thank Fielding's family for sharing their wonderful father with me.

The people at the agency were very happy to try to help me reconnect with the family, but I think they were really surprised when I told them I had been matched with Fielding in 1935!

In the 1920s my father died when I was sixteen months old, leaving my mother to raise me alone. We moved from a small town in Illinois to St. Louis so that my mother could find work to support us. Then in 1934 Mom became ill with cancer and died. I was a twelve-year-old orphan.

Originally, I was shuffled between the homes of different people we knew, but the Great Depression was raging on. People barely had the money to take care of their own families, never mind having another mouth to feed and a growing boy to clothe.

I moved into the Thomas Dunn Memorial Home for Boys, a two-story building with forty-eight boys housed in two large dormitory rooms. It was run by a lovely couple named Mr. and Mrs. Hyndman, who arranged for the boys at the home to be matched with Big Brothers. I was immensely lucky to be given Fielding Childress as my Big Brother.

Fielding was truly one in a million. He was the president of the Mississippi Valley Barge Line and a director of the Mercantile Commerce National Bank. Not only was he extremely bright and savvy about the ways of the world, but he was also very kind and an excellent listener. When I was with him he gave me his full attention, and I felt cared for.

We did many fun things, like going to sports events, playing basketball, and going to the opera. We also did many practical things, like working on my schoolwork. The important thing to this young boy was the feeling that there was a man who believed in me and cared enough about me to spend some of his free time to ensure that I would be able to succeed when I became a man.

Fielding took me places on weekends so I wouldn't be alone. He brought me to his family's home for dinner and exposed me to a world that I probably would have never seen were it not for his kindness.

My Big Brother instilled lessons in me that became part of the fiber of who I am. Fielding had an intense work ethic and an equally intense belief in the need to generously share our blessings with others. He taught me both of these lessons in an interesting way. He owned three cars, beautiful machines that were the high-end cars of that time. He hired me to wash and wax the cars and paid me $5 for each car. In today's money it may not sound like much, but in the Depression $5 was a man's wages for several days. To pay a thirteen-year-old boy that kind of money for washing a car was extremely generous.

Flush with the money Fielding paid me, I would take all forty-seven of my Boys' Home brothers out for ice cream cones. What a feeling of joy that gave me! Fielding's generosity allowed me to experience the joy of giving multiplied forty-seven times!

Fielding was my mentor, my adviser, and my friend. I could call him whenever I had a problem, and he was always there—a steady hand stabilizing a sometimes erratic adolescent. He bolstered my confidence when it sagged and let me cry when the tough times of my young life overwhelmed me.

After school, I had part-time jobs at a gas station and later a pharmacy, earning twenty-five cents an hour. Fielding's words to "share what we have" rang in my ears. I used the money to buy shoes for my fellow Boys Home brothers.

I enrolled in night school to learn to become a welder. After three years of schooling, I was employed as a welder and was making enough money to support myself. Even though I wasn't eighteen yet, I left the home to make room for another needy boy. World War II came shortly thereafter, and I enlisted in the Army Air Corp, hoping to earn my wings.

I lost track of Fielding during this time, but his influence never left me. I too was a successful businessman, ultimately becoming sales director for the northwestern United States for a large multinational company. I was married to my beautiful wife for forty-five years before she passed away four years ago. I have a wonderful daughter and stepson. I had a tough start to my life, but I have lived a great life.

When you get older you start looking back at your life, thinking about the people who influenced your journey. I was blessed to have many terrific influences in my life, but the one who stands head and shoulders above the others was Fielding Childress—a man who befriended an orphaned boy for no other reason than that his kind heart wanted to help me grow into a good man.

It was too late for me to go back and thank Fielding personally for the enormous way he touched my life. I knew, though, that it was payback time. I had to find a way to thank his family for sharing this great man with me. That is when I called the BBBS agency and asked for help contacting Fielding's children.

The agency arranged a meeting, and we went to a baseball game, reminiscent of many times with my Big Brother. Fielding had wonderful children. Would you have expected anything less from a man like Fielding? I would have known that even if I had never met them.

By C. Ed Harrison as told to Beth Barrett

The Power of Small Things

Big Brother Steve West and Little Brother Tony Carter

You have probably heard the expressions that small things matter, people make a difference, and being a friend and mentor can save the life of a child. I can tell you, without any reservation, that they are true.

I am testament to the power of small things. I am living proof that one person can make a difference. My life was changed, maybe even saved, because my mother wrote a letter, because Big Brothers Big Sisters was there to help, and because Steve West volunteered to be my Big Brother.

I will be forever thankful to Big Brothers Big Sisters, to Steve, and especially to my mom. She is a very wise woman; she was a great role model; and she kept me on the right track. But she was a single mother; she knew I needed the influence of a man in my life, and she wasn't ashamed or embarrassed to ask for help.

The letter she wrote to Big Brothers Big Sisters was short—not even a hundred words. It was a small thing, but it had a very big effect. At the most important time in my life, when I was only nine years old, I was matched with Steve.

For the last thirty years, Steve has been a friend and mentor, a Big Brother I admire and trust, a teacher who has expanded my understanding of life, and a role model who inspired me to be a better father to my children, a friend and mentor to the children I coach, and a member of the Cincinnati police force.

What Steve did still amazes me. He was young, just out of college, and he was white. It was 1970, and racial tension enveloped the community. There were a lot of other things Steve could have done with his time, but he spent it with me. We played basketball; we read books; and we talked. We talked a lot about my grades and the importance of education. We talked about treating all people the same regardless of their skin color, their religion, where they lived, or what they looked like.

When I told Steve that I had never been camping, he took me camping. There was an electric fence, and I learned that it's never a good idea to hang your sweatshirt on an electric fence. Despite the near-death experience, we did a lot of camping.

When I told Steve that I didn't know how to swim, he took me to the YMCA. I jumped into the pool and went straight to the bottom. Steve had to pull me out. Despite a second near-death experience, we did a lot of swimming.

No matter what we did, I never felt like I was a burden or an embarrassment, and the fact that I was a black male child and he was a young white man didn't stop us. It wasn't even an issue. We were just friends. He was my Big Brother.

I think this experience made me the type of person I am today. I don't believe in stereotypes. I know that people are people. My experience as a Little Brother taught me to judge the individual, not the race. And it gave me a thirst to pass this knowledge along.

I chose law enforcement as a career so I could serve the community. I've worked hard to do my job well, to be a role model for kids, and to succeed at my profession. In fourteen years, I've been promoted from police officer to lieutenant, and I hope my success is the inspiration that will lead someone else to work just as hard as I have.

I coach youth sports so I can give kids the benefit of my experience. I have two daughters in high school now, and I've been coaching their soccer teams since they were little girls. I was the Soccer Commissioner for West Chester and Liberty Township; we had 1,400 kids in the program. This summer Cincinnati started a baseball league for at-risk inner-city youth, and I coached one of those teams.

When I got involved in police work and when I started coaching I never thought about why I was doing it, but I'm sure it was the influence of my mom, Big Brothers Big Sisters, and Steve West. It's my payback. It's my turn to do something positive for someone else.

I want to do the little things, just like my mom did. I want to give time to my kids the same way Steve gave his time to me. I want to be a mentor and a role model for my daughters and my players like Steve was for me. I teach them to play hard, to fight fair, to make the most out of the talent they were given, and to have fun. I want them to know they cannot win every time.

Success cannot be measured by the amount of money they make, the possessions they have, or the promotions they get in their careers. It's about effort. Always do your best. Don't take anything for granted. Work hard. Never quit. Enjoy what you have. Help others when you can. I hope my example inspires each of them to become a Big Brother or Big Sister.

Children today need mentors and role models. Too many kids are from broken homes and single-parent families. Too many kids are at risk. One parent can't give a child everything. My mother was great; she kept me out of trouble. But she knew I needed a strong male role model.

I needed someone I could look up to, someone I could talk to, someone who had life experiences to share.

That's what Steve West did for me. He became the friend, mentor, and role model I needed. I want to thank him from the bottom of my heart. He proved that one person can make a difference.

By Tony Carter

December 21

Big Brother Jeff Haynes and Little Brother Matthew Pearson

December 21, 1998, my twenty-second birthday. I had just graduated from the University of Tennessee the day before, and I felt that I could neither enter adulthood with its cubicles, memos, and office parks nor salvage what was left of my childhood. My roommates and I were moving out of our apartment, and I knew that when I left Knoxville the next day I could never return. The town would continue to change, welcoming new freshmen, convincing them that the best years of their lives would never end, or, worse yet, convincing them that these would indeed be the best years of their lives.

I had tried hard to avoid all that. While some fall prey to get-rich-quick schemes, I evaded the confines of cubicle prison with get-mature-quick schemes, instant adulthood, Hollywood style, complete with a soundtrack and voiceover: "Matthew was at a low point at this time, but little did he know that he was about to stumble upon the experience that would change his life forever."

My quest for instant adulthood had begun exactly seven years earlier on December 21, 1991, my fifteenth birthday. That day my mother and little brother Adam were killed in a car accident, and I was the victim of some very bad advice.

Among the highlights:

- "You're the man of the house now."
- "You have to be strong."
- "You're going to have to grow up fast now."

Please, resist the urge to give any version of the above advice to any child who has lost a parent. My response, which became mantra, was likely worse than the advice: "Well, when something like this happens to you, it will inevitably change you, and I figure that it can either change you for the better or for the worse, and I want this to change me for the better." Then I would stop and smile and wait for the recipient to tell me what a mature young man I was. That praise became a thin substitute for the way my mother's loving kindness used to make me feel good.

Instant maturity would come (I hoped) in the form of a semester in the wilderness with the National Outdoor Leadership School (NOLS). My Big Brother, Jeff Haynes, had promised me that he would send me on one of these wilderness adventures when I graduated from college, and the day had finally come.

I was matched with Jeff Haynes a little more than eleven years before, in the fall of 1987. Jeff, I am happy to say, was not one of the people who hammered the machismo grieving process on me. He was compassionate and empathized with the crippling devastation a fifteen-year-old boy feels when he loses his mother and only sibling in one horrifying second.

I had yet to understand what Jeff had taught me over all those years. There were plenty of lectures, to be sure, but, without a lifestyle that exemplified the values that he was trying to impart, the lectures would have amounted to nothing. From the day I met Jeff, he had risen, gone to work, and come home to spend time with his family every day of the week. His life, by most standards, is quite ordinary. I spent the early part of our relationship admiring him from a distance, but I was also determined never to own as many neckties as he did or, worse yet, a station wagon.

While I learned a lot on that NOLS trip, it didn't "make me a man" like I had hoped it would. Neither did leaving for college a year early; nor joining the Marines a semester later (I was sure that one was going to work); nor moving to Europe for a year. It did, however, make me realize how far I was from being the man I wanted to be. Being confined to the company of the same twelve young men for three months will reveal things to you that you may never know in the context of friends, who have the luxury of leaving you when they are annoyed with you.

In the end though, the knowledge I gained from that experience was invaluable preparation for my life with the very first person I met upon arrival back into civilization—the woman I would marry a year later.

Today is December 21, 2003. I have been happily married for three and a half years, and I have an almost two-year-old daughter who outshines any accomplishment or experience in my past or future. Although I am still far from being who I want to be, I am, for the first time in my life, happy with who I am. In the end, it wasn't the few extraordinary days that made me the man I wanted to be; it was the many ordinary ones. I have finally realized the thing I needed so badly was the thing I had spent the greater part of my life running from—the mundane. The ordinary experiences are where life, where reality, is encountered. Even if we try to escape it, it catches up with us by the law of diminishing returns, and the extraordinary becomes ordinary.

Accepting the inevitable, though, is more comforting than scary. My Big Brother Jeff's greatest contribution to my character was forged over many ordinary ice cream cones and nights eating pizza and watching baseball or watching him fulfill his responsibilities to his family and his job even when he didn't feel like it.

Attaining my master's degree over the first three years of my marriage, most of it with a young child, meant going to school and working afternoons at a coffee shop while forging time for my wife and daughter. Jeff taught me that a man's character is not tested on a rock face hundreds of feet above the ground. Character climbs by being a responsible husband and father and fulfilling your responsibility to those to whom you are committed, even when you don't feel like it. That is when love is bared of feeling and mandates more than what is merely convenient.

Jeff, my wife, and many others in my life have loved me when it was inconvenient and mundane. That is largely why I am who I am today, and that is why I am happy with it, even though I have plenty of room for improvement.

I am not, of course, saying we should not follow our dreams, just that our dreams should not get in the way of our responsibilities. My dream is to become an economist, and I am pursuing a degree to that end right now. Pursuing my dream while upholding my responsibilities is costly, but I do it daily. I have seen that strength firsthand in Jeff Haynes. And, while I don't have as many neckties, yesterday I bought my first station wagon.

By Matthew Pearson

My Christmas Gift

Big Brother Fred Schmidt and Little Brother Sean Barnette

When I was four, my biological father died from a self-inflicted gunshot wound to his head. My mother remarried when I was six, and while she was attending college and working two separate jobs, I was physically abused by my stepfather for approximately six months. The abuse caused permanent nerve damage in my left ear and left physical scars on my body. He had threatened to kill my mother if I told her what had taken place, so I became very good at making excuses for the injuries.

Needless to say, once my mother learned the truth, she left her husband, and we tried to start all over. I distinctly remember feeling emptiness and a void that was caused by not having a positive male role model in my life.

When I was twelve, my mother was diagnosed with a rare form of cancer. The treatments made her very sick, and as with any serious illness, no treatment was guaranteed to work. Things looked grim not only for my mother's future, but for mine as well.

That year, 1993, as Christmas neared, my mother asked me what I wanted. I told her I would think about it and get back to her. That afternoon while watching television, I saw an ad for Big Brothers Big Sisters. It was like a lightbulb went on in my head, and I told my mother I wanted a Big Brother for Christmas. It seemed to be the perfect solution, since money was tight that year. I was matched on December 15 at 7:05 P.M.

There are moments when you know that your entire life is going to change. Meeting Fred was the biggest moment to date. The first thing Fred did upon meeting me was to give me the biggest bear hug.

Having a Big Brother instilled confidence, raised my self-esteem, and made me feel like I was living, rather than just going through the motions of life. Here are a few examples of what Fred has done for me. We were the support team for a two-week journey through the Hells Canyon National Recreation Area with the off-road motorcycle club that Fred belonged to. We made an attempt to climb Gannett Peak, visited Mount Rushmore, went to the geological center of the United States, and climbed the highest points in North and South Dakota—and we did it all in three days!

The first time I ever went skiing was with the Big Brothers Big Sisters group. You couldn't have wiped that smile off my face if you had tried. Fred taught me how to ride a motorcycle and drive. We have gone shooting, hunting, backpacking, climbing, and running. We have literally "been there, done that," as Fred likes to say.

Where am I in my life today? I am a firefighter for the United States Air Force. Values such as confidence, compassion, and dedication that Fred taught me have helped immensely with my chosen profession. If I had never met Fred, I honestly don't know where I would be in my life, but I feel from the bottom of my heart that I would be nowhere close to where I am today. As far as I am concerned, Fred is my blood brother.

My wish is that every child who needs one could find

an adult who is willing to share the magic and change his or her life. Big Brothers Big Sisters is the program that can make that happen.

I am eternally grateful for what Fred and Big Brothers Big Sisters have given me. Mere words cannot express what this program has meant to me. The little moments Fred spent with me were magical. Thank you for the best Christmas gift a boy could ever get!

By Sean Barnette

Art by Big Brother Brett Turk

Three Little "Bothers"

Big Brother Ben Shamberger and Little Brothers Carl Leach and BJ Lofland

My Big Brother's journey began in 1981. Twenty-three years, and three Little "Bothers" as I jokingly call them, later, the program continues to enrich my life. I was in the Air Force, stationed at Dover Air Force Base in Delaware, when I first volunteered. I was just starting my own family with my wife Charlita and two-year-old daughter Stacy.

I wanted to be a Big Brother because of the many great memories of my own biological big brother Herb. He is six years older than me, well liked and respected in our neighborhood, and I was proud to be called his little brother. I wanted someone else to feel what I felt.

My first Little Brother was eleven-year-old Carl. We immediately connected with each other because of our love of dogs. Carl had a very large mixed-breed dog named Dusty that was his best friend. I'm not sure who loved to play Frisbee more, Carl or Dusty!

By the time Carl entered high school, he was like a member of my family. My daughter Stacy looked up to him as her big brother. Carl always treated her with kindness and respect.

In high school Carl started hanging out with the wrong crowd. His friends were planning to do some serious mischief at a neighborhood school basketball game where my daughter was a cheerleader. That was the turning point for him. Carl said, "I was afraid that Stacy would think I was part of a bad crowd. She looked up to me, and I couldn't stand the thought that she and Ben and his wife might find out. I felt a responsibility to them. Right there I broke off with that crowd and never hung out with them again. I know that one of them is in jail now, and the others haven't done anything with their lives. That could have been me."

Instead, Carl graduated from high school and joined the U.S. Marines, where he spent ten years. I was so proud of him. I remember the first call I received from him after he arrived at boot camp. He said the training was hard, but he remembered the stories I'd told him of my boot camp experience in the Air Force. I was quick to remind him that the Marine Corps was much harder than the Air Force! I still proudly display his military picture on my desk. Carl and I have remained friends over the years. I can always count on a visit when he comes home.

During our match, we made a coffee table for his mother, Helen. The top of the table was made of ceramic tile that spelled her name. Carl was proud when we completed the table and took it to his mom. She was so proud; she would tell all her friends and family that her son and his Big Brother made her a special table, and she *still* uses it!

Carl is now thirty-two, with a wife and son and another baby on the way. He works as a systems administrator for a defense contractor. In looking back at our relationship, Carl said, "My relationship with Ben was never about what he said; it was about what Ben did. I looked at what he did and how he behaved, and I wanted to be like that too. I looked at his family and corrected my actions according to the way his family conducted themselves. I look at Ben like a brother. I love him. He's always there for me; he's always shown me love. It's as simple as that."

After Carl, I was matched with Little Brother Chris, and then I was matched with my latest Little Brother, BJ, when he was six. I knew that being a Big Brother was a family affair, so I wanted a Little Brother close in age to my son Ben, Jr., so we could all have fun together.

BJ lived with his mom and older sister in a pretty tough neighborhood. At an early age he had a reputation for never backing down from a fight, even though he was quite small for his age.

Our first meeting was quite memorable. BJ was very outgoing and enjoyed an audience. After the initial formalities, I asked if he would like to come home with me to meet my family. As we started driving to my house, BJ became very quiet. He seemed nervous, but he wouldn't admit it. I continued to drive, telling him about my son. I glanced over and he was crying! I told him it was okay; he didn't have to come to my house until he was ready.

We turned around and I brought him back home. I felt it was understandable—after all, he was only six—but his mom was upset! She told him that if he didn't go the next time, he couldn't have a Big Brother. The next day I could hardly keep him out of the car! He never cried again. It's been twelve years since that first day, and we still laugh about the experience.

He spent almost every weekend at my home and often weeks during the summertime. Although he was always shorter than my son, he was much more athletically gifted. I watched in amazement as they both learned about friendship. BJ could easily beat Ben at most sports, but he never had a fight with Ben for fear of disappointing me. Their competition turned into a team—usually against me!

There was one sport in which Ben had the upper

hand—fishing! Ben caught his first fish at the age of four and has never stopped. Ben quickly showed BJ all the secrets and tricks of the trade. I remember a magical moment that happened shortly after we were matched. We had visited a friend's pond several times to fish, without success. Then one day, the conditions were perfect. The joy of watching BJ catching his first fish was indescribable! His best buddy Ben was right there by his side, cheering him on. They both caught a pile of fish that day and still boast of their great fishing skills.

In 2003 I was nominated as Big Brother of the Year. The application required a letter from the Little Brother stating why he thinks I should be chosen. The words sixteen-year-old BJ wrote will stay with me forever. He wrote, in part, that I was always there for him, providing direction, helping him stay on the right track. He said that he could always talk to me about anything, that I was more than just his Big Brother, I was his best friend.

I cried when I read the letter he wrote about me. It was greater than *any* award I could ever receive. I have been rewarded with the love and friendship of three wonderful Little Brothers. I am a lucky man!

By Ben Shamberger

I Never Knew

Big Brother Michael Schuster and Little Brother Dwayne Porter

Being a Big Brother has been one of the most positive things I have ever done in my life. I was a senior at a Catholic high school where I needed to do twenty hours of community service before graduation. I chose to become a Big Brother. Little did I know this decision would have such a huge impact on my life.

Dwayne Porter was my Little Brother, and he was eight years old when we got together. We would go out two to four times a month for anywhere from two hours to all day. His mom told me how much better he was doing in school and how much confidence he had gained as a result of the time we spent together. All I knew was we had a great time together, and I enjoyed it just as much as he did.

We lost touch after he turned sixteen. I always had fond memories of doing things with him and often wondered what he turned out like. Well, as fate would have it, we ran into each other about a year ago. He is now twenty-six years old, getting married, and he just bought a house.

We went out to dinner with his fiancée and, as we drove to the restaurant, we passed a field where he reminded me we used to fly kites. We passed a park that reminded him of the days we would hop into one of my old muscle cars and drive to a park to picnic.

After dinner he pulled me aside to give me a heartfelt thanks for being his Big Brother. I replied with the usual "No problem," and he said, "No, Mike, I really mean it. Thank you. You made a huge impact on my life. You helped guide me in the right direction, and I don't know where I would be without you." I said, "Wow, I never knew." Dwayne said, "I don't think you will ever know the influence you had in my life. I would not be the person I am today if it weren't for you."

It's a great day when someone tells you of the difference you made in his life. I had forgotten a lot of the things we had done, but seeing Dwayne again made me realize the impact an adult can have on a child. This small accomplishment in my life could be one of my greatest achievements.

A year has passed since Dwayne and I have reconnected, but I have now decided to hire him to work for my family-owned business. He is really excited about working with me and my father, and I feel as if I am hiring one of the family.

Dwayne recently asked me to be in his wedding. I was so proud! It's amazing how a small gift of time given so many years ago has paid me dividends over and over again.

By Michael Schuster

She Changed My World

Big Sister Randon Randolph and Little Sister Mary Dooner Griffin

When I was a young child, I was extremely shy, quiet, and introverted. I came from a very large, poor, and dysfunctional family. We were, however, very fortunate to have been assigned a social worker named Pearl Logen who suggested to my mother that I get a Big Sister.

When I was around eleven or twelve years old, I was introduced to Randy, the woman who would be my Big Sister for years to come. Randy was my escape from the misery at home. As an adult, I realized the magnitude of her influence; my Big Sister changed my world.

Randy did so much for me. She subtly pointed out the dysfunction in my family and its destructive behavior. She taught me to be an independent thinker. She asked me what I thought—and why—and affirmed my right to have my own feelings. Randy took me to museums, plays, and the ballet. She encouraged me to read, and she took me to the library often, sometimes more often than I appreciated at the time.

My Big Sister showed me how to open a bank account and encouraged me to save. Randy introduced me to the YMCA swimming and community boating programs. She stressed the importance of higher education and the idea of making sacrifices for the sake of long-term goals.

Randy took me to the beach and to the movies. She took me on a picnic in the Boston Public Gardens and to a couple of her college classes to show me what college was like. Randy even took me on a couple of dinner dates, where I learned about proper etiquette.

She enlightened my mother and encouraged her to have my teeth fixed. Randy told her how it would affect my self-esteem, confidence, and future. The list goes on and on, but, most importantly, Randy was my sole source of nurturing. She made me feel I was a good, worthwhile, intelligent individual who could determine my own destiny. She showed me I was important and special by giving me her time, attention, and commitment.

Even after a few years, when Randy moved away, she continued to write. Eventually, geography, time, and hectic lives took their toll, and we lost contact. There have been many times over the years that I've spent in reflection. Sometimes in times of turmoil and emotional stress and in other times of happiness and contentment, my thoughts have turned to Randy.

I wished I could let her know how much she had affected my life. I wanted her to know how grateful I am to her for giving me reason to hope for happiness and fulfillment. In my head, heart, and soul, I know she saved me. Randy was the one person in the whole world who gave me a chance. She validated my existence.

My Big Sister gave me the opportunity to pursue a life that could somehow resemble normalcy despite coming from a family in chaos. Randy was a wonderfully positive female role model and my only mentor.

I have often wondered if she knows how much I appreciate having her in my life. I tried many times to find her to tell her so. In the process, I contacted the Big Sisters

Association and conveyed my appreciation. I researched further and eventually wrote a letter to her last known address. The letter reached her in Florida, where she now lives, and we have since reconnected and regularly keep in touch.

I've let her know how much her time, thoughts, and efforts mattered. I am who I am because of her. I'd be afraid to know what my life would have been like without her. My Big Sister has made a difference not only in my life but in the lives of everyone I touch as well.

I'm thirty-eight years old now, and I'm a high school teacher in a Boston public school. I see myself in so many of my students; I see how so many of them have identical needs. I try to change their worlds in the same way Randy changed mine.

By Mary Dooner Griffin

The American Dream

Big Brother Donald Cummings and Little Brothers Phanny, Phanna, and Dane Prep

As amazing stories of survival go, the saga of Cambodian native Sokhom Sen and her three sons, Phanny, Phanna, and Dane Prep, is about as dramatic as it gets.

In November 1978 Sokhom Sen visited her husband, Phay Prep, who was in a forced-labor camp created by the Khmer Rouge, a brutal, ruthless regime in power in Cambodia at the time. Little did she know that it would be the last time she would see him.

Three months later, when Vietnam invaded Cambodia, Sokhom and her three young sons—Phanny, four; Phanna, two; and Dane, two months—were ordered by the regime to leave her aunt's house, where they had been living. At first they traveled by boat and by truck. When the truck they were riding in ran out of gas, they had to leave all their possessions and walk.

By April they reached a village where relatives lived. They stayed for five months, but the village had little to eat and no medical care. So Sokhom decided, for the sake of her sons, to move on. Traveling by ox-drawn cart, they spent the night in a foxhole as Vietnamese bombs fell around them, killing many people in the village where they had relocated. Yet Sokhom would not give up her dream to find a better life for her sons.

Fortunately, the Red Cross arrived and evacuated the refugees to Thailand, where they were given food and canvas for shelter. Sokhom and her sons lived at the refugee camp for several months. While there, she met a man who knew her parents. His nephew was living in the United States, and he vowed to help Sokhom and her family. Eventually, the nephew sent them airline tickets to the Philippines, where they stayed for six months, learning to speak some English.

In 1982 Sokhom and her sons arrived in Rhode Island, thanks to airline tickets provided by the International Institute. The family also received money for food, rent, blankets, and clothing. They had finally made it to America; the place Sokhom had dreamed of.

With the help of Don Cummings, a thirty-two-year Big Brother veteran, one chapter in their amazing story was thankfully closing, and another was about to begin. Don, a past president of Big Brothers of Rhode Island, met the family in 1987, when he was matched with Phanny, Sokhom's oldest son.

"Phanny was very happy to be getting a Big Brother," says Sokhom, who is now, along with her sons, a U.S. citizen. "It was the beginning of a very special relationship between Don and my family."

Special may be an understatement. When Don came by to pick up Phanny for a weekend outing on the first visit, he asked Phanna and Dane if they wanted to go along. They did, and they all had a great time! Don soon informed the Big Brothers agency that he wanted to have all three boys as his Little Brothers. It's unusual, but in this case the agency agreed.

"I couldn't have been more delighted," Sokhom says.

Don told Sokhom that he was very sorry about their

horrendous experiences before coming to America, and he wanted them to feel safe in their adopted country.

"He didn't want us to worry about anything. He said he would always be there for us," she says. "Those words were very comforting."

Of course, Don and the boys enjoyed many of the activities shared by Bigs and Littles in organizations throughout the country. But Don's care went beyond weekends at the ballpark, camping trips, and movies. For the past six years, he has rented the lower half of his house to the family. Sokhom and Phanna still reside there. Don says, "I vowed to ensure their fulfillment of the American Dream."

When the matches finally ended as the three boys turned eighteen, they had decisions to make. Cummings was there to help them.

After Phanny graduated from LaSalle Academy in Providence, he enrolled at Rhode Island College. But financial pressures caused him to consider other options. He discussed joining the military, and Cummings encouraged him. He joined the Air Force in 1998 and is still serving, first stationed at Hill Air Force Base in Salt Lake City, Utah, and now in Okinawa.

Dane, the youngest brother, followed his older brother's footsteps into the U.S. military, though he joined the Marine Corps. Phanna is a college student, living at home with Sokhom.

Looking back on his years as a Little Brother, Phanny is particularly thankful to Don Cummings and all his efforts on the family's behalf. "That period of time definitely instilled the values and principles that will guide and direct me during my entire lifetime," Phanny says. "Don and my family will always remain close."

For their part, in fact, the boys are still very much a

part of Don's life, and vice versa. "Although they have been out of the program for a while, we remain very close," Don says. "With all they have done, especially with Sokhom's courage, it's like a Hollywood script."

According to their Big Brother, all three of the boys are fantastic examples of what a role model should be in today's world. And they, along with their mom, are testament to the fact that you should never give up, no matter what the odds.

Sokhom is forever grateful to the role Big Brothers and Don have played in their lives. "My heart is filled with love and gratitude to this wonderful organization," she says. "They have been a Godsend for us. Thanks to Big Brothers, the American Dream is a reality for our family."

By Tom Starner

Basic Life Training

Big Brother Ralph Ledgerwood and Little Brother Kyle Kiper

Much of what I am today I attribute to the early training I received from my Big Brother. The death of my father when I was four, leaving mom and me barely subsisting on survivor's benefits, had me headed for trouble. Although I had a loving family and a sainted mother, I was quickly becoming a thug and may have eventually ended up in prison or dead.

By matching me with the right man, a man equipped for a little fighting, Big Brothers helped mom save and raise one boy.

I was initially matched with a pizza restaurant manager. He was a good first match, a nice man named Richard who taught me how to make pizza and gave me unlimited credits on the jukebox, but he became too busy to continue the match.

The second match lasted one day. I didn't like him, and Big Brothers listened to my feedback.

Match number three was the charm. His name was Ralph Ledgerwood, a single guy, fresh out of the Army, college, and a commission in the National Guard; he was full of "cool" knowledge about guns, camping, fishing, and other stuff that a boy in Arkansas should enjoy.

Ralph immediately struck me as an honest and sincere person. I was a tough city kid who walked to school through some of the rougher parts of Little Rock and often fought my way home. He was from Ozark, Arkansas, in the mountains and forests, and he knew stuff that was foreign to a boy from the capital city.

His experiences grabbed my interest, though. He had lived in Germany, been a paratrooper, completed Army Ranger School, and knew survival techniques, medical procedures, and leadership—things that turned up later in my life. We built model planes and ships while making pizzas at his apartment, which was adorned with military mementos.

The church was also a big part of his upbringing, and he often involved me, the rebellious grandson of a minister, in his church functions. Looking back, it seems that mom jumped on approving those trips more then the shooting and camping variety, but she went along with most everything except the request to go skydiving together. She said no, and Ralph said, "Yes ma'am." I didn't get a vote.

I'm not sure the Army prepared Ralph for the combat theater he was entering. I was street smart and fancied myself quite the tough guy. My mouth and temper matched my Irish and German lineage.

When he picked me up, Ralph would confirm our plans to see a movie, but would add, "First though, we've got some work to do at the church." My responses landed me back on my mom's driveway until I sorted it out and decided that the movie was worth having to sand a church bus or wash a car. I don't know how he managed to not kill me, but I'm still here. I think it was the "pick your battles" philosophy.

One of my favorite stories, the one my son can repeat verbatim, is when Ralph was going to take me on my first camping trip. I was a Little Rock kid, skilled in many survival techniques involving stalkers, robbers, and switchblades, but bears and mountains were a whole different story.

A few days before our adventure, Ralph gave me an old backpack, which I stuffed with most of my earthly belongings. When the day arrived, he removed most of my possessions and left me with a couple of warm things, a flashlight, water, and toilet paper.

I had anticipated an arrival at a campground, maybe a walk of ten or so feet to our camper, some rudimentary rough days of only basic television and mediocre air conditioning, and then a return to civilization. No. We hiked, we climbed, we crossed streams, we hiked more, we crossed logging roads, we rested, and we climbed more. I complained, we hiked even more and, finally, after hours, reached a clearing near the top of a mountain and set up camp.

I was tired, disinterested, bored, sore, and itching. Ralph ignored my fuming and, after dumping our packs, told me to grab a flashlight and a jacket and took me to the peak of the mountain. We watched the sunset that night over the valleys and mountains of Arkansas. I made sure he knew that I was not impressed. I doubt my disinterest was genuine, though, because it's one of the most vivid memories of my childhood—one that I think about when I think about America. After the sun went down, we ate MREs, made hot chocolate, and lived out in the wild for a while. I've never been able to recreate that feeling.

Such experiences served to provide me with a basic understanding of what was important in life and how a man should act while working toward his goals. Ralph married, and they eventually moved away, but I've held onto the things I learned from him. I've raised a stepson who now is the envy of all the parents in town because I've repeated some of what Ralph taught me.

Although my eyes kept me out of the military, I served ten years as an EMT and utilized many of the skills that I learned from my Big Brother. I'm now losing my vision completely because of a genetic blinding disease, but I still somehow have an indomitable spirit and have "fallen back, regrouped, and moved out" by returning to college, studying here and in England. I have started two businesses, and I will soon earn my counseling license and my doctorate.

One of my goals is to work with the Department of Veterans Affairs to assist our troops who return to civilian life with disabilities. A veteran worked hard to help me get my start, and I can't think of a more deserving segment of our population for returning the favor and helping them to get their lives restarted.

Back when he met me, if Lt. Ralph Ledgerwood had been hauled off into a *Twilight Zone* screening room and shown a clip about who I am today, he would surely have given the film two thumbs down as unbelievable. But maybe I'm wrong. One doesn't see too many military officers giving the thumbs-down sign, since that would mean defeat. Ralph won the battles; and, although he may have moved on to new frontiers during the most recent actions, he ultimately won the war.

Thanks, soldier.

By Kyle Ryan Kiper

Chapter 10

Speaking From The Heart

A Brotherly Bond That Beat the Odds

Big Brother Bill Plaschke and Little Brother Andrew Fishbein

He was so small. Expecting to meet a little boy, I had just been introduced to a stick figure. His jeans hung loosely around dental-floss legs. His T-shirt swallowed the rest. I reached for his hand and grabbed him clear up to his elbow. I had just agreed to be Andrew's Big Brother, yet there was nothing there. A commitment of three hours a week, each week, for the next year? What could an active twenty-two-year-old man possibly do with a seven-year-old shadow? What could we ever share besides an awkward stare?

I had been told that Andrew was suffering from cystic fibrosis, a genetic predator that kills young. But an overeager counselor whispered, "Don't worry, you can't tell." One look at Andrew's stunted growth and I could tell. One ugly cough, and I could hear. I had just met a boy to whom I was morally bound for the next year, yet I couldn't figure out how to spend the first minute. "So, um, what do you like?" I finally asked this little thing hugging his mother's legs. It was then I realized I had missed something: two eyes, flickering under a mop of blond hair, eyes now bigger than all of him. "Sports," he said, his small voice booming, and I'll remember this as long as I remember anything. "I like sports."

We like it, hate it, embrace it, denounce it, talk about it for hours, watch it for weekends, rip it for days. We teach with it, blame it, try fruitlessly to play it and hopelessly to understand it. The one thing we never do, it seems, is pause and be thankful for it. For me, for sports, this day works as well as any. This is trying to be a Thanksgiving sports story, but not about sports as names and numbers, winners and losers. It's about sports as language, as one of this country's most important means of communication, spanning generations, crossing economic classes, giving our diverse people something in common. It's about how sports connected me with Andrew.

I wasn't trying to save the world. I was trying to save myself. I had just graduated from college and was working in the swamp bureau for a newspaper in Fort Lauderdale, Florida. I was covering bowling and shuffleboard and hoping for the day when somebody would consider me good enough to cover high school football. I lived in a one-room apartment with a bed in the wall and roaches on the ceiling. My life lacked any sense of order or importance. I figured the Big Brothers Big Sisters program would give that to me.

I met Andrew Fishbein at a Christmas party in 1980. He said he liked sports. "What do you know?" I said. "So do I." On our second visit, I tentatively dumped a pile of baseball cards on the floor. He dropped to his knees and ran them through his hands like money. "Do you know how to play?" I asked. He didn't, so I taught him a game I had learned when I was young. Soon we were sprawled out on the carpet, shouting together at little pieces of cardboard, Big and Little now shoulder to shoulder. And so the language of our relationship had been established, the currency set.

We played soccer as long as his clogged little lungs could handle it. We pitched baseball until it was time to go home for his medicine. I was promoted to covering high school basketball, so he attended his first live sports event, Boyd Anderson High versus Dillard High, sitting next to me in the stands, cheering as if it were the Bulls and the Jazz. Sports was like this for us. A language of laughter and lessons, a bridge between distant lives.

A year passed, and my formal commitment to Andrew ended, but our visits continued. Sports had given us a new world—big enough for only two—that neither was willing to leave. There was always another miniature golf course to play, another pretend Super Bowl to enact with a rubber football on the scrubby field behind his townhouse.

Then in the fall of 1983, I landed a job as far from that world as Andrew thought possible. I was going to cover the Seattle Mariners, 3,500 miles away. I still remember watching Andrew collapse in tears on the floor of his mother's townhouse. To him, I was just another man who had come and gone. "You'll come see me, I'll stay in touch, I promise," I said quickly. "I'm covering baseball, remember?" I'm sure he didn't believe it. I don't know if I believed it. But it was baseball, remember?

Within a year, Andrew, by then ten, had worked up the courage to fly cross-country by himself to spend long summer days with me and my wife. Or, more to the point, to spend an afternoon with the Mariners, running the outfield during batting practice, hanging out in the clubhouse, chaperoned by an unforgettable pitcher named Roy Thomas.

As we grew older, through vastly different situations on different sides of the country, it was sports that gave us both the incentive to keep our relationship strong. At least three times a year, we would get together, seemingly always to watch a sporting event or to hang out near a sporting event I was covering. Our reunions were, therefore, usually marked by big happy crowds, and our separations usually occurred against the echoes of cheers. When Andrew was thirteen, a basketball assignment took me close enough to Florida so I could give the toast at his bar mitzvah, a wonderful celebration of manhood for a child not expected to live long past his eighteenth birthday.

When Andrew graduated from high school, another milestone for a kid whose lungs and digestive system were weakening by the day, he received a congratulatory phone call from Orel Hershiser. I've never asked an athlete for anything like that before or since. But Hershiser never held it over my head because he understood the death sentence hanging over Andrew's.

Cystic fibrosis is a genetic, terminal disease affecting about thirty thousand children and adults. It causes the body to produce abnormally thick mucus that clogs the lungs and obstructs the pancreas, affecting everything from breathing to digesting.

The language of sports, of course, includes none of those words. It's about life, and I privately rejoiced that the topic of Andrew's prognosis never came up. We were too busy arguing who was better, the Dolphins or Seahawks, the Heat or Lakers. Many times, for a boy who underwent daily chest-pounding therapies and biannual lengthy hospital stays, sports was also the language of healing.

Despondent over his situation as a freshman at the University of Florida, Andrew once swallowed enough pills to kill himself. Fortunately, a fraternity brother found him in time. When I was finished being furious, I bought him World Series tickets, and we stayed up all night in Atlanta, talking about comebacks.

It was his first of three World Series games, one baseball All-Star game, one Super Bowl, one national college football championship, one NCAA regional basketball championship. He has been with me everywhere from Seattle to St. Petersburg, with stops in places like Cincinnati, New Orleans, Charleston, S.C., and even Dodgertown.

He has survived two major surgeries—half of his lungs have been removed—with that same language. Sitting at his hospital bedside, I would read him the sports pages. Phoning his room from across the country, I would ask which game he was watching, and turn my TV to the same game, and we would shout at it together, even if he couldn't always shout.

The years passed, and I became a balding middle-ager, and the stick figure became a strong, handsome adult. Yet we stayed together until, at some point, it stopped being all about sports and started being somewhat about us. That point was reached this fall, when I was scheduled to fly to Boston to cover what became one of the most dramatic Ryder Cup golf tournaments in history. I flew to Jamaica instead.

It was there, on a beach, that his mother and I gave Andrew away at his wedding. On Wednesday, he flew to join me for this Thanksgiving with his new bride, Sigrid. Sure enough, the little guy has finally rumbled his way out of the corner and back up field.

Andrew is twenty-six. He is a successful real estate agent. He undergoes countless daily therapies and painstaking hospital stays, but he works out at a gym and is cut like a body builder. Scientific advancements have pushed the median age of an individual with CF to thirty-one, and here's betting he doubles it.

Today he will hug my wife as if she is his second

mother, which she is. He will roll around the floor with my three children like one of their favorite uncles, which he is. And with me? What do you think? Today we'll watch football, eat turkey, watch football, watch more football, then fall asleep in front of the TV while watching everything replayed in thirty-second video bites on the highlight show. Some might call us lazy sports nuts. We just call ourselves brothers.

By Bill Plaschke

Editors Note: Bill Plaschke is a sports columnist for the Los Angeles Times. *This was his column on Thanksgiving Day 1999. Andrew still resides in Florida.*

The PR Man

Big Brother Tom Boyle and Little Brother Dave Wright

Sometimes forty years seems like a long time ago. Then there are times when it seems like yesterday. Today, as I put these words together, is one of the latter times.

In 1959 I was six years old and the youngest of four boys living in Detroit. My mother was a nurse, not a well-paying profession then. My father had health issues that were never resolved. Taking care of four boys and an ill husband and working a full-time job was an overwhelming task. Mom needed some help raising her boys.

She found it in St. Francis Home for Boys. We lived there full-time, got a Catholic education from the Sisters of St. Joseph, and received discipline training through the school's military program. There was a mix of boys at this school—kids from family situations similar to ours, kids from broken homes, and orphans. It wasn't a perfect scenario, and I can only hazard a guess at how long Mom agonized over the choice.

The nuns tried their best to make the environment as warm as possible, but there was one thing they absolutely couldn't do—provide a little boy with some male companionship. Luckily, one day in the mid-1960s Tom Boyle became my Big Brother.

We went to events like Detroit Tigers baseball games, University of Detroit basketball games, and movies. We bowled and ate pizza. Tom gave me reasons to laugh and, when needed, let me cry as well.

Tom worked for the PR department of Ford. We didn't get a lot of mail at St. Francis, so it was a big deal when I got a postcard from Minnesota where he was on assignment. Minnesota seemed like the other side of the world to a twelve-year-old living in a home in Detroit. As I was to discover later, it wasn't far away.

Eventually, I moved on to high school and college—the latter, ironically enough, in St. Paul, Minnesota, where I live today. As frequently happens in these situations, I lost contact with Tom and his wife Corinne. But the lessons I learned from Tom lingered, even though I didn't know it at the time.

I went on with my life and didn't think a lot about Tom for many years. Occasionally, when I read something about Ford, I would wonder what happened to him. For the most part, however, I busied myself with my life.

Then, a few years ago, I was hired by United Way St. Paul to develop their in-house PR campaign. For inspiration, I looked at the list of agencies that work with United Way. And there it was, big as life—Big Brothers Big Sisters. Four decades ago, I had been involved with a United Way agency and didn't even know it. The material flowcd casily aftcr that.

I thought about one of my early jobs. In high school, and later in college, I worked on the staff of Columbus Boys Camp in Orillia, Ontario. I taught—and learned things from—kids aged seven to seventeen. We laughed and cried a lot. In a way, I had taken on Tom's role in my life, and the kids had inherited my old role for five glorious summers. Even though the most money I ever made there was $500, it was—and still is—the best job I ever had. I still love working with children. Now, I volunteer in a reading program as a mentor to grade schoolers.

It all reminded me of Tom and made me wonder again if I ever thanked him properly for being my friend.

Thinking about him, I realized how much my old friend had affected me in other ways as well. I majored in journalism in college and eventually moved into a career in media/public relations. Was it something Tom had told me years before that led to my career? I can't say for sure, but it can't be a total coincidence.

Tom said I had an excellent speaking voice and recommended a career using my voice. Like a lot of little boys, I loved sports. I found a job where I could combine the two interests. In high school, I began to do public address work for our hockey games. I continued that part-time job in college and now handle nearly a hundred games a year in several sports, working state high school and national college tournaments. And even though I've lived in Minnesota for over thirty years, I still search for the University of Detroit basketball scores in the paper—Tom's team.

But the question still lingered in my mind—how are Tom and Corinne doing? I asked Big Brothers Big Sisters in Detroit if they could help me find them so I could write a note thanking them for all they did for me so long ago. A few weeks later, Ford sent me my Big Brother's current address.

Funny, for a fellow whose business it is to write a lot of words, I suddenly didn't know what to say. Finally, I cobbled together 338 words and sent it to Tom. I wanted to write more, but it didn't seem right to intrude after such a long absence. The essence of the note was that I didn't know if I had ever thanked him properly for being such a good friend a long time ago. I wanted to do so now and, if he wanted to, would like to restart the friendship begun so long ago.

The response came the next day in an e-mail. Tom had moved to Atlanta twenty years ago, retired from Ford, and was now teaching at Georgia State University. He wrote, "I have tears in my eyes. What a great surprise to hear from my Little Brother of forty years ago. I have thought of you often. I simply didn't know how to reach you. We *will* get together."

Three days later, I heard a very familiar voice on the phone. Within minutes, the clock seemed to have turned back, and we were talking like old times, exchanging family information and bad jokes. Tom's oldest son has become involved in Big Brothers also. We talked for about a half-hour until, realizing that no time machine can catch someone up in one night, we called it a night. We promised to talk again and plan a reunion.

For a brief time, the clock rolled back forty years, and then it sprang forward with unbridled joy. But isn't that the way it is with dear old friends?

By Dave Wright

She Hears Me

Big Sister Jane Bracken and Little Sister Stacy Mier

Typically when you meet someone for the first time, you usually say hi or offer to shake the person's hand.

The first time I met Jane Bracken, who was about to become my Big Sister, I chose a much less direct way to communicate. I hid under the table.

Let me explain. Nearly ten years ago, I was a rattled, scared second-grade kid who was completely unsure of how to deal with the fact that I was going to have a new Big Sister.

Jane, twenty-five at the time, had volunteered for the Big Brothers Big Sisters program in Cincinnati. When she came to meet me, I wasn't ready, so I hid under a table as she came up the walk. Today, it's very different. Two people couldn't be more comfortable with each other than Jane and I are.

As is the case in many Big Sister matches that I read about, I really do consider her my sister. I don't even call her my Big Sister anymore, just my sister.

Like most kids in the Big Sisters program, I come from a single-parent home. I am an only child whose dad moved out of state when I was just seventeen months old.

When I was five, I began losing my hearing. The doctors had no idea why. To add to those trying times, when I turned six, one of my older cousins, who had served as a big sister to me, moved away to New York. My mom Donna worked two jobs (full-time and part-time) and was concerned about how to raise a daughter under such stressful conditions. Due to my hearing problems, I began to see a speech therapist who recommended Big Brothers Big Sisters to my mom.

My mom's main concern was finding someone she could trust, which is easy to understand.

So when Jane needed a new Little Sister (her first Little's family moved away, and her second Little dropped out of the program), I was one of the kids who needed a Big Sister.

In 1994 Jane and I were matched. My hearing problems were never a stumbling block for Jane. I wore hearing aids for a time, and I learned to read lips. Jane made sure that she stood in front of me when she spoke so there would be no communication issue.

We did many of the things Big Sisters and Little Sisters do together. We went to parties and picnics sponsored by Big Brothers and Big Sisters. We hit the museums, zoo, and parks in the area. We enjoyed ice cream. We even volunteered for Make a Difference Day, a local volunteer event. I guess our most memorable experience together came in the summer of 1996, when we went to Atlanta Olympics together. Jane even took on the thankless job of helping me with my homework (ugh).

Back in the fourth grade, I faced another hearing-related challenge. As I grew older, my hearing worsened. Hearing aids no longer worked, so my mom looked into cochlear implant surgery, which is pretty complicated and challenging. During that entire time, I really appreciated Jane's caring, supportive manner. Right before I started fifth grade, I had the surgery, which I am happy to say was a smashing success. Today, I only have mild to moderate hearing loss.

As I became a teenager, there wasn't much that Jane and I couldn't talk about. If you know teenagers, you know it's important to have someone who listens and offers advice and counseling. Jane is not shy. In fact, she often asks personal questions about my teenage life and warns against drinking, sex, and all the things that are really on a teenager's mind. Jane and I often talk about things that happen to me or one of my friends. When it comes to listening and understanding, it's hard to beat Jane.

Because of Jane's example as a volunteer, I am also becoming more interested in volunteering myself. Whether that means handing out food in a homeless shelter or visiting an orphanage in West Virginia, I know it will be a really rewarding experience. And when I am old enough, I plan on being a Big Sister to keep Jane's tradition going. I know that makes her proud of me, and I appreciate it.

My life isn't the only one that's changed during my match with Jane. She married Bob, himself a Big Brother, in 1996, and I was lucky to serve as a junior bridesmaid in their wedding. A few years later, I was honored to be one of the first to know that Jane was expecting twins. Born in August 2001, Benjamin and Anna today are happy and healthy toddlers. I think of them as if they were my own and love them completely. Jane will never need to look far for a babysitter.

Despite the twins, Jane hasn't wavered in her commitment to me as her Little Sister. In fact, she's told me that, by the time she had the twins, she was convinced we would always be sisters. Jane even tells people that she sees me more than many of her good friends from high school and college—and more than some family members.

One recent event really hit home for me. In April 2003

Jane gave a Toastmasters talk about being a Big Sister and our relationship. She talked about me, the little girl who developed into a happy, healthy young woman, getting good grades and looking forward to a bright future. As she talked to the group, she began to cry.

"You just don't imagine how much this fulfills your life," she said to the audience.

From where I sit, the feeling is completely mutual.

By Stacy Mier as told to Tom Starner

Art by Little Sister Candace Hale

A Brighter Day

Big Brother Rob Fernandez and Little Brother Tim Ellis

There are times in our lives when we experience trials and tribulations. I believe they are God-given to help make us stronger, and I also believe God blesses us with angels that help us get through the tough times. In my case, I was blessed with a Big Brother who cared enough to be there then and will most certainly be there for years to come.

Mixed Latino and American, I grew up in the very racist projects of South Boston. I was involved with a street gang, and I was in trouble at school. If something wasn't done, I quite possibly could have been in a jail for a very long time, or worse. When my mom introduced me to the idea of getting a Big Brother, I was hesitant at first, but I finally gave in.

When I met Rob Fernandez, I was probably eleven or twelve years old, and I was into all kinds of bad things with the gang. But Rob and I hung out, mostly playing basketball or going to the movies. He didn't wear fancy clothes or drive a BMW, but I looked up to him.

My mom was always at my throat since my father's never been around, so I always looked forward to the weekends, because that's when Rob and I hung out. I probably would not have seen much other than Boston if it weren't for Rob. We went to a beach house in Rhode Island a few times and even took a day-trip to New York City.

I spent a week in Telluride, Colorado, due to my involvement with the Big Brothers Association. My first Celtics and Red Sox games were with Rob. I've done so many fun things with Rob that I never would have had the chance to do without him. I was doing so much better in my life thanks to Rob's influence.

Recently, my mom died. She wasn't a perfect mom, but she was the only parent I had and I loved her. I went into a serious downward spiral following her death. I was an angry, depressed sixteen year old, and I was once again headed for destruction. I was getting into much more trouble than I ever did before.

Rob tried to help, but I was so lost and confused that I pushed my best friend in the world away. I decided that I didn't need him or anyone else in my life. Big, tough guys, like I thought I was, don't need anyone in their lives. It was stupid behavior, I know, but I ended up doing something even more stupid.

My behavior was that of a criminal. I'm seventeen years old now, so I was treated like a criminal and thrown into the Suffolk County House of Correction. I spend twenty-two hours a day in a cell that is no bigger than the average bathroom. For a while, I demonstrated the same mentality I had on the streets—nobody cares, and I don't trust anyone. Deep down in my heart, I truly felt this way, and it would take a miracle to change my life around again.

In my first two weeks in jail, I received a letter from Rob. In the letter, he expressed his compassion and care for me, which was very comforting. He said to pray to God for guidance and direction, which I did. I got on my knees to pray, and moments later I was in tears while opening myself up to God.

From that day on, I pray at least once a day and read the Holy Bible daily. I'm closer to God now than I ever was before, and it's because of Rob.

There was a time when I had lost all hope and accepted this as my destiny. I believe an angel came to me and I've had an epiphany. Three-hundred sixty degrees of opportunity is what is promised to me when I'm released. I'm still in jail, and, due to the nature of my offenses, I could quite possibly spend a while here, but there's a difference now. Now there is hope for a brighter future. Only God sets the limits of what I can do. I am so grateful for this knowledge.

Is it magic? No, but I'll tell you what it is. It's a soul that was lost but now is found. It's a mentor who did much more than what was in the job description.

It's a life saved. All praise due to God Almighty. It's an unconditional friendship that has achieved much more than ever expected. Thank you, Big Brothers Big Sisters of America for such a wonderful friend, and thank you God for sending me an angel named Rob.

By Tim Ellis

My Rudder in Life

Big Brother Sam "Bud" Miller and Little Brother Ambrose Rojas

Bud Miller probably knew his whole life that teaching was his raison d'être. Little did he know that his twenty-eight years in the classroom would significantly change thousands of children's lives, including mine.

Coming from a needy family situation isn't easy. My mom is a stalwart lady with drive, ambition, and integrity, but let's face it, when you live in a rough neighborhood, are very poor, and have no help from a father who is serving time in a correctional facility, raising five kids can be overwhelming.

Knowing that my four sisters' and my mom's influence wasn't enough for a ten-year-old boy, my mom took the advice of a coworker and called the local Big Brothers Big Sisters agency. She didn't know that I was skeptical because I felt that my shyness would surely ruin any potential friendship. Luckily, she made the phone call that ended up changing my life forever.

Bud Miller is my best friend. At age ten he was my rudder in life; and now in my thirties, he is still in my veins as a constant reminder that I can do anything I set my mind to. Bud once asked me to peel a banana with my feet. I didn't realize at the time that he was teaching me a critical life lesson, but I now know that giving anything a try at least once is good for you. Not only did I successfully peel that banana, but have since asked others to try it as well—it is good for the soul to have fun trying.

Bud is not a typical man. He is a genuine, caring, loving man who took a boy who couldn't see beyond his immediate community and offered more than hope. Bud taught me through example that the world is a wonderful place and that our only limitations are self-prescribed. Bud was literally my steady ripple of motivation in the still pond of self-doubt.

When I first met Bud, I didn't do any homework, hadn't read a book, and certainly didn't know that I had a brain. But by sixth grade, after being matched with Bud, I was receiving standing ovations for science presentations. Bud taught me to work with a passion and to love learning. I remember going to the public library for the first time to research my science project and discovering a true curiosity and thirst for knowledge. Even my teacher saw the dramatic change in me as she awarded me an A with twelve plus marks!

It is safe to say that I took to Bud's approval and positive influence like a duck to water! He became my ray of sunshine with every new experience he introduced me to. It seemed that Bud handled every situation with incredible grace and kindness.

At one of my Little League baseball games, our coach got so frustrated that he stormed off the field and left my team wondering what to do. Bud didn't skip a beat. He ran onto the field. He was the glue our team needed. Not only did he buy us matching green team shirts, but he taught us that quitting wasn't an option. Oftentimes we were short a ninth player, so Bud took an extra glove and invited a boy from the stands to join us. That was my best season ever!

As a Latino boy, I was surprised to learn that it was okay for a man to be sensitive and thoughtful. It was an important realization for me because Latino machismo was not an intrinsic part of my makeup, and this helped me feel comfortable about myself.

Bud taught me this valuable lesson when we went out to dinner one night. I remember eating a ton because it was an all-you-can-eat Mexican buffet. Unfortunately, I ate too much and got sick in the parking lot. Bud turned a very embarrassing situation into a fond memory just by being gentle and kind. It wasn't the last time I threw up either—so Bud had several opportunities to teach kindness through example!

Although a gentle man at heart, Bud believes in a tough work ethic and expected a high standard of discipline. In fact, when I was eleven, he enrolled me in an Arizona State University summer class in industrial arts. The experience was exactly what I needed to erase some built-in fears. I became familiar with the campus environment and felt that I belonged.

In 1975 Bud graduated from ASU, and I was a part of the celebration. I was so impressed and excited that I knew for certain that I would return to ASU as a student. Sure enough, many years later, I'm proud to say that I am an ASU business graduate and own my own company.

I'm very proud of my business not only because it is one of the top property appraisal firms in Phoenix, but because it represents all that I learned from Bud—especially his creativity and ingenuity. In his honor, my company, Miller Anderson, is named in part after Bud Miller.

My professional and educational ambitions are direct results of Bud's influence. I make no room for questioning this statement; if it weren't for Bud, I wouldn't be where I am today. He is my family and my lifelong friend, and whether we are attending retirements or just having lunch at the local cafe, we will always remain close friends.

A Chinese proverb best exemplifies Bud's impact on me: "Give a man a fish and you feed him for a day. Teach a man to fish and you feed him for a lifetime." Bud changed my life and the lives of my family. I can only hope that this tribute somehow expresses the depth of my gratitude. Thank you Bud! Love, Ambrose.

By Ambrose Rojas as told to Denice Riffey

The Inspirational New York Jets

Big Brother John Cori and Little Brother Lawrence Davis

Watching the New York Jets football team was never as inspirational to me as it was one special day in 1987. As I sat with my two brothers, Mike and Brian, a United Way commercial spoke to my heart. Freeman McNeil, a leading rusher for the Jets at the time, spoke about Big Brothers and their need for volunteers. I had lost my brother Chris to cancer a couple of years earlier, and I somehow knew that this experience would fill a gap and hopefully make a difference.

What I didn't know is that, seventeen years later and after many visits to the hospital, I would still be Big Brother to the same Little Brother, Lawrence. I really had intended to join Big Brothers for just a year and then to move on with my life.

I have moved on with my life all right. I married my beautiful wife Lucy, had two children, Chris and Victoria, built a rewarding career, and still managed to take Lawrence along for the ride.

Lawrence and I were paired together when he was eleven. For the most part, we were average Joes enjoying one another's company. Like all guys, we enjoyed hanging out—going to Mets games and movies, eating ice cream, sharing families, and talking. What became less ordinary, however, were the times we spent together in the hospital as Lawrence learned to cope with irreversible kidney failure.

Usually, a first meeting between a Big Brother and Little Brother entails something exciting, like going to Coney Island. That's what I had planned anyway. Instead, I visited Lawrence in the hospital and got to know him in a much more vulnerable way. I quickly found that as an only child who had experienced his father's death at age nine, Lawrence could really use a dependable friend. Knowing that I could stand by his side made me stand a little taller. I had found a purpose more rewarding than occasional ice cream outings.

As time passed, Lawrence and I realized that our relationship was bigger than the confines of a hospital. We were bridging gaps we didn't know could be bridged. Our ethnicities proved more apparent to others than to ourselves, and our friendship was a way to show others that diversity could be unifying. A special testament to this point happened when I was asked to attend Lawrence's grandmother's wake.

As an Italian-Irish Catholic, I had only attended wakes that were very solemn and private. I had no idea what to expect when I headed to Jamaica, Queens, one night after work. As I hurried to make it on time, I remembered the advice Lawrence gave me, "Be careful!" Even Lawrence recognized the danger of my venturing into a neighborhood that I wasn't typically "allowed" to enter. Cultural diversity aside, I wasn't going to let Lawrence down.

The wake was alive with song, hallelujahs, and members getting up to talk about the late Mrs. Staten. I found myself underdressed and unprepared. As the minister concluded the service, Lawrence's mom requested that I say a few words. Thank goodness Lawrence was by my side offering support, as I was the only white guest present and felt a need to do a good job as Lawrence's friend.

I was received graciously then, and I have since marveled at how our cultural and racial differences through those uncertain 1980s taught us so much. Lawrence, who was educated in a private elementary school, entered a tough public high school, where many of his beliefs about race and friendship were put to the test. The extreme peer pressure to support same-race athletes made it almost impossible for him to openly admire his favorite San Francisco 49er, Joe Montana. All I could say was, "Go with your heart, and do what you think is right."

Those typical teenage struggles were further complicated because Lawrence's peers told him that our friendship should not have been so meaningful. I kept hanging in, knowing that time would prove to Lawrence that our relationship was worth believing in. I'm proud to know that in a small way some prejudices and misconceptions have been put to rest for Lawrence, me, and our friends and families.

I feel so lucky to have made a friend in Lawrence. He allows me the chance to do something that really makes me feel good *just* by being his friend! Like so many other Big Brothers and Big Sisters, I almost feel guilty that I have gotten just as much out of our friendship as I hope I have given. Lawrence grounds me, keeps me real, and helped me make one of the biggest decisions of my life.

One afternoon I took my then-girlfriend Lucy on an outing with Lawrence. Lawrence was quick to inform me, "Yep, that's the girl you're going to marry." His intuition proved right on target, and I'm so glad that I listened to him!

Now that Lawrence deals with life as an adult, I sit back and watch how he makes mature decisions—like moving forward with his commitment to his wonderful girlfriend, thinking about having kids and what it means to be a father, being an older brother and mentor to his adopted little brother Julian, being a good son to his wonderful mother, and, of course, continuing to deal with challenging health issues.

What a good guy Lawrence is. His smile and the smiles of the children at Big Brothers Big Sisters keep me motivated. Life is fragile; what better way to embrace joy than by helping others meet a potential that is sometimes hard to see at first glance?

As I told Lawrence a long time ago, "Go with your heart, and do what you think is right." I'm glad I did!

By John Cori as told to Denice Riffey

One Match, Two Voices

Big Brother Jim Basham and Little Brother Matt Brickey

Big Brother Jim's Story:

I grew up in a very stable home with wonderful parents and three older brothers. I was twenty-six, had a good job, had just graduated from engineering school, and was dating my wife-to-be. Life was really good, and I wanted to give a little back.

The one-to-one mentoring concept of Big Brothers Big Sisters really appealed to me. What I had not considered was the impact it would have on my life.

Matt was a short, stout, eight-year-old with freckles and bright red hair. He was so shy when we first met that he basically didn't talk. I think I heard him squeak occasionally in response to questions.

Initially, I wondered if I would be able to relate to this kid and his world. I grew up in a *Leave It to Beaver* type home, and he lived in a trailer park with his brother and mom. I did not know how to help him.

But Matt was a sweet kid, and I didn't have the heart to make him wait any longer for a match. So I decided to make a one-year commitment and move on. It didn't work out that way.

Matt is now twenty-four, and we've been together

sixteen years. Even though he's now bigger than me, he's the little brother I never had. We both love sports, the outdoors, reading, and learning new things. He's one of the smartest people I know. If I had placed an order, I couldn't have received a better friend than Matt.

When people find out I'm a Big Brother, they usually commend me for this wonderful thing I've done, and they want to know why we've stayed together for so long.

Big Brothers certainly made a great match. I like being around Matt because he's a dreamer who goes after his dreams. In high school Matt lettered in football, wrestling, and track while maintaining a 3.9 GPA. He was voted Most Athletic and received many honors and scholarships. In college he played football at Georgetown College, was an academic All-American, and graduated cum laude in environmental sciences. He's now preparing to enter medical school. It's exciting to hang around someone like that.

The best part is that I know I've been blessed ten times more than I've given. It has always been fun. Matt just needed a male role model to learn from and give him encouragement as he grew into a man.

Matt is now part of my family, a good friend to my wife Janice, a big brother to my son Harry, and a life-size teddy bear to my daughter Sara.

There is one story that best sums up our experience. When Matt was about nine, he asked me, "Jim, if you could have anything in the world you want, what would it be?" Without hesitation I answered "A '57 red Corvette convertible." Matt responded, "Well Jim, one day when I'm rich and famous, I'm going to get you that Corvette!"

I had forgotten that conversation until a couple years later, when we were exchanging Christmas presents. When I opened the little box Matt had given me, I was amazed to find a 1957 red Corvette convertible ornament! I don't know where that little boy found such an ornament, but it was one of the best surprises I ever had.

Every December that ornament finds a special place on our Christmas tree. Over the years, I've thought a lot about it because it reminds me of the value of this relationship and how I wouldn't trade that little car for all the life-size Corvettes in the world!

Little Brother Matt's Story:

I'm often intrigued when people are interested in the fact that the friendship between my Big Brother Jim and me has lasted sixteen years. They always want to know how we did it, and what made it possible to stay friends for so long. In all honesty, I never quite know what to say. It seems that time has a peculiar way of passing so quickly that the past may be crystal clear yet hazy and vague concurrently.

I first met Jim at a White Castle when I was eight. However, now it seems as if Jim has always been around. The truth of the matter is that I base the success of our friendship solely on the fact that Jim is such a giving and supportive person. I would like to think I've impacted Jim's life in the same magnitude he has mine, but I doubt I could actually offer back half of what he provided me as an adolescent.

Jim was the father figure and male role model I unconsciously needed at the time. He was always there for me, through the good times and the bad. He was never too busy to talk to me when I had a problem. He offered me advice on everything from academics and athletics to girls. Jim had faith in me when I didn't have faith in myself. He believed in me so much growing up that I started to believe in myself.

He helped me gain a more positive self-image when I was young, short, stubby, and rounded like a potato. He was there at football games when I played youth league, and he encouraged me to play high school football as a freshman when it seemed like everybody was bigger than me.

Jim also provided the example I needed when I first considered going to college. At the time, he was the only person I knew who had actually been to college. He made it clear that college was not only available, it was very attainable. Eventually I went away to college, and although we didn't get to see each other often, we still remained in close contact.

Jim and his wife, son, and little girl made numerous trips to see my football games. He would even come and sit on the frigid, iced-over December bleachers to support me.

Now as I pursue medical school, his support is still unwavering. He's never judgmental or condemnatory, even as I sporadically find myself wandering into trouble. Jim has faith in me. It's because of the way he has treated me that I think our relationship has matured beyond friendship into a bond between true brothers—a bond that has lasted sixteen years, a bond that deserves my respect and loyalty. Jim has refracted my life like light through a prism. He has helped me develop my life into something more brilliant than I could have ever planned.

By Jim Basham and Matt Brickey

Art by Little Sister Rachael Rust

Empathy's Call

Big Sister Angela Gustafson and Little Sister Nicole Horn

I was eighteen years old and fresh out of high school when a radio commercial for Big Brothers Big Sisters piqued my interest. Growing up with a brother who was eight years older than I, the thought of having a Little Sister was very exciting. At my first interview with BBBS, I not only discovered that it would it be fun to have a Little Sister, but I also realized how much I had to offer a little girl.

As a teen I had lost a very close friend to cancer. BBBS asked if I would be interested in choosing a girl whose mother had cancer and was in remission. They thought that, in case her mother should become ill again, maybe I would be better able to help her deal with the situation. I immediately wanted this special girl. Little did we know that their suggestion would change the course of both of our lives.

When Nicole and I were first matched, both of us were very shy. To break the ice, I typed up a questionnaire that we could fill out for each other. The questions asked birth dates, favorite color, favorite food, movie, etc. We filled the questionnaires out while sharing our first pizza.

Immediately we realized that we had more in common

than expected; we even had the same birthday!

Nicole was just nine years old when I met her and her mother, Kathy Horn. They lived a few short blocks away from my parents' home, where I lived at the time. Kathy and her daughter had always been very close, and Nicole matured early, surrounded mostly by her mother's friends.

Within months of the beginning of our match, Nicole began expressing concern that her mother was not telling her as much as she always had in the past, and I also noticed that her mother had become more reclusive. As a result, Nicole and I spent more time together and grew closer.

After returning from dinner one evening, I got a call I will never forget. Answering the phone I heard Nicole crying on the other end. She said, "Angie, you need to come to the hospital right now; my mom's heart stopped today."

I was immediately at her side.

It became painfully clear that her mother had been much more ill than anyone had thought. Kathy had requested that she not be placed on life support. All we could do at that point was wait and pray.

A few hours later , I was hugging Nicole when suddenly there was silence. Her mother passed away right before our eyes.

Nicole and I held each other for a long time. The priest asked where Nicole was going to go for the evening. No one really knew, so the priest asked her where she wanted to go. Her response was, "With my Big Sister," and so she did.

We spent Nicole's first night without her mother at my house. We spent moments crying, talking, and just being silent. Nicole was safe and not alone, and that was all that mattered.

Now it is 2004. Nicole has turned out to be a more

wonderful sister and young woman than I had ever imagined that she would. She has grown to be independent, responsible, mature, loving, and considerate. I love and respect her.

Almost nineteen, Nicole is optimistic and very active. She spends most of her time working for her family's business, and she has enrolled in a school for culinary arts. However, her pride and joy are the two horses she keeps in a stable in her backyard.

Living in Waupaca with JoAnn and Galen Heier, who became her guardians, Nicole has been given a life and a family she had not known before. She has been there for seven years now, and we visit as much as distance and schedules permit and talk on the phone.

What if I had not heard that commercial, or called that phone number, or met Nicole? What if I had missed any of those moments, or those memories?

For those of you debating whether to get involved as a Big Sister or a Big Brother, remember that each and every one of us has something special to offer. But until we take the steps to volunteer, we will never experience the joy that comes from sharing our hearts. I know I didn't.

Every one of us can help a Little make memories he or she will cherish for his or her entire life. For some, those memories are all they have to help them through. The great thing is, those same memories help us make it through sometimes too.

By Angela M. Gustafson

David

Big Brother Michael Bowler and Little Brother David Leone

The call came while I was at work. I'm a high school teacher, and it was the last day of school in June 2003. The call came from David's grandfather. "There's been an accident," his cracking voice informed me. "David's at UCLA in intensive care." My heart stopped and I held my breath. "What happened?" David had been with friends. They had been drinking and were driving out to the beach.

David's friend, the driver, was drunk. He lost control at 80 mph and the car spun through a brick retaining wall and wedged against a tree. The driver was unhurt. David had stopped breathing. Some passersby worked frantically to revive David until paramedics arrived. He was rushed to UCLA with a fracture at the rear of his skull.

Though I wanted to rush to David's side, I had committed myself to graduation ceremonies that afternoon and Grad Night at Disneyland that same evening. That June 19 was one of the longest days and nights of my life. I kept in touch with David's mother via cell phone and got middle-of-the-night updates while I ambled around Disneyland in a daze.

Thank God David was not dead! Thank God he was no longer critical! Thank God, period! The moment I returned to school at 7 A.M. the next day, I drove to UCLA and went straight to the ICU. David was conscious and very happy to see me. I was never so happy to see him smile as on that warm summer day.

My match with David began when he was seven years old. David was hard of hearing, as I am, but his disability is much more severe. His left ear was useless and his right possessed approximately 10 percent hearing amplified by a hearing aid. David had been termed by some teachers and camp counselors "incorrigible" because of his seemingly callous disregard for the feelings of others and repeated bad behaviors.

He was a hyperactive child, literally the Tasmanian devil from *Looney Tunes* brought to vivid, unforgettable life. I had two other Little Brothers at the time, Edgar and Matthew, and often the three of us had difficulty containing David's vast stores of frequently misdirected energies. Of all my little brothers, David seemed to take the longest to really bond with me. I feared it might never happen.

As David grew older, the two of us grew closer, and, as a teenager, he wanted to spend more time with me rather than the expected less. Over the long years, David and I developed a friendship that was more father-son than big brother-little brother. But, until that day when I almost lost him, even I didn't realize how much I loved him.

Over the years I was able to redirect his energies in more positive and productive ways. He loved and respected me. Often I accomplished more with him than his family did. Until the crash, David, like most twenty year olds, had not given much consideration to safety or mortality. Thankfully, and perhaps due to my obsessive adherence to the rule over the years, David had been wearing his seatbelt. That habit saved his life.

It did not save his hearing. David had cracked the

temporal bone behind his right ear, the good one, and was now completely deaf. The doctors told him he would never hear again. He was devastated, and I was in shock. I stayed with him the rest of that day and tried to be strong. But what can you say to someone who's been told he would never hear again?

David had the ability to read my lips with near perfection so we could still communicate—as long as I remembered to look directly at him.

The doctors assured David that a cochlear implant would restore some hearing in that ear, but a freakish-looking, artificial-sounding device is nowhere near the real thing, no matter how poor the real thing was. That weak, inefficient real thing, his small amount of hearing, made David feel human. "Now I'll be like a machine," he lamented.

David and I talked at length about the implant during his lengthy recovery. Never have I spent so much time with him as during those months. I'd be at the hospital or his house several times per week. I had to help him walk, because the head injury had caused extensive dizziness. We watched videos with closed-captioning. I took him to captioned movies in theaters, and went to the gym with him when he was finally allowed to exercise, all the while trying my hardest to make him laugh and feel human.

Yet I wondered how it felt to be deaf. Being hard of hearing my whole life, I had often feared total hearing loss. During my time with David, I wanted to get a sense of how he felt, so I watched movies wearing earplugs and reading captions. I never finished one movie. I couldn't stand it. But David did it every day, and he has managed to survive without going crazy.

He has been by turns frustrated, angry, depressed, and regretful. Yet he has endured, and I have never been so proud of him. He has displayed a level of patience and maturity I am not sure I could have under the circumstances. But I have done my best to stay by his side. That's what a Big Brother is for, right?

Four months after the crash, David finally had his cochlear implant surgery. All went well according to the doctors. I was with him before he went under and with him when he woke up. He knows I love him, and that knowledge buoys him. But the device has not yet been turned on. We do not yet know how his brain will adapt to this foreign object. First there was trepidation about the surgery and now there is the worry over the quality of life and sound.

That he will hear is a given. But will those he loves sound the same to him, or will they resemble the computer voice on *Star Trek*—or worse, Donald Duck? Will he hear well enough to attend movies and other social activities? Will he be able to attend college and do the kind of work he wants to do? These are questions yet to be answered. But the one question he could put to me, he doesn't. He already knows the answer. Will you be with me for the journey? The answer is, of course, absolutely.

By Michael Bowler

In My Father's Footsteps

Big Brother Cliff Taylor and Little Brother Ross Godwin

One terrible morning, my mother woke up next to my father who had died in his sleep. It was December 5, 1989, the day before my fourth birthday.

When I turned eighteen, I commemorated both events surrounded by family and friends. Among them was the face of the stranger who rang our doorbell eleven years before and quite possibly saved my life.

My dad's death hit us hard. My mother was left alone with two energetic little boys. She tried to be cheerful, but I knew she was crying every night, and I ached to be the man of the house. Within a few years, I had plunged into a massive depression. I didn't want to live. I couldn't get out of bed, and I stopped eating and playing. A couple of hospitalizations and a long recovery awaited me.

For me, the turning point came when a man named Cliff Taylor walked through my front door, holding a bouncy ball. Cliff and I were matched by Big Brother Big Sisters of the National Capital Area, which serves the Washington, D.C., metropolitan area. The whole idea seemed a bleak reminder that my dad was gone forever, and I pushed Cliff's buttons endlessly those first weeks. I was pretty terrified, even though I may not have shown it.

I think I was testing: "Is this man really here for me? Will he hurt me? Is he patient?"

But Cliff and I grew very close that year. We read all of C. S. Lewis's books together. He took me to movies and horseback riding. He taught me card tricks, mnemonic devices, and tons of riddles.

At the end of the first twelve months, Cliff asked if I wanted him to stick around. I said, "Yes!" Cliff has a demanding career, a nice wife, and a house in Arlington, and yet he makes time for me every Saturday. I get help with schoolwork, and he gives me a lot of life lessons from a man's point of view. His favorite opener for one of our deep talks (usually precipitated by one of my screwups) is: "I speak from experience. Don't go down that path."

A teenager's broken heart can hurt like hell, and Cliff understood that. (I really did love that girl.) He taught me that there is joy in life, but some days sorrow outweighs the joy. God is always there, in good stuff and bad. He taught me that, too.

Cliff showed me how to be a man. Once I admired a stuffed Thumper at the Disney Store, and he solemnly bought it for me. I was ten years old, but he kept a straight face.

One of Cliff's gentle reassurances when we met was "I am not going to replace your dad." But that's what he has done—everything a father would do. For nine years, he came to all my baseball games. In bad situations, he is a problem solver and a peacemaker. There are heated debates and bear hugs. Some real fathers never share those moments with their sons. He knows everything about me. No subject is off limits, not even sex.

One day I put my brother's Rollerblades on Cliff and dragged him down to Rock Creek Park. It was his first time on blades, and he fell and sprained his ankle. Later he bought his own pair. He did it for me; that's pretty much what it was about. I don't think Cliff has ever had a bad day, because he's thankful for everything that happens.

Today, I am a high school senior with good grades and many friends. I even ran for the Maryland state champion cross-country team. And soon, my life will change forever. I'm doing the Great Mailbox Stakeout, awaiting decisions from colleges and looking forward to that challenge. Cliff and I both know it will never be the same. But because he had the courage to walk into my life all those years ago, I will be okay.

Happy one hundredth birthday, Big Brothers Big Sisters of America. And thanks, Cliff, for everything you have done and for all the help you've given me. I love you. I couldn't have made it without you.

P.S. I still have Thumper. He's sitting on my bed. I might take him to college, but I want to leave enough stuff behind so they can't turn my room into a guest room.

By Ross Godwin

Originally printed in The Washington Post, *February 2, 2004.*

Just Like Phil

Big Brother Phil Fink and Little Brother Morgan Hassler

Many moons ago, when I was six, my parents and I moved from Maryland to Texas because my father accepted a new job. Soon after, my mother gave birth to twin girls, and my grandmother moved in with us to help take care of the babies.

My father was consumed with work and didn't spend a lot of time at home. When I was nine, my parents divorced after my father had exhausted all of our financial resources. Suddenly I was the man of the house. The last thing I did every night before going to bed was check all the doors and windows to ensure that everything was closed and locked tight. I felt responsible for protecting my baby sisters, mother, and grandmother. Fortunately, shortly after the divorce, my mother moved us back to the Baltimore area, where we had an established support network of family and friends.

My mother was concerned, though, that I was growing up without a male role model. She learned about the Jewish Big Brothers and Big Sisters League program and suggested that I try it. I was upset and insulted by her suggestion I needed a male role model. Didn't she realize that I, like most nine-year-old boys, was a prodigy? I had already acquired all the knowledge necessary to live the rest of my life, and there wasn't *anything* I didn't already know. I had done just fine without a man in my life!

After a period of arguing that lasted several days, the battle was over. My mother resorted to the most powerful weapon in her arsenal, guilt. Being a Jewish mother, she used guilt with surgical precision. Mom prevailed.

When we applied, the BBBS caseworker told my mother that there would be a delay due to the long waiting list. When my mother told me this, I feigned disappointment. Inside, though, I held out hope that I would remain on the waiting list without a match long enough for my mother to come to her senses and realize that this was totally unnecessary.

Every warning by the caseworker that it might take a long time to be matched kept my hope alive that I wouldn't have to be matched. When the agency called and said they had a match, Mom was very excited. The caseworker brought the prospective Big Brother, a tall man with a beard and glasses named Phil Fink, to our house to meet me.

Phil was much more enjoyable than I had anticipated, and we started doing things together. As it turned out, we shared many interests.

We took day-trips to the aquarium and amusement parks. Phil got on all the fun rides with me, unlike my mother, whose favorite ride was always the bench. We enjoyed the same types of movies, especially James Bond, and like 007 we both loved auto shows.

We enjoyed simpler activities too, like playing chess, building model cars, and putting puzzles together. Not all the models were completed, nor were all the puzzles put together in their entirety, but we still enjoyed spending time together.

The relationship continued to build over the years. It

didn't take me long to realize that my mother had been right—again. Phil and I enjoyed taking long drives on winding country roads, short local hikes, and walks around the neighborhood. He was supportive of all of my activities; came to watch my ballgames and karate demonstrations; helped me with my homework; attended important school functions; and supported my interest in learning the art of magic.

To me, Phil was a perfect blend of a role model and best friend. He helped me study for my bar mitzvah and stood next to me on the bema when I read from the Torah. As a special bar mitzvah gift, Phil took me on a road trip down the East Coast to Disney World, Busch Gardens, and Gatorland. We were gone for several weeks and had a fantastic time.

Phil is an accountant, and as a result I became interested in accounting. Phil helped me get hired as a part-time after-school employee at the accounting firm where he worked.

My ambition as an adult, though, was to become an accomplished law enforcement professional. Again, Phil was there, attending my graduation from the police academy.

I am presently a violent crime detective in the Baltimore County Police Department. After working as a uniformed patrol officer for several years, I became a detective at the age of twenty-four and was accepted to the hostage negotiation team the same year.

It has been twenty years and counting since our first meeting, and we continue to have a very close relationship. Nobody will ever know or be able to calculate the ways Phil contributed to my development as a child, teenager, adult, and professional. There is no way to measure the positive impact he had on my life, other than to say that it was significant. It is clear that Phil played an important role in my life and will continue to do so. Phil helped in many subtle ways to develop me into the person I am today.

To this day, I am as grateful for my mother's persistence as I am for Phil. I am overwhelmed by emotion as I sit and write this story. How would things have been different without Phil? Who would have been my role model? Who could I talk to about my most private thoughts? Who would have instilled confidence in me as a young person?

Fortunately, I don't have to answer these questions. Phil may not be my biological father, but if I could special order one, he would be just like Phil.

By Morgan Hassler

Chapter 11

Little Moments, Big Rewards

In Tribute

Big Brother Senator John Ensign and Little Brother Donzale Butler

I still think of him as a sweet little boy, but in the seven years that I have been Donzale's Big Brother, we've both grown more than I could have ever imagined. As he now stands nearly as tall as I, I can't help but think about the physical growth spurt I've witnessed as well as the emotional growth we have shared.

As young children, my brother, sister, and I were raised by our mom. She did an incredible job raising us. However, when her new husband adopted us when I was fifteen, I learned what it really means to be a father. Genetics has little to do with it. Someone like my father, who took on three children unrelated to him—that is being a father. My dad's generosity and love for us always inspired me to give something back.

Big Brothers Big Sisters seemed like the perfect opportunity for me to reach out to a young boy without a father and try to make a difference in his life. I got much more than I bargained for because I feel like my Little Brother has given me more than I could ever give him.

Our first meeting was right after Donzale finished fourth grade. He was a very shy, quiet, and sweet little boy, and I was looking forward to developing a relationship with him. We went to the library because I wanted to determine what level he was reading at and assess some of the ways I could help him. I was stunned to learn that this soon-to-be fifth grader literally couldn't read a *Cat in the Hat* book. I was shocked and saddened. Here was a kid who had been passed from grade to grade, and he couldn't read.

I knew we had a lot of work to do. We got him a series of Dr. Seuss books and put him into a reading-focused program, and I read to him as much as possible when we were together. Reading to children and being read to by them makes a huge difference in so many aspects of their lives.

One of the aspects of my relationship with Donzale that I am most proud of is how our two separate and different families have made us each so welcome. My three children absolutely adore Donzale. He's like another member of the family to my kids. They get so excited when he is coming over. They love it when we all go swimming or skiing or just hang out. Now that Donzale is growing up and we're not able to spend as much time together, my kids really miss him, but I hope that they always have that closeness.

As for Donzale's family, he has three brothers and a new baby sister. His mom Rhonda and I have a great relationship. I respect her for how hard she works as a parent. As a former welfare mom she has struggled mightily, but she is teaching her kids a good work ethic and emphasizing the importance of education. I know that being a single mom is an incredibly difficult situation—I saw how hard it was for my mom.

I always keep in mind that Donzale's father is absent from his life, and I try to engage him in father-son conversations because I know how important that is when you are growing up. We talk about a lot of moral issues and what it means to be a man. Donzale is almost sixteen, and he is entering a new stage of life with new responsibilities. He has a job, and he's learning a work ethic there. But being a teenager and a young man is not easy. I have tried to be a strong and consistent figure in Donzale's life, and I can only pray that he feels this has had a positive impact.

As for my life, Donzale has affected me in ways that I can't even put into words. He has taught me to be a better father and a better person. I have gotten more out of the relationship than I ever put in just by seeing how appreciative he is to have a mentor and friend in his life.

It's hard to believe that Donzale is growing up so quickly. Just as I do when I look at my own children, I wonder where the time has gone. I look forward to seeing what the future holds for Donzale. My hope is that he will learn to love God with all his heart, mind, soul, and strength. I want him to reach his goals while understanding what it means to be a man. Most of all, I hope he becomes a loving, responsible, and respectful human being and member of society. And when Donzale eventually has children, I hope that he will be a good father.

Being Donzale's Big Brother is the finest tribute I can think of to my father. He taught me you can voluntarily enter a child's life, and with love, guide him toward being all he was born to be. It was too good a gift to not pass on.

By U.S. Senator John Ensign

My Little NBA Star

Big Brother Dewy Forbes and Little Brother Brad Miller

When I first volunteered to become a Big Brother back in the early 1980s, I had no idea how it would change my life. One day, my wife and I were reading a newspaper article that touched us both about a sad youngster in the Fort Wayne area who needed a Big Brother. A few days later, I visited the agency to offer my services in helping that boy.

My first Little Brother had knee problems and underwent surgery that encased him in a cast on both legs from his waist down. We had a van at the time, so we could handle his special needs. They set up the match, and it started out well.

His parents were divorced, and he lived with his mom. About a year into the match, he visited his dad, and after deciding that he and his dad could have a relationship, he left the Big Brothers program.

I was disappointed, of course, but the agency asked me if I would consider a second Little Brother. I agreed, and in 1985 they passed along the names of a few boys whose moms had signed them up for the program. One of those kids, Bradley Miller, was eight years old. Brad was tall for his age, but not a giant. He played YMCA basketball, and he was pretty good at the game. Little did I know then that Brad would grow into a seven-foot-tall NBA all-star center, currently playing for the Sacramento Kings. Well, that's exactly what happened.

When we met in 1985, Brad was a shy, laid back youngster. Brad's mom and dad were divorced, but he had a very solid family life, living with Rosie, his mom, Renee, his sister, and his grandmother Mary Ann Heitz. As the only male in a female household, Brad needed a role model to help him along. That was where I came in.

We did the guy things that most boys do with their Big Brothers, including going to ballgames, hunting, riding motocross, and camping. We live on a lake called Big Long Lake, and we have a Bass boat and a speedboat, so we did a lot of fishing, skiing, and tubing when Brad was a kid.

At the time, I was playing softball all around the Midwest with a couple of different city teams, and I did a lot of traveling. Brad tagged along on those trips.

In 1986 my wife and I adopted a newborn baby named Dane and then had two more children, Dylan and Danica. But my match with Brad kept on going.

Throughout Brad's high school basketball career, we went to most of his games. After he earned a scholarship to play for Purdue University, we traveled to many of those games too. When Brad turned eighteen, the agency called to tell us that the match had officially ended. But that didn't matter; we kept up the friendship. In our hearts he is our fourth child.

Brad was named Honorable Mention All-American by the Associated Press after his senior season at Purdue in 1997–1998, and he is one of only three players in Purdue history to top 1,300 career points, 700 rebounds, and 200 assists. He also was a member of the 1998 U.S. men's basketball team that earned bronze at the World

Championships in Athens, Greece.

Brad wasn't drafted by the NBA graduation, but he never considered quitti instead to play in Italy during the 1998 NBA soon as the strike ended, Brad was picked up Charlotte Hornets, and then went to the Indiana Pacers, where he was named to the All-Star team during the 2002–2003 season.

No matter how well Brad has done in the NBA, he's always remained the same small-town guy he was when we first met him. His genuineness is one of the best things about him. He never developed an attitude of being above anyone in Kendallville. Even as a kid, Brad never got into trouble. He was always a kid you could count on.

Of course, that's because he comes from a very good family. And we like to think that his being part of our family was a factor too. After all, you can only be around someone so long before they are part of you. To Brad, our kids are like his little brothers and sisters. Brad bought his mom a house not far from our place on Long Lake, and he also owns a house there, along with 200 acres of land.

Looking back more than twenty years, being Brad's Big Brother was an immense pleasure. The instant we met, we got along. And no matter how things changed around us, Brad and I always shared a strong bond, almost like father and son.

When he was traded from the Indiana Pacers to the Sacramento Kings last season, I was concerned because California is so far away. But it doesn't matter, because as soon as the season ends, Brad is back in Indiana, right where he belongs.

By Dewy Forbes as told to Tom Starner

Sharing the Magic

Big Brother Sy Sternberg and Little Brother Ed Michaels

It all began with a phone call I received some thirty years ago. The person on the other end of the line asked if I would make a charitable donation to a group that provided mentors for young people. As she described the program, I began to get more interested. I asked her what I thought was a simple, innocent question: "What exactly do you have to do to become a Big Brother?"

The next thing I knew, I was being interviewed. Then I was invited to learn more about the program. And before long, there was another phone call; they had matched me up with a seven-year-old boy who would be my new Little Brother.

I'll never forget the first time I walked up to the front door of his family's house. Stepping inside, I wondered what I had gotten myself into. There in the living room sat Ed, his eyes glued to the TV set. I don't think he even noticed me enter the room. At that moment, neither one of us had a clue that we were about to embark on an adventure that would change both of our lives.

Ed lived with his mother and his two sisters. After losing his father, he no longer had a male role model in his life. He didn't know it, but he really needed a Big Brother.

So for the next several years, I visited with Ed twice a week. I'd often take him out for burgers after school, or sometimes on the weekends we'd go on outings like picnics, fishing, or ballgames with other Big and Little Brother matches. I realized Ed was beginning to depend on me for empathy and advice.

Actually, I think it was his mother who first noticed that I had been adopted by her son. A couple of years into our match, she said, "I'm worried about Ed. He has been acting very hostile and rude to the man I am dating. Please see if you can talk to him; you're the only one he will listen to."

I understood why Ed was reacting badly to someone who, in his mind, was trying to take the place of his father. I explained to him, "You owe it to your mother to be courteous to this man. You don't have to like him. But you must be courteous."

Ed puzzled over this for a moment. "I don't have to like him?" he asked. "No," I said, "you don't."

And that was that. From that moment on, Ed was respectful to the man who would soon become his stepfather. It didn't surprise me when that respect later turned into affection.

I stayed matched with Ed through junior high and high school. He was a good student. When I asked him about his plans for college, Ed said, "I want to study engineering, just like you did."

So Ed and I visited college campuses together, and I helped him choose a school. We stayed in touch all through his college years, and I couldn't have been more proud when he graduated, with honors, in the top 20 percent of his class. And he had more good news to tell me: "I have two job offers! And one of them is from the same company that hired *you*, when *you* graduated college."

Remarkably enough, not only was it the same company I had worked for, it was the same division and the exact same location. I know Ed looked up to me as a role model, but I had to advise him to take the other job offer instead. "It's not a great place to start your career," I told him. "You won't be happy there."

This time he refused to listen to me. Ed's dream was to grow up to be like his Big Brother. As it turned out, after a few months with this company, he knew it was a mistake. Finally, he admitted to me, "Sy, you were right again."

You see, it never really ends. I will always be Ed's Big Brother. He will always be my Little Brother. I love that feeling.

But my story is by no means unique. Talk to any Big Brother or Big Sister. They will all tell you the same thing; there are few things in life more rewarding or more life changing than the mentoring relationships fostered through this organization.

That is why I brought the Big Brothers Big Sisters Workplace Mentoring program into my company, New York Life, where I am chairman and chief executive officer. Some of our employees have been involved in mentoring their Little Brothers and Little Sisters for more than five years—and I have no doubt that there are many relationships being built, like my own, that will last a lifetime.

Even though Ed has his own family now, we still find the time to get together for our occasional weekend visits, just like the old days. Last month, we had a Big Brother Little Brother outing to the beach. If I remember correctly, we hit Bally's, Caesar's, and the Trump Plaza. Hey, *someone* has to supervise the kid!

When I signed up as a Big Brother all those years ago, I thought it couldn't hurt to give a little bit of my time to this organization. But now I know it is an uneven bargain: I received far more than I ever could have given.

Big Brothers Big Sisters gave me a buddy. They gave me an extended family; and they gave a wonderful boy a man who will be his champion for life.

Thank you to all the Bigs and all the Littles who make this miracle happen again and again. And thank you, Ed. I will always be proud of you.

By Sy Sternberg

The Little Toothbrush

Big Sister Alice Abbott and Little Sister Chris Colley

The first time I met Alice, she drove up to my house in a big, burgundy Cadillac. It was 1975, and in those days that was a huge car. Alice had long, straight, dark hair; she carried herself in a sophisticated manner. I had never seen anyone so fancy, and I kept thinking, "She's *mine*!" We drove to Baker's Sweet Shoppe and had ice cream, and I thought that having a Big Sister was going to be fabulous.

The next time Alice came to pick me up, she was driving an old safari-style Jeep, with her hair in a bun and a dog in the back seat. I honestly didn't recognize her. But we went out and had a great time, and I concluded that I'd gotten two sisters in place of one.

Of course, in those days, at the age of ten, I didn't realize that *one* sister like Alice would be more than I could ever have hoped for. I was the proverbial middle child, a girl sandwiched between two brothers. My parents were divorcing; I was losing my dad; my mom was going back to work full-time; and I was lost in the shuffle.

Alice was in her late twenties, a homemaker with no children and a husband who was immersed in his work. Big Brothers Big Sisters matched us because we shared a love of animals. I was soon attached to her dogs and her huge, monster parrot.

We spent a lot of time together in the first years of our match. We took the dogs to the beach or the park and threw sticks. We attended Big Sisters agency activities, playing games and doing crafts on Saturday mornings. We participated in walk-a-thon fundraisers. Sometimes Alice took me to the movies. I still remember that *Saturday Night Fever* seemed very risqué and grown-up. Sometimes I'd ride in the back seat of the Cadillac, and she'd let me fiddle with all the buttons and knobs. Eventually she took me to a rural area and let me drive the Jeep on a dirt road. It was pretty simple stuff, but our time together meant the world to me.

More than anything, Alice made me feel special. Once she gave me a toothbrush—a red-and-black-checkered toothbrush with a really wide handle and natural bristles. I thought, "This is the fanciest thing I've ever seen in my life." I knew she really cared about me to give me a gift like that.

We had been matched about four years when I went through some monstrous teen years. My mom had remarried, and we'd moved to a farm north of Seattle. Alice and I weren't able to see each other as much. I was in and out of school and definitely running a bit wild. At fifteen I ran away from home, and even after I went back, I had a hard time telling Alice. Finally we made plans to meet back at Baker's Sweet Shoppe. I was nervous, sure that she would judge me or be disappointed in me.

"I've got to tell you something," I confessed, "something I did that's really bad." Alice heard me out and thought for just a moment. Then she said, "I need to tell *you* something. I ran away from home too." She explained that she had left her husband and was getting a divorce. Instead of judging me, Alice had once again demonstrated that it was okay to confide in her.

In 1982 Alice remarried, and when I was almost eighteen, her daughter, my niece, was born. By that time I had earned my GED, and we began to spend a lot of time together again, as I could drive into town to visit her. The next year Alice presented me with a nephew, and I watched her become a wonderful mother, hoping that someday I would be as good a mom as she was.

Within another year, I was married and had my own son; my daughter soon followed. Together we tackled the toddler years, and I tried to emulate her parenting skills. We enrolled our children in the same preschool and my closest friends came from that experience.

Once my kids were a little older, I enrolled in a community college, completed nursing school, and now work full-time in Seattle's trauma center. That experience has finally given me the opportunity to give something tangible back to Alice after all these years.

Now that her children are grown, Alice has gone back to school herself. She's attending the same community college I did and studying management. Recently she told me, "I would never have thought it was possible to go back to school at my age if I hadn't seen you do it so successfully."

Alice sees me as this big, strong person now. But I don't know if I would have grown up this way without her. It's hard to say how my life would have been different. I just know that Alice gave me one-on-one time I otherwise would not have gotten. She was always there for me; I knew I could rely on her. She made me feel special. It didn't involve anything extraordinary—just being together and that little toothbrush. They meant the world to me.

By Chris Colley as told to Tisha Frank

Art by Little Sister Aaliyah Clarkson

Starring Doryen

Big Brother Bruce Hunter and Little Brother Doryen Chin

For some reason I've always had an interest in being a Big Brother. But like many other people, I spent most of my life being too busy, and being a Big was just something I hoped to do one day. When I moved to Phoenix in 1997, I had no social circle, no outside everyday demands, so it seemed the perfect time to start.

After starting the process with Big Brothers Big Sisters, I promptly got significant new responsibilities at work, started an evening MBA program and a weekend leadership program, began golf and singing lessons, bought a new house, and, in my spare time, built a social life. My golf and singing are still sub par, but the decision to become a Big has changed my life as much as it has changed my Little's life.

I had no real idea what it meant to be a Big Brother. On the one hand, I had images of parks, baseballs, footballs, and in-line skates. On the other hand, I had images of taking a small dysfunctional child and making him better—fixing him.

When I first met Doryen, he was a precocious, adorable twelve-year-old kid. He spouted, nearly correctly, physics facts. He spoke proudly of his having descended from the

Chin dynasty, founders of China. He told me about his girlfriend and how, in just six years, they were going off to college together and getting married. We proudly posed for pictures for our case manager, me easily lifting him with one arm as he held his Styrofoam airplane.

We then bravely got into my car and launched off together. It was an early summer day, probably in the mid-90s, and the first thing Doryen did was to roll up all the windows in my car. He quickly proclaimed his disdain for the outdoors. I was shocked. No outdoors meant no baseball, no football, no in-line skates!

As the summer went on, I began to understand the extent of the challenges Doryen was facing. I found out that he spent the majority of his days alone at the kitchen table, reading, drawing, and isolating himself from the world. I began to understand that he was a brilliant ninety-pound twelve-year-old with the self-image and social confidence of a stray cat.

That summer we began to develop our pattern of seeing every bad science fiction movie, some of them more than once. At that point in his life, Doryen was going to be a movie director when he grew up.

While waiting for movies to start, he would amuse me with the movies he planned to direct. We agreed that in all of them, regardless of theme, I would play the-man-in-the-park-who-was-eaten-by-a-T. rex. Suddenly, in the middle of a starship battle, Doryen would break to the park where I would be eaten by a T. rex. There, in the middle of an enchanting love scene, Doryen would break to the park where I would be eaten by a T. rex. . . . People would stop me in the street, "Are you the guy who got eaten by the T. rex?"

It was at about this point in our match, long after I had given up on the golf lessons and singing lessons, long after my empty life had become full enough to be stressful, that I stopped looking at being a Big as another thing to do or simply another responsibility. I began to see Doryen as an excuse to have at least a minimum of balance in my life. Imagine *having to* take a break from fault-tolerant computer systems, UNIX operating systems, and macroeconomics to go play laser tag, watch a lousy science fiction movie, or simply spend time letting a fabulous child know that he is fabulous!

About two years into the match with Doryen, I got a huge surprise. We had volunteered to speak to Tempe Cares, a collection of about two hundred volunteers and bystanders from across Tempe. It was at this point that I finally expressed what I had learned about the program and learned from my relationship with Doryen.

I had entered the program wanting to fix Doryen. I thought he was somehow broken and it was my job as a volunteer to help cure Doryen of whatever problems he had. I also told them how I had figured out that there was nothing wrong with Doryen. I simply had to give him space to grow up. If I needed to feel heroic, perhaps I would say one simple thing that he would remember and that would make a difference. I was thinking something along the lines of Hamlet's Polonius: "Be true to yourself."

Then came the surprise. Doryen stood up, took the microphone, looked at the two hundred people in the audience, including the mayor and city council, and completely commanded the audience. I do not remember what he said, but I remember how closely the audience listened to him and how comfortably he took over that room. In two short years, he had gone from someone who had trouble commanding the kitchen table to someone who could command a room and make city council members listen.

Then, perhaps six months later, an even bigger surprise happened. Doryen reminded me that I had once said that I was hoping to say one thing that would make a difference. "That was it," he said. "Huh?" I said eloquently. "That was it. You saying you wanted to make a difference. That was it." I didn't immediately understand what he was saying, but the point became clear. He was saying that I had made a difference in his life by simply being someone who wanted to make a difference. I didn't need to fix him; he simply needed to see that somebody thought he was worth fixing. I never thought watching terrible movies could be such a worthwhile thing.

I can no longer lift Doryen, let alone lift him with one arm. Now that he is nineteen instead of twelve, I stand on my toes when we hug. And he comes to pick *me* up. He is not a movie director. He's not in college and married to the girlfriend from 1997. But he's feeding himself, paying his own rent, and just now entering into his own as a young man who has a sense that he matters.

By Bruce Hunter

Lessons from the Little

Big Sister Tammy Sepeck Rundle and Little Sister Jana McLaughlin

I met my Little Sister Jana on Saturday, March 28, 1998. I remember the excitement and nervousness I felt when she opened her front door to me for the first time. Was I wearing the right clothes? Did I look the part of a Big Sister? Would I fulfill the expectations she had built up in herself about my becoming her Big Sister? Would we click as soon as we began to converse? Would her mother approve of me? Would I feel comfortable in her home? Would I know what to say to her when we first had the opportunity to be together?

When Jana looked at me, her first words to her social worker Valerie were "Is she mine?" Never in my life had I felt more welcome, needed, and appreciated than I did at that moment. From that point on, I knew that my fears and apprehensions would subside because Jana's excitement and anticipation of having a Big Sister were greater than my insecurities about my ability to perform as one.

My relationship with Jana has been a truly enriching and rewarding experience for me. She has taught me lessons about myself—both personally and professionally—that have enabled me to grow and mature in a more positive way. From a professional viewpoint, my training as a guidance counselor has been positively enhanced through my abilities to communicate effectively with Jana.

It is often difficult for adolescents to share their thoughts, concerns, and dreams with others. I have been able to develop a rapport with Jana that has made her feel safe to share these things with me. Through my conversations with her, I have learned a great deal about the issues facing our youth today, and this information will be invaluable to me as I further my career in counseling.

On a more personal note, Jana's friendship has taught me two very valuable lessons about life. The first lesson is to be grateful for the many gifts and blessings in our lives, and not take them for granted. The second lesson, simply stated, is not to take ourselves so seriously!

As adults, we often criticize our upbringing for one reason or another. We complain that we did not have the perfect *Leave It to Beaver* families, that our parents—in some way or another—failed us. We cast blame on people in our lives and on circumstances and experiences that somehow allegedly crippled our development.

While each person grapples with defining his or her own self-identity and finding his or her place in the world, without Jana's presence in my life, I would still be distorting this reality in my own life. Without a doubt, I have learned that families are not perfect entities, and that to arrive at a place of peace and inner harmony within myself, I must concentrate on defining my family's strengths and blessings. That is what I try to instill in Jana as well.

The second lesson infused by Jana's friendship was totally unexpected. As a Big Sister, I have learned how *not* to take myself so seriously. I have always worked very hard in my academic and professional realms. I have always strived for perfection in all that I do. As assets, my motivation and drive have enabled me to accomplish great successes in life, yet, as a detriment, I have always been too hard on myself when perfection is not realized. Jana has taught me to keep sight of the truly important things in life—love, friendship, and humor.

My outings with Jana have enabled me to learn to be a kid again. I had forgotten what it was like to have someone with whom to play just for fun. We have been to an amusement park, a county fair, an art museum, Saturday matinees, ceramics studios, miniature golf, nature walks, and more. Jana's carefree sense of humor has been a breath of fresh air for me.

During our girl talks, it amazes me that I confide in her and ask her for advice about situations in my own life. She has become a true friend to me, and I no longer perceive my relationship with her as an act of charity. Instead, our friendship is genuine, open, and above all *fun*.

Having Jana as my Little Sister has helped me to grow, mature, and improve in more ways than I ever could have imagined. During our Big Sister training, we were told that we may never know how our relationships with our Littles will influence their lives. It is a wonderful feeling to know that this influence is reciprocal and that my Little Sister has been a source of strength and support for me. I decided to become a Big Sister because I wanted to make a difference in a young girl's life. I never imagined that she would do the same for me.

By Tammy Sepeck Rundle

Social Lives

Big Sister Tina Krejci and Little Sister Tammy Schenk

A transplanted urbanite, I found the Big Horn Basin in north-central Wyoming to be a quiet place when I first arrived more than ten years ago. I had known that living here would be a big change from the constant activity I grew up with, and I expected that it wouldn't be that much different from Laramie, where I attended college. But I'd never lived anywhere without an event center where I could see concerts and shows on a whim, and I had always dwelled near scads of young people who mingled at local restaurants, bars, or nightclubs.

Determined to survive here, I adjusted. I got a community concert schedule, kept up with the high school events, and watched the paper to see where and when live musicians played. Brief forays into local nightlife quickly fizzled when I discovered that clubbing in the basin meant more drinking and driving than socializing, so I joined community groups like the reading council and the conservation district. I coached Special Olympics. But the best thing I did was to become a Big Sister.

I had volunteered with Big Brothers Big Sisters in Laramie, so the experience wasn't completely new to me. Tammy, my new nine-year-old Little Sister, wasn't that different from the kids I spent time with in college. She was typically shy at first, then eager to spend time together. My social calendar soon filled with after-school activities, weekend get-togethers, and daily phone calls.

Always having had a hard time sitting still, I shared with her my passion for activity. I taught her to play tennis, took her cross-country skiing, and made regular walks a part of our routine.

She loved music and going for drives. I'd pick her up after school, and we'd wander our favorite routes or pace the high school halls when the weather was bad. Other times we'd load up my car and hit the road, radio cranked up, singing along. We played ball and danced. She creamed me at bowling.

One day during the second year we were matched, Tammy said she would have to miss our next regular time together. When I asked why, she said she was going to Blind Camp.

"Blind Camp?" I said. "What are you doing going to Blind Camp?"

She laughed in that infectious way she has. "You know I'm legally blind." She thumped me on the arm with her fist. "What? Did you forget?"

I knew Tammy suffered visual impairment, as anyone could probably tell from her thick glasses and the way she craned her neck to see what was happening around her. We'd talked about the magnifying machine she used to read in her classroom, and we practiced her math facts out loud because it was easier than writing them. We bought fluorescent pink tennis balls because she could track them better. If dusk descended on our ski trail, I'd go fetch the car to give her a ride the rest of the way. But if anyone had ever told me that Tammy was legally blind, I had honestly forgotten.

"Well," I said. "I'll bet you're the only kid at Blind Camp who plays tennis." We laughed ourselves breathless.

That was seven years ago. Last May, Tammy graduated from high school. Our connection through Big Brothers Big Sisters had been closed the fall before, when she went to live with her mother, but just because the paperwork declared our match closed didn't mean that we had stopped being friends. We don't see each other as much as we used to, especially since I have another Little now, but we try to get together whenever possible and talk on the phone regularly.

Over the years, I tried to teach Tammy to give her best effort even when she wasn't skilled at things. She taught me to appreciate the abilities I'm blessed to have and to enjoy country music. But, most important, she showed me how the activities people fill their time with are best spent with real friends—even if they're not exactly what we expected.

By Tina Krejci

The Great Triumvirate

Big Brother Neil Young and Little Brothers Eric and Lyle Green

A friend riding the Rapid Transit to work one day saw an advertisement for Big Brothers Big Sisters. He called to see if I was interested in learning more. I quickly went through the interview process, and within a couple of months I found myself in the office of the Jewish Big Brothers Big Sisters Association of Cleveland.

It was a cold, blustery day in December 1978, but the moment I met Eric, then eight and a half years old, and his seven-and-a-half-year-old brother Lyle, the room filled with warmth. The boy's mother had asked to have one Big Brother for both boys. Although the agency had never done this before, they agreed to give it a try. When the caseworker presented the double match to me, I agreed to accept, but only for a six-month trial period. I never looked back!

My desire to become a Big Brother stemmed from losing my father to cancer when I was thirteen years old. I knew what it was like to grow up in a single-parent household. Eric and Lyle's father passed away when they were just four and five years old. I thought this connection was a good one, because I had lived what they were going through and I could relate to it. Eric and Lyle have said that if anything good could come from losing their dad, for them it was getting me as a Big Brother.

"Do you like football?" was Lyle's first question to me. I was never really much of an athlete, but I knew "no" was the wrong answer. "To play or to watch?" I replied, knowing it was only buying me some time before I had to answer his question. "Both" they blurted out together. I did not let the secret out of the bag, as I did not want to disappoint them at our first meeting. I told them I was not a very good player but I did like football.

Some of my best memories of our match include the numerous football games we played in their front yard, watching them play on their high school football team, and going to Cleveland Browns games. A trip to Pittsburgh to watch the Browns play the Steelers was topped off by our staying in the same hotel and on the same floor as the team. Eric and Lyle got many players to autograph the football books I had given them at the start of our trip. The smiles that beamed from the boy's faces were magical!

Over the years our activities ranged from helping with school studies and cleaning garages to celebrating birthdays, going for walks, overnight trips, talking over lunch or dinner, movies, playing board games, and watching TV. Just being together was what was special to all of us.

I watched two young boys grow up, and I played a major role in their lives as they had no local family and no adult male role model. I was with them as they left home dressed in tuxedos for prom night, and I was there for them when their feelings were hurt by someone or they were left behind on a school field trip. The boys knew I cared about them, and I knew they cared about me.

Special? You bet—and Cleveland's *PM Magazine* thought so too. We were featured on a segment of the TV magazine show in 1984 to promote Big Brothers Big Sisters during the organizations eightieth anniversary. That was a magical moment the boys remember well.

We celebrated holidays together, and my family welcomed them as part of the family. I watched as they each received high school and college diplomas. Their graduations were such joyous occasions as I watched these confident young men march across the stage and hugged them afterward as their proud Big Brother.

Eric and Lyle both stood up for me at my wedding in April 1988. I did the same for Eric when he got married in June 2000, and in October 2004 I will be honored once again when I stand up for Lyle at his wedding. In December 2002 Eric and Dania made me a Grandbig when their daughter was born.

My involvement with the Jewish Big Brothers Big Sisters Association of Cleveland consisted of holding numerous offices, including president, but I enjoyed my fundraising activities the most. My favorite fundraiser was the Bowl for Kids Sake in 1997, when Eric and Lyle flew to Cleveland for the weekend and the three of us bowled a true bowl-a-thon. We vowed to knock down one pin for every dollar we raised. The three of us raised over $5,000, and we bowled for over five hours straight to keep our word to our contributors. What a proud feeling it was to have Eric and Lyle back in town for this worthy cause!

Today, twenty-five years after we met, the boys introduce me as their Big Brother. My children, who adore them, call them Uncle Eric and Uncle Lyle. Even though Eric lives outside the Philadelphia area and Lyle lives in Los Angeles, we talk regularly. While never enough, we visit often as well.

I know I made a difference in Eric and Lyle's lives. The gratification I get from that feeling is never-ending. I didn't go in with the expectation that my Little Brothers would become my best friends. The love and caring I get from them has proven to me that becoming a Big Brother was the best decision I made in my life. While a Big Brother is intended to be a special friend to his Little, I found exceptionally special friendships with Eric and Lyle that have filled the last twenty-five years of my life with magical moments, and will continue to do so every time we talk or get together—for another twenty-five years!

By Neil Young

Having a Positive Role Model ... Priceless

Big Brother Jim Berry and Little Brother Dave Taillon

I was born and raised by my mom in Schenectady's low-income housing, subsisting on food stamps and other public assistance my mom received to feed and cloth my two sisters and me. Few would have bet that I'd earn a civil engineering degree and eventually a master's degree, and that I'd have a successful career as a professional engineer.

People point to a variety of systems and services that helped me escape the cycle of poverty, drugs, and crime that many of my Steinmetz Home peers never left. And many elements did contribute to my successful exit. But nothing I can think of was more important to me than the consistent presence of a positive role model—someone who exposed me to a vision, who helped me see beyond my daily grind of poverty and glimpse a life that existed on the other side.

Jim Berry, who managed the Mohawk National Savings Bank in Rotterdam, was my Big Brother for more than three years. He and I spent countless hours together doing things that sound particularly unexceptional, but that at the time meant the world to me: sharing a laugh over a cheeseburger, fries, and a soda; playing Ping-Pong in his basement; playing tennis; learning to play golf at Whispering Pines; having dinner at his house with his wife; and so on. To this day, I think of Jim while I'm playing tennis or while I'm spending some time on the golf course.

I remember vividly the excitement I felt in school knowing that I was to spend the afternoon after school with Jim. My end of the bargain required me to stay out of any formal trouble—in and out of school—and earn decent grades. Staying out of trouble was a good thing, but it paled in comparison to the positive benefits I experienced from Jim's friendship.

I was really proud to have such a great guy as my Big Brother. For once in my life I had something that no one else had. I wasn't used to having something special given to me. In those critical years between ages eleven and fourteen, having Jim in my life was a priceless gift.

He inspired me to do the right thing, not because of anything he ever directly said, but because he gave me a reason to work hard, to make someone proud. My confidence, my desire, and my abilities came alive as a result of his small contribution of time once a week. I wanted Jim to be proud of me, and I didn't want to disappoint him by getting into trouble or not doing well in school. He believed in me, and I didn't want to let him down.

Nearly a decade ago Jim died from cancer. He never did get to see the positive turn my life took. Perhaps he knew all along. Sometimes I think he would have put his money down on me—and perhaps that's what he was doing once a week.

Today I spend much of my time recruiting others to consider volunteering as Big Brothers or Sisters. The commitment is a small amount of time, and the benefits are infinite. As a Big Brother, I have learned firsthand what Jim used to claim—that the mentor reaps the largest rewards from the relationship. For inspiration, I often read the following quote that I keep on my desk:

A hundred years from now it will not matter what my bank account was, the sort of house I lived in, or the kind of car I drove . . . but the world may be different because I was important in the life of a child.

I have come a long way from where I started forty years ago, and much of that road I was able to travel only because I had a positive role model in my life. When my time is up on this Earth, I hope I can say what Jim Berry was able to say—that someone's life was more fulfilling because I was important in their life.

By Dave Taillon

Three Sisters' Big Smiles

Big Sister Kristin Halverson and Little Sisters Kristy Paulson and Breona Foulk

Six years ago I married my best friend, Steve Halverson. Like most bridal couples we were enveloped by the excitement, anticipation, and love of the day. The special moments of our October 25, 1997, wedding were captured by the hired photographer. As we thumbed through the photos a few weeks later, one particularly caught my eye. Six years later, it remains my favorite photo from that day.

No, it is not the picture of Steve and me looking lovingly at each other, nor is it the picture of my niece up to her elbows in our wedding cake. It is the picture of me with my other two best friends—Kristy Paulson and Breona Foulk—in my arms. The love, devotion, and pride I feel for both of my Little Sisters from the Big Brothers Big Sisters program, and the love they feel for me, shines through that snapshot like lightning.

Breona, just eight and wearing her favorite faux fur coat, was a new addition to my life then. She and I had just been matched the spring before. Her smile is magic, and her personality fills a room like laughter. I had asked Breona to tend my guest book and welcome my friends and family into the church that morning.

As soon as Steve and I emerged from the sanctuary, she bounded into our arms—ahead of everyone else, including my parents. Her excitement was contagious, and Kristy dashed up to join in the sisterly hug.

Kristy, then seventeen, wore the bridesmaid dress I picked out with her in mind when Steve and I got engaged. Aside from my own sister, I knew that the most important person standing up with me that day would be the little girl who first came into my life ten years before and who had become my friend and sister in the decade since.

All three of us are wearing smiles bigger than our faces in the photo snapped at that moment. We were happy for each other and happy to be with each other—a Big Sister family formed of fun and friendship and made to last forever.

In the years since that photo was taken, my smile has only widened when I think of the adventures Kristy and Breona have brought to my life, the lessons we've learned together, and the laughter we've shared. We hiked and biked and talked one hundred miles. We baked and burned a thousand cookies, glued hundreds of pieces of felt and wood and paper together, carved dozens of pumpkins, visited zoos and museums, traveled to the mountains and the sea, laughed until we couldn't stand up anymore, and even cried a time or two.

I estimated just the other day that in the seven years Breona and I have been matched, we have spent more than six hundred hours in the car together going to and from our houses and our destinations. Kristy and I, matched eleven years, certainly surpassed the thousand-hour mark. Yet the journey never seemed long. Cars are, after all, a good place to talk or at least get up to speed on the newest rap music sensation. Had I not been a Big Sister, I never would have heard—much less know all the words to—

music by such stars as 50-Cent!

In all those miles, I've watched Kristy and Breona grow from little girls with big dreams into beautiful, caring, and intelligent young women determined to make those dreams come true.

Breona is a sophomore in high school now, a cheerleader and a volunteer in her community. She wants to be an art teacher and has the talent, personal drive, and wit and wisdom to help tomorrow's generation paint their dreams.

Kristy graduated college last spring and is a specialist in the U.S. Army, serving in Fort Drum, New York, where she cooks for thousands, serves our country, and fine-tunes her skills.

Kristy also keeps busy serving others, as she's always done since before I met her. Not long after my wedding, Kristy called to tell me some exciting news—she was becoming a Big Sister too! The lump in my throat made it impossible for me to respond when she said that she had wanted to give back the great experience she had with me to someone else. She was matched with a little boy named Travis in Wisconsin for two years. Since transferring to Fort Drum, Kristy has been matched with a little girl, Antisia, and she still keeps in weekly contact with Travis.

When Kristy calls to fill me in on their adventures or on her concerns for her Littles' futures, I get that lump back in my throat again. Once in a while, Kristy says, "You can't imagine how I feel when . . ." or "I can't believe I worry about this, but. . . ." I listen quietly and knowingly, and I smile at the memory of those same feelings I had for Kristy when she was the Little Sister looking up at me from the passenger seat of my car all those hundreds of miles ago.

We take many journeys in our lives. I've been blessed

to travel the world and walk down the aisle, but few journeys will ever be sweeter than the miles I've walked—and certainly driven—with my Little Sisters. My choice in the fall of 1986 to become a Big Sister and my choice in early 1997 to do it all over again were the best two decisions I've ever made. The experiences of being someone's Big Sister have changed me, improved me, in ways that no trip or job or trophy could ever do.

The fun I have, the pride I feel, the happy tears I've shed over Little Sister memories, and the love and friendship I share, sustain and rejuvenate me still. Nothing could feel as warm and as strong as the Little hug I got on my wedding day. Our Big smiles say it all!

By Kristin Gilpatrick Halverson

Beth Barrett

Beth Barrett was a successful trial attorney for eighteen years—initially on Park Avenue in New York City, and then in Connecticut.

Six years ago that exciting, hectic world came to a screeching halt when she had an accident which shattered her left foot and worsened a nerve disease that already required her to walk with crutches or to use a wheelchair. Always optimistic, she believed that this forced slow-down was an opportunity to find out what her life purpose and mission was.

What an adventure that turned out to be! What could have been the worst years of her life have turned out to be the best. Beth knows that her purpose in life is to inspire people to live more joyful and fulfilling lives, despite whatever challenges they may face. She speaks and writes about living a joyful life, as well as on the joys of mentoring.

Her next book, called "*Soaring Beyond Limits: Ten Lessons on Living a Joy Filled Life for the Physically Challenged*," will be published in 2005.

Beth was Connecticut's Big Sister of the Year for 2003. Her story "Big Sisterhood" about her relationship with her legally blind Little Sister Karen Hays, was published in *Chicken Soup for the Volunteer's Soul.*

The publication of that story made her a natural fit as lead author of *Little Moments, Big Magic* and co-creator of the publishing company. Beth feels incredibly blessed for the amazing synchronicity of events that guide her to fulfill her life mission.

For further information about Beth contact:

PO Box 915, Southbury, CT 06488-0915
(203) 264-8804 Fax (203) 267-7142
bbarrett@magicalpublishing.com

Visit our web site at www.magicalpublishing.com

Alan Annis

Alan Annis is a pragmatic entrepreneur, business owner, and leader. He has owned three different companies and has been a successful small business owner for the last ten years. He is a loving, caring, motivator with a vision to make the world a better place.

Alan was instrumental in helping build a successful Electronic Cash Register (ECR) service center. The service center was built from a small customer base and grew into the largest service center of its type in the U.S. Alan became a world renowned expert in his field and has authored and published six comprehensive service guides for the ECR industry.

With the success of his career, Alan looked for new and different ways to contribute and to give back. He found it in Big Brothers Big Sisters and quickly signed up to be a mentor. Soon after, Alan also accepted a role to serve on the Board of Directors for Big Brothers Big Sisters of Central Arizona. He later stepped in and became an interim Vice President for the Agency as well.

Alan has had an amazing experience with BBBS. As a result of serving as a mentor, a Board member, and Vice President, he has had the chance to connect with, meet, and share magical moments with some wonderful people. That developed into the opportunity to create this book and build a new publishing company. What an incredible and very fulfilling experience it has been! Reflecting back, he knows it all came from that one kind act of wanting to give a child a little of his time. One kind act can change your life!

For further information about Alan contact:

aannis@magicalpublishing.com

Denice Riffey

Denice Riffey is a three-time Big Sister and marketing/development professional for Big Brothers Big Sisters of Central Arizona. For eight years she has spent her time creatively and enthusiastically sharing the mission and passion of mentoring with Arizona communities, corporations and outstanding volunteers.

As a mass communications/public relations major from Mesa State College in Grand Junction, Colorado writing has been a life long love and professional ambition.

Denice is most proud of her family. After twelve short years, her and her wonderful husband share the joy of parenting Rachel, Madison and baby Rebecca. Together they conquer sleepless nights, high-energy days and the constant challenges of balancing family, church, work and dreams – what a life!

For further information about Denice contact:

driffey@magicalpublishing.com

Permissions

We would like to acknowledge the following publishers and individuals for permission to reprint the following material:

The Turning Point. Reprinted by permission of Dr. Kenneth S. Saladin. ©2003 Dr. Kenneth S. Saladin.

No Limits. Reprinted by permission of Beth Barrett. ©2003 Beth Barrett.

Food for Thought. Reprinted by permission of Beth Barrett and Todd English. ©2004 Beth Barrett and Todd English.

Giving Us a Future. Reprinted by permission of Manuel Carrasco. ©2004 Manuel Carrasco.

The Little with Big Dreams. Reprinted by permission of Ty Le'Var Eiland. ©2003 Ty Le'Var Eiland.

Caring from the Heart. Reprinted by permission of Brenda Clark. ©2003 Brenda Clark.

Service Before Self. Reprinted by permission of Denice Riffey and Peter Grossenbach. ©2004 Denice Riffey and Peter Grossenbach.

The Road to Success. Reprinted by permission of Sashe Dimitroff. ©2004 Sashe Dimitroff.

A Beautiful World. Reprinted by permission of Robin Palley. ©2004 Robin Palley.

Words from a Little. Reprinted by permission of Darius Murray. ©2003 Darius Murray.

My TV Star. Reprinted by permission of Tom Starner and Todd Kulaga. ©2003 Tom Starner and Todd Kulaga.

Big Impact. Reprinted by permission of Richard S. Greif. ©1997 Richard S. Greif.

Beautiful Colors. Reprinted by permission of Jossette Kelly. ©2001 Jossette Kelly.

Ray, Me, and Fee. Reprinted by permission of Robert Drozda. ©2003 Robert Drozda.

Our Common Language. Reprinted by permission of Arlene Schneider. ©2004 Arlene Schneider.

My Little Brother Pete. Reprinted by permission of George D. Wood. ©2004 George D. Wood.

The Little Brown Porsche. Reprinted by permission of Tom Starner and James Copes. ©2004 Tom Starner and James Copes.

The Haircut. Reprinted by permission of Shane Miskell. ©2004 Shane Miskell.

Double O Little Bro'. Reprinted by permission of Greg Balogh. ©2003 Greg Balogh.

Worth Fighting For. Reprinted by permission of John Sias. ©2004 John Sias.

Friendships for a Lifetime. Reprinted by permission of Julie Johnson. ©2003 Julie Johnson.

Our Vietnamese Brother. Reprinted by permission of David Denman. ©2003 David Denman.

I Am Blessed. Reprinted by permission of Hoagan Powell. ©2003 Hoagan Powell.

Sisters for Life. Reprinted by permission of Dave Taylor. ©2003 Dave Taylor.

The Carver Rule. Reprinted by permission of John D. Carver. ©2003 John D. Carver.

Making Our History. Reprinted by permission of Tom Hargis. ©2003 Tom Hargis.

Forty Years and Counting. Reprinted by permission of Bill Lynch. ©2003 Bill Lynch.

From Six to Private First Class. Reprinted by permission of Gregory A. Hearing. ©2003 Gregory A. Hearing.

Brothers for Fifty-Eight Years. Reprinted by permission of Deanna Petersen. ©2003 Deanna Petersen.

It Started Innocently Enough. Reprinted by permission of Larry Bailey. ©2003 Larry Bailey.

We Will Never Forget. Reprinted by permission of Alan Annis and Sara Sparks. ©2004 Alan Annis and Sara Sparks.

Forever, Rob. Reprinted by permission of Beth Barrett and Rob Neal. ©2004 Beth Barrett and Rob Neal.

My Son Michael. Reprinted by permission of Marilyn Miller. ©2004 Marilyn Miller.

Finding Victory. Reprinted by permission of Melissa Tabolsky. ©2003 Melissa Tabolsky.

The Magic of John's Brothers. Reprinted by permission of Margaret LeRoux. ©2003 Margaret LeRoux.

Michaela's Life. Reprinted by permission of the Houston Chronicle. ©2003 Houston Chronicle Publishing Company. All rights reserved.

I Wouldn't Trade a Second. Reprinted by permission of Tom Starner and Paul Oberg. ©2004 Tom Starner and Paul Oberg.

Big, Little, for Life. Reprinted by permission of John Kador. ©2004 John Kador.

Four Generations and Room for More. Reprinted by permission of Beth Barrett, Stephanie Block and Chris Craig. ©2003 Beth Barrett, Stephanie Block and Chris Craig.

What's Age Got to Do With It. Reprinted by permission of Courtney Hunkins. ©2004 Courtney Hunkins.

The Compassion Cycle. Reprinted by permission of Clifton Sherrod III. ©2004 Clifton Sherrod III.

Giving Back. Reprinted by permission of Jennifer Perez. ©2003 Jennifer Perez.

To Be Continued. Reprinted by permission of Dawn Huibregtse. ©2003 Dawn Huibregtse.

You Can Have All of This. Reprinted by permission of Julie McAllister and Jennifer Grimsley. ©2003 JulieMcAllister and Jennifer Grimsley.

From Little to Big. Reprinted by permission of James A. Gaillard. ©2003 James A. Gaillard.

Making a Difference. Reprinted by permission of Tracy Dieterich. ©2003 Tracy Dieterich.

Little Brother and a Sister Too. Reprinted by permission of Tom Smith. ©2004 Tom Smith.

The Sky's the Limit. Reprinted by permission of Judith Saint-Sommer. ©2004 Judith Saint-Sommer.

Big Benefits. Reprinted by permission of Rick Rosu-Myles. ©2003 Rick Rosu-Myles.

My Road to the NFL. Reprinted by permission of Tom Starner and Ben Nowland. ©2003 Tom Starner and Ben Nowland.

Thank You for My Scholarship. Reprinted by permission of Brian Lopez. ©2003 Brian Lopez.

Camping, S'mores, and GT Mustangs. Reprinted by permission of Cindy Glover. ©2003 Cindy Glover.

My Reading Teacher. Reprinted by permission of John Johnson. ©2003 John Johnson.

What a Lucky Girl. Reprinted by permission of Tom Starner and Jami Jensen. ©2003 Tom Starner and Jami Jensen.

A Hand Up. Reprinted by permission of Kevass Harding. ©2004 Kevass Harding.

My Guide in Life. Reprinted by permission of Tom Starner and Ruth Ponce. ©2004 Tom Starner and Ruth Ponce.

Someone Like Jeff. Reprinted by permission of Jackie Watson. ©2003 Jackie Watson.

The Rest of the World. Reprinted by permission of Jennie Mustafa-Julock. ©2004 Jennie Mustafa-Julock.

The Costume Party. Reprinted by permission of Mitch Sibley-Jett. ©2004 Mitch Sibley-Jett.

My Buddy. Reprinted by permission of Beth Barrett. ©2003 Beth Barrett.

The Christmas Glow. Reprinted by permission of Amy McDade. ©2003 Amy McDade.

Hawaii's First. Reprinted by permission of Beth Barrett, the Honolulu Star Bulletin and Honolulu News. ©2003 Beth Barrett, Honolulu Star Bulletin and Honolulu News.

It Takes a Village. Reprinted by permission of Marsha Ammerman Nee. ©2003 Marsha Ammerman Nee.

1968. Reprinted by permission of Gwendolyn Andrade. ©2004 Gwendolyn Andrade.

A Mother's Point of View. Reprinted by permission of Yvonne Rogers. ©2003 Yvonne Rogers.

Twenty-Five Years. Reprinted by permission of Denice Riffey and Carole Beath. ©2004 Denice Riffey and Carole Beath.

Thank You, Mark Griffin. Reprinted by permission of Diana Vest. ©2003 Diana Vest.

From Mother to Son. Reprinted by permission of Mary Powell and Jason Powell. ©2004 Mary Powell and Jason Powell.

Roger's Story. Reprinted by permission of Susan White. ©2004 Susan White.

My Officer and a Gentleman. Reprinted by permission of Marie Garside. ©2004 Marie Garside.

Little Brother Ed. Reprinted by permission of Beth Barrett and C. Ed Harrison. ©2004 Beth Barrett and C. Ed Harrison.

The Power of Small Things. Reprinted by permission of Tony Carter. ©2003 Tony Carter.

December 21. Reprinted by permission of Matthew Pearson. ©2003 Mathew Pearson.

My Christmas Gift. Reprinted by permission of Sean Barnette. ©2004 Sean Barnette.

Three Little "Bothers". Reprinted by permission of Ben Shamberger. ©2004 Ben Shamberger.

I Never Knew. Reprinted by permission of Michael Schuster. ©2003 Michael Schuster.

She Changed My World. Reprinted by permission of Mary Dooner Griffin. ©1998 Mary Dooner Griffin.

The American Dream. Reprinted by permission of Tom Starner. ©2004 Tom Starner.

Basic Life Training. Reprinted by permission of Kyle Ryan Kiper. ©2003 Kyle Ryan Kiper.

A Brotherly Bond That Beat the Odds. Reprinted by permission of The Los Angeles Times. ©1999 Los Angeles Times.

The PR Man. Reprinted by permission of Dave Wright. ©2003 Dave Wright.

She Hears Me. Reprinted by permission of Tom Starner and Stacy Mier. ©2003 Tom Starner and Stacy Mier.

A Brighter Day. Reprinted by permission of Tim Ellis. ©2004 Tim Ellis.

My Rudder in Life. Reprinted by permission of Denice Riffey and Ambrose Rojas. ©2004 Denice Riffey and Ambrose Rojas.

The Inspirational New York Jets. Reprinted by permission of Denice Riffey and John Cori. ©2004 Denice Riffey and John Cori.

One Match, Two Voices. Reprinted by permission of Jim Basham and Matt Brickey. ©2004 Jim Basham and Matt Brickey.

Empathy's Call. Reprinted by permission of Angela M. Gustafson. ©2003 Angela M. Gustafson.

David. Reprinted by permission of Michael Bowler. ©2003 Michael Bowler.

In My Father's Footsteps. Reprinted by permission of Ross Godwin. ©2004 Ross Godwin.

Just Like Phil. Reprinted by permission of Morgan Hassler. ©2004 Morgan Hassler.

In Tribute. Reprinted by permission of Senator John Ensign. ©2004 Senator John Ensign.

My Little NBA Star. Reprinted by permission of Tom Starner and Dewy Forbes. ©2004 Tom Starner and Dewy Forbes.

Sharing the Magic. Reprinted by permission of Sy Sternberg. ©2004 Sy Sternberg.

The Little Toothbrush. Reprinted by permission of Tisha Frank and Chris Colley. ©2004 Tisha Frank and Chris Colley.

Starring Doryen. Reprinted by permission of Bruce Hunter. ©2003 Bruce Hunter.

Lessons from the Little. Reprinted by permission of Tammy Sepeck Rundle. ©1999 Tammy Sepeck Rundle.

Social Lives. Reprinted by permission of Tina Krejci. ©2003 Tina Krejci.

The Great Triumvirate. Reprinted by permission of Neil Young. ©2003 Neil Young.

Having a Positive Role Model...Priceless. Reprinted by permission of Dave Taillon. ©2004 Dave Taillon.

Three Sisters' Big Smiles. Reprinted by permission of Kristin Gilpatrick Halverson. ©2003 Kristin Gilpatrick Halverson.

Index

<u>Places - U.S. States</u>

<u>Schools / Universities</u>

Sports / Activities

Let Us Know

Do you have any comments, feedback or stories you want to share with us? We would love to hear from you! Please share with us:

By email: authors@magicalpublishing.com

By mail: Magical Moments Publishing
PO Box 915
Southbury, CT 06488-0915

Would you like to volunteer as a Big Brother or a Big Sister or enroll your child in this wonderful program? Would you like to donate to keep BBBS growing for another hundred years?

Please visit: www.BigBrothersBigSisters.org

Or call: 1-800-412-BIGS to be connected to your local BBBS agency.

If you are an alumni of BBBS and would like to reconnect with your Big or Little, join the on-line reunion at:

www.BigBrothersBigSisters.org

Magical Moments
PUBLISHING LLC

Share some Little Moments and Big Magic with someone special!

Order books: from your local BBBS Agency; or
from www.BigBrothersBigSisters.org;
OR

❑YES, I want______ copies of *Little Moments, Big Magic* at $19.95 each plus $4.50 shipping and handling per book.

My check or money order for $_________._____ is enclosed.

Please charge my credit card:
❑MasterCard ❑VISA ❑American Express
❑Discover

Card #______________________________ Exp. Date__________

Signature____

Name____

Address____

City / State / Zip_______________________________________

Phone___________________________ Email________________

Please make your check payable and return to:

Magical Moments Publishing, LLC.
PO Box 915
Southbury, CT 06488-0915

Or order by:

Phone: Toll-Free 1-877-778-5958

Fax: 203-267-7142

Email: order@magicalpublishing.com